Flash® CS4

FOR

DUMMIES®

054397

Flash® CS4

FOR

DUMMIES®

**by Ellen Finkelstein
and Gurdy Leete**

WILEY

Wiley Publishing, Inc.

Flash® CS4 For Dummies®

Published by
Wiley Publishing, Inc.
111 River Street
Hoboken, NJ 07030-5774
www.wiley.com

Copyright © 2008 by Wiley Publishing, Inc., Indianapolis, Indiana

Published by Wiley Publishing, Inc., Indianapolis, Indiana

Published simultaneously in Canada

For general information on our other products and services, please contact our Customer Care Department within the U.S. at 800-762-2974, outside the U.S. at 317-572-3993, or fax 317-572-4002.

For technical support, please visit www.wiley.com/techsupport.

Wiley also publishes its books in a variety of electronic formats. Some content that appears in print may not be available in electronic books.

Library of Congress Control Number: 2008934804

ISBN: 978-0-470-38119-9

Manufactured in the United States of America

10 9 8 7 6 5 4 3 2 1

WILEY

About the Authors

Ellen Finkelstein has written numerous bestselling computer books on AutoCAD, PowerPoint, and Flash. She also writes articles for Web sites, e-zines, magazines, and her own Web site (www.ellenfinkelstein.com). The nine editions of her *AutoCAD Bible* have sold more than 125,000 copies in the United States and abroad. She writes at home so that she can take the bread out of the oven on time.

Gurdy Leete has been working as a computer animator, computer animation software engineer, and teacher of computer animation since 1981. He has been teaching Flash and other computer animation programs for 17 years at Maharishi University of Management, where he is an Assistant Professor of Art. You can see his art on the Web at www.infinityeverywhere.net.

Dedication

To MMY, for explaining that life is meant to be lived in happiness and teaching us how to realize that reality in daily life.

Authors' Acknowledgments

Ellen Finkelstein: This book was very much a group effort. First, I'd like to thank my co-author, Gurdy Leete, without whom I could not have completed this book nor even thought of writing it. Gurdy is always a pleasure to work with, always in a good mood and helpful. He's a brilliant artist and a programmer, too, while I am neither. I've been quite impressed.

At Wiley, I'd like to thank Steve Hayes, our acquisitions editor, for his ongoing support. Great kudos go to Nicole Sholly, our project editor, for a great job of organizing and keeping us on track. And special thanks to Teresa Artman and Heidi Unger for whipping the text into shape.

Personally, I'd like to thank my husband, Evan, and my kids, Yeshayah and Eliyah, who helped out and managed as I wrote every day, evening, and weekend. I love you all.

Thanks to Adobe, for supporting Flash authors during the beta period while we were learning the new features of Flash CS4, testing Flash, and writing, all at the same time.

And now, a few comments from Gurdy.

Gurdy Leete: I'd like to echo all of Ellen's words and thank her for being such a great collaborator. She has such a talent for explaining things with the simplicity, precision, and humor that are so characteristic of the deeper workings of the cosmos. I'd also like to thank my brilliant former students Alek Lisefski (www.bluesheepstudios.com) and Benek Lisefski (www.benekdesign.com); as well as intrepid research assistants Nutthawut Chandhaketh, of Thailand; Radim Schreiber, of the Czech Republic; Burcu Cenberci, of Turkey; and Praveen Mishra, of Nepal; whose research activities on the Web were so helpful in writing this book. Thanks to my omnitalented former student Mike Zak for the wonderful collection of clip art drawings that he created in Flash for the companion Web site. And thanks to my adorable wife (Mary) and my children (Porter and Jacqueline) for being so supportive during the many hours I spent working on this book.

Publisher's Acknowledgments

We're proud of this book; please send us your comments through our online registration form located at www.dummies.com/register/.

Some of the people who helped bring this book to market include the following:

Acquisitions, Editorial, and Media Development

Project Editor: Nicole Sholly

Executive Editor: Steve Hayes

Copy Editors: Heidi Unger, Teresa Artman

Technical Editor: Danilo Celic

Editorial Manager: Kevin Kirschner

Media Development Project Manager: Laura Moss-Hollister

Media Development Assistant Project Manager: Jenny Swisher

Media Development Assistant Producers: Angela Denny, Josh Frank, Kit Malone, and Shawn Patrick

Editorial Assistant: Amanda Foxworth

Sr. Editorial Assistant: Cherie Case

Cartoons: Rich Tennant (www.the5thwave.com)

Composition Services

Project Coordinator: Patrick Redmond

Layout and Graphics: Stacie Brooks, Carrie A. Cesavice, Reuben W. Davis

Proofreaders: Linda Quigley, Amanda Steiner

Indexer: Rebecca R. Plunkett

Publishing and Editorial for Technology Dummies

Richard Swadley, Vice President and Executive Group Publisher

Andy Cummings, Vice President and Publisher

Mary Bednarek, Executive Acquisitions Director

Mary C. Corder, Editorial Director

Publishing for Consumer Dummies

Diane Graves Steele, Vice President and Publisher

Composition Services

Gerry Fahey, Vice President of Production Services

Debbie Stailey, Director of Composition Services

Contents at a Glance

Table of Contents

Introduction

*W*elcome to *Flash CS4 For Dummies,* your friendly Web animation companion. In this book, we explain in plain English how to make the most of Flash to create stunning, animated Web sites. We aim to give you all the information you need to start using Flash right away — with no hassle.

About This Book

As though you hadn't guessed, *Flash CS4 For Dummies* covers the powerful animation product Flash CS4, from Adobe. (The preceding version was Adobe Flash CS3. You're holding the 6th edition of this book.) Flash CS4 is the latest version of the popular software used on some of the coolest Web sites on the planet.

We comprehensively explain the Flash features, including

- Working with the Flash screen, toolbars, and menus
- Creating graphics and text in Flash
- Adding sound and video
- Using layers to organize your animation
- Creating *symbols,* which are objects that you save for repeated use and animation
- Animating graphics (the key to Flash)
- Creating interactive Web sites
- Publishing Flash movies to your Web site

How to Use This Book

You don't have to read this book from cover to cover. We provide just the information you need, when you need it. Start with the first three chapters. Then play around with graphics until you create what you need for your Web site. You might want to check out Chapter 6, on layers, to help you organize it all, and Chapter 7, which covers symbols. Then feel free to jump right to Chapter 9, on animation, to create your first real Flash movie. Chapter 13 tells you how to get your movie on your Web site. Then fire up your browser, sit back, and marvel.

You'll want to check out other chapters when you need them so that you can create text and buttons, add sound and video, and build an interactive Web site. Chapter 12 provides some ideas for putting all the Flash features together for your best Web site ever.

Keep *Flash CS4 For Dummies* by your computer while you work. You'll find that it's a loyal helper.

Foolish Assumptions

We assume that you're not a master Flash developer. If you want to use Flash to create high-quality Web sites and you're not an expert animator, you'll find this book to be a great reference. *Adobe Flash CS4 For Dummies* is ideal for beginners who are just starting to use Flash or for current Flash users who want to further hone their skills.

Because people usually add Flash movies to Web sites, we also assume that you know some of the basics of Web site creation. You should know what HyperText Markup Language (HTML) is and understand the process of creating and structuring HTML pages as well as uploading them to a Web site.

If you want some help on the topic of Web sites, you might want to take a look at *Web Design For Dummies,* 2nd Edition, by Lisa Lopuck (Wiley).

Conventions Used in This Book

Sometimes it helps to know why some text is bold and other text is italic so that you can figure out what we're talking about. (A typographic convention is *not* a convention of typographers meeting to discuss the latest typography techniques.)

New terms are in *italics* to let you know that they're new. When we suggest that you type something, we show you what we want you to type in **bold**. Messages and other text that come from Flash, including programming code, are in a `special typeface, like this`.

When we say something like "Choose File⇨Save As," it means to click the File menu at the top of your screen and then choose Save As from the menu that opens. When we want you to use a toolbar or panel button (or tool), we tell you to click it.

The new Flash interface features an item for changing values that's like a combo text box and slider, except that there isn't any text box when you first see it. If you click the value, a box appears in which you can type and then press Enter (Windows) or Return (Mac). Alternatively, you can also click and drag upward or downward, like a traditional slider even though no slider is visible. Calling it a text box seems misleading because you don't see a text box. For this book, this is how we generally describe this new way of doing things: "Click the value, type a new value, and then press Enter (Windows) or Return (Mac), or drag to specify a new value."

How This Book Is Organized

We start by presenting an overview of the Flash universe and then continue in the general order that you would use to create a Flash movie. More basic material is at the beginning of the book, and more advanced material (but not too advanced!) comes later.

To be more specific, this book is divided into seven parts (to represent the seven states of consciousness — okay, we don't have to get too cosmic here). Each part contains two or more chapters that relate to that part. Each chapter thoroughly covers one topic so that you don't have to go searching all over creation to get the information you need.

Part I: A Blast of Flash

Part I contains important introductory information about Flash. In Chapter 1, we tell you what Flash is all about, show you what the Flash screen looks like, and explain how to get help when you need it most. You also find instructions for starting a new movie and opening an existing movie, and we give you a list of steps for creating your first animation. If you're new to Flash, running through these steps will give you a great overview. Chapter 2 explains in more detail the steps for creating a Flash movie. We also explain some basic concepts that all Flash users need to know.

Part II: 1,000 Pictures and 1,000 Words

Part II explains all the tools available for creating graphics in Flash. Chapter 3 explains the unique drawing tools included in Flash. We also explain how to import graphics if you don't feel like creating your own. Chapter 4 shows you how to edit and manipulate graphic objects, and Chapter 5 is all about creating text. Chapter 6 explains *layers,* which help you organize your graphics so that they don't interfere with each other.

Part III: Getting Symbolic

Symbols are graphical objects that you save to use again and again. Whenever you want to place an object on a Web page more than once, you can save the object as a symbol. You can also group together many individual objects, making them useful when you want to manipulate, edit, or animate them all at one time. Chapter 7 explains creating and editing symbols. Chapter 8 describes how to create buttons — not the kind that you sew, but rather the kind that you click with your mouse.

Part IV: Total Flash-o-Rama

Part IV explains how to put all of your graphics together and make them move. Chapter 9 covers animation in detail — from frame-by-frame animation to *tweening,* where Flash calculates the animation between your first and last frames. Tween movement to make your objects move or morph into new shapes. You can also tween color and transparency.

Chapter 10 shows how to create interactive Web sites that react to your viewers. For example, when a viewer clicks a button, Flash can jump to a different part of a movie or go to a different Web page entirely. To create interactivity, you use *ActionScript,* Flash's JavaScript-like programming language. We tell you how to put ActionScript to work.

Chapter 11 is about adding multimedia — sound, music, and video — to your Flash movies and buttons.

Part V: The Movie and the Web

This part helps you put all of your animated graphics and cool buttons together and publish your work on the Web. Chapter 12 outlines the various techniques that you can use to create a great Web site by using only Flash.

Chapter 13 explains how to test your animation for speed and suitability for all browsers and systems. Then we cover the details of publishing movies as well as the other available formats, such as HTML and GIF. You can also create *projectors* — movies that play themselves.

Part VI: The Part of Tens

What's a *For Dummies* book without The Part of Tens? Chapter 14 answers some frequently asked questions about Flash and introduces some special techniques, such as synchronizing sound with motion and dynamically loading music from the Web. Chapter 15 provides you with the ten best resources for Flash (besides this book, of course). Chapter 16 points you to the work of ten fabulous Flash Web designers.

Icons Used in This Book

Icons help point out special information. For example, sometimes they tell you that you don't care about this information and can skip over it without fear.

This icon flags new features in Flash CS4. If you have been using Flash CS3 or even an earlier version, you may want to skim through this book and look for this icon to help you quickly get up to speed in the new version.

Look for this icon to find all the goodies on the companion Web site, at www.dummies.com/go/flashcs4fd.

This icon alerts you to information that you need to keep in mind to avoid wasting time or falling on your face.

Flash has some advanced features you might want to know about — or skip entirely. This icon lets you know when we throw the heavier stuff at you.

Tips help you finish your work more easily, quickly, or effectively. Don't miss out on these.

Uh-oh! "Watch out here!" is what this icon is telling you. If you skip this icon, you never know what might happen.

Where to Go from Here

If you haven't already installed Flash, check out the complete instructions for installing Flash in on this book's companion Web site, www.dummies.com/go/flashcs4fd. Then open Flash, open this book, and plunge in.

Here's some of the cool stuff that you can find on the Adobe Flash CS4 For Dummies companion Web site:

- A library of geometric, fanciful, and artistic vector graphics ready to be instantly opened in any Flash movie.
- Flash movies that you can dissect.

Your own personal library of vector graphics

We've created more than 50 vector graphics that you can use in your Flash movies. Some are geometric shapes that are hard to create in Flash. We added fun shapes . . . some practical and others whimsical, such as our thought bubble and explosion. Finally, we included some art drawings of everyday objects. We hope you like them! (Please keep in mind that these files are provided for your personal use and are not to be sold or redistributed.)

To download the library of graphics, point your Web browser to www.dummies.com/go/flashcs4fd and click the download link to download the zip file for this book. When you unzip the file, you'll see a file named `Flash CS4 For Dummies Library.fla`. All that you see when you open this file in Flash is a blank screen. To see the graphics, choose Window⇨Library. To use these shapes in another Flash file, choose File⇨Import to Library and choose the file named `Flash CS4 For Dummies Library.fla` from the location where you saved it on your computer.

An even better idea is to copy the `.fla` file from wherever it is on your computer to the Libraries subfolder of your Flash CS4 folder. (In Windows, you find this at `Program Files\Adobe\Adobe Flash CS4\en\ Configuration\Libraries` on your hard drive. On the Mac, you find it in `Applications/Adobe Flash CS3/Configuration/Libraries` on your hard drive.) Then you can access this file at any time by choosing Window⇨Common Libraries.

Flash movies galore

Throughout this book, we refer you to the companion Web site to look at Flash movies as examples of the features we are explaining. These movies are organized by chapter. They help you understand some of the more complex capabilities of Flash that are hard to explain or show in a figure. Some of these movies are real-world Flash movies that come from active Web sites. Others are examples we created for you to isolate a Flash feature. Either way, we hope that you can use them to further your understanding of Flash.

To examine and use these movie files, you need to first download them to your hard drive. Point your Web browser to `www.dummies.com/go/flashcs4fd` and download the zipped file. When you unzip it, you can open the file you want. Here are a few troubleshooting tips to keep in mind when you use the Flash movie files provided on the Web site:

- **The Flash movie doesn't play.** Sometimes when you open a Flash movie, nothing happens when you try to play the animation. Choose Control⇨ Test Movie to see the animation.

- **The fonts look different.** If some of the fonts required by the Flash files aren't available on your system, you might see less-than-satisfactory substitutions when you play the Flash Player files. You might also see a message asking you to substitute fonts. You can click Default or choose any fonts you want.

We would love to hear your comments about this book. You can contact Gurdy Leete at `gleete@mum.edu` or Ellen Finkelstein at `ellen@ellen finkelstein.com`. Please note that we can't provide technical support on Flash. (If you need technical support, check out the resources we list in Chapter 15.)

Enough of all this talk. It's time to move into the real part of this book and start creating cool Flash movies! Enjoy!

Part I
A Blast of Flash

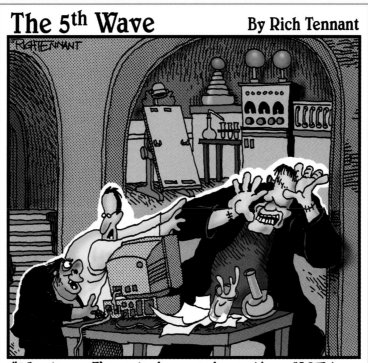

The 5th Wave   By Rich Tennant

"You know, I've asked you a dozen times NOT to animate the torches on our Web site."

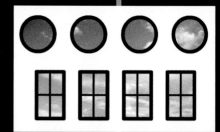

In this part . . .

*I*n this part, you discover what Flash can and can't do and start to make your way around the Flash world. In Chapter 1, we introduce you to Flash, show you what it looks like, and explain how to use its toolbars, menus, and panels. You find out about the Stage and the Timeline, two central Flash concepts. Play your way through your first animation to get firsthand experience in the power of Flash.

In Chapter 2, you get an overview of the entire process of creating a Flash animated movie, from developing your concept to publishing your movie in the format a browser can display. We explain how to set properties that affect your movie as a whole and how Flash works with various kinds of graphics. We close with the steps for printing your movie on paper. This part provides the foundation for future success.

Getting Acquainted with Flash CS4

*O*nce upon a time in a galaxy that seems far, far away by now, there was the Internet, which contained only plain, unformatted text. Then came the Web, and we gained text formatting and graphics. Then the Web grew up a little, and Web page graphics got fancier with things such as small animations in banner ads. But people, being used to movies and TV, wanted an even more animated and interactive Web experience. Along came Flash.

Flash, once from Macromedia but now from Adobe Systems, is the software that runs some of the coolest Web sites around. When you surf the Web and see sites that contain animation across the entire page or buttons that do spectacular stunts when you click them, you're probably seeing some Flash magic. If you create a Web site, you can use Flash to rev up the basics and actively respond to users' choices so that your viewers will say, "Wow!"

In this chapter, you find out what Flash is all about, what the Flash screen looks like, and how to use Help. Then you create your first, simple animation so that all the rest of this book makes sense.

Discovering Flash

Flash offers a powerful system for creating animation for the Web. In a nut-shell, here's an overview of how you use the system:

1. **Create a Flash movie by creating graphics and animating them over the duration of the movie.**

   Besides animated graphics, you can add navigational buttons, check boxes, and other user interface elements. You can add a few Flash components to a Web site or create an entire Web site.

2. **Use the Publish command in Flash to publish the movie into a Flash Player file that a browser can display.**

   At the same time, Flash creates the appropriate HyperText Markup Language (HTML) code that you need for your Web page.

3. **Insert HTML code into your HTML document that references the Flash Player file.**

   It's similar to adding a graphic to a Web page. Or you can use the HTML code alone as a new Web page for a fully Flashed page.

4. **Upload the new or edited HTML document and the Flash Player file to the location where you keep other files for your Web pages.**

5. **Open your browser, navigate to your Web page, and presto! — there's your cool animation, navigation, or other Flash element on your Web page.**

You need the Flash Player to see the effects that Flash creates. These days, the Flash Player comes installed with most computer systems and browsers, so most people can view Flash-driven Web sites immediately without any special download or preparation. When you display a Web site that contains Flash effects, your system uses the Flash Player to play the animation. Users who don't have a Flash Player can download it for free from Adobe at www.adobe.com/go/flashplayer.

Web sites are getting more and more sophisticated. By using animation, special effects, and interactive techniques, you can distinguish your Web site from the also-rans. Creating animation isn't hard, and you don't have to be a professional graphic artist, either. Anyone can create simple animations to enhance a Web site; it just takes a little time.

To find Web sites that have successfully used Flash, check out the Adobe site at www.adobe.com/products/flash/flashpro/productinfo/customers and look at some of the examples. Don't get discouraged by seeing some of the truly sophisticated results at these sites. You can start with a simple, animated site and go from there. (Chapter 16 lists ten great Flash designers and where you can find their work.)

Understanding What You Can Create with Flash CS4

You can use Flash CS4 to create simple animation to add to your Web page. Or you can create an entire Web page or site with Flash and incorporate text, graphics, interactive buttons, user interface components, and animation. You can even program applications in Flash.

This book helps you use Flash to create a simple or complex Web site. The following list describes some ways that you can manipulate text, graphics, and sound by using Flash CS4:

- **Create still or animated text on your Web page.** You can choose to stop the animation after a few seconds or repeat it while your viewers view the page.

- **Use Flash tools to create your own graphics for your Web page or to import graphics.** You can lay out an entire Web page graphically or add graphics to only a part of a Web page, as shown in Figure 1-1.

Thanks to the New York Philharmonic, www.nyphil.org, for permission to display its Web site.
Photo by Chris Lee

Figure 1-1: The New York Philharmonic Web site uses Flash to create an ever-changing display on its home page.

✔ **Animate graphics and make objects appear and disappear by using the transparency feature.** Objects can move, get bigger or smaller, or rotate. Flash also lets you *morph* — that is, transform — shapes into new shapes.

✔ **Fill shapes and text with *gradients*, which are colors that gradually change into new colors.** You can even fill shapes and text with bitmap images that you import into Flash. For example, you could fill the letters of your name with dozens of flowers. (You aren't a flower child any more?)

✔ **Create Web page buttons that not only lead your viewers wherever you want them to go but also change shape or color at the same time.** You can make buttons change when you pass your mouse over them. People who view your page can click a button to display a movie (animation) or start a small application.

✔ **Add sound or video to your movie.** It's easy to add sound effects in Flash. You can control how long the sound or music plays and whether it loops to play continuously. You can play video files as well.

✔ **Create menus that viewers can use to navigate your site.** You can create navigation tools as well as forms, check boxes, and other interface elements that look a lot more stylish than plain HTML ones.

As you can see, you can go far with Flash if you want. And why not? It's great fun!

Determining When Not to Use Flash CS4

If Flash CS4 is so wonderful, why doesn't every Web site designer use it? Why aren't most Web sites created completely with Flash?

Here's the other side of the story.

Although the vector graphics and animation of Flash load quickly, they don't load as quickly as plain text and simple graphics. Adding a movie to your Web page creates some overhead. There's no point in using Flash if you want simple pages consisting of mostly text and a few graphics that you want to stay put and not move.

You can create certain graphic effects more easily by using bitmap graphics. Painted brush stroke and textured effects are examples. Artists create these types of graphics by using graphics editing software, and the results are bitmaps. Similarly, to add photographs to your Web page, you need to scan the photographs as bitmaps. Flash creates *vector graphics* (defined mathematically), which are different from *bitmap graphics* (defined by lots of dots). However, you can import bitmap graphics into Flash. Find out more about bitmap and vector graphics in Chapter 2.

If you want simple animation, such as a few blinking dots or a marquee effect, animated *GIFs* (the animated bitmap graphics that you often see on the Web) might be smaller than Flash movies, so they load faster. You can create animated GIFs by using animated GIF editing software.

Some sites don't lend themselves to animation. Animation can distract from your content, and overdoing animation can make a serious site seem silly. Animation is great, but it has its place. Also, although Flash has some features that allow accessibility for people with disabilities, it still isn't as accessible as plain HTML. You need to determine whether animation is right for your Web site.

Getting the Right Start

Well begun is half done, as the saying goes. The easiest way to begin using Flash CS4 is with a shortcut or alias right on your desktop. Double-click the Flash icon, and you're on your way. (See this book's companion Web site for information on installing Flash.)

Starting Flash on a PC

Whether you installed Flash from the DVD or by downloading it from the Adobe Web site onto your PC, you might or might not have a shortcut on your desktop. To create one, choose Start➪All Programs➪Adobe Flash CS4. Right-click the Adobe Flash CS4 item and choose Create Shortcut from the pop-up menu that appears. The new shortcut appears on the menu. Drag that shortcut to your desktop.

To rename the shortcut, click the shortcut on your desktop. Then click the text beneath the icon. Type **Flash CS4** (or whatever you want) and press Enter. Just double-click the icon to open Flash.

Starting Flash on a Mac

You might find it handy to add the Flash CS4 icon to your Dock for easy launching. To do this, click the Finder icon on the extreme left of the Dock to bring up a new Finder window. Navigate in the Finder window to the Applications folder, and in the Applications folder, double-click the Adobe Flash CS4 folder to open it. Click and drag the Flash CS4 application icon to the Dock. A copy of the Flash CS4 application icon appears on the Dock.

Creating a new movie

Files that you create by using Flash are commonly called *movies.* When you start Flash, the startup screen appears (by default), as shown in Figure 1-2.

In the Create New section, click one of several options to immediately open a new movie file. These options let you create movies for various types of uses, such as mobile devices and further programming. For the purposes of this book, we assume that you want to create a general-use movie using the latest technology, which is the Flash File (ActionScript 3.0) option. (ActionScript 3.0 is the latest version of Flash's programming language.)

If you have already opened a movie and have the menus available, choose File⇨New. In the New Document dialog box, select Flash File (ActionScript 3.0) on the General tab and then click OK. You usually start by creating or importing some graphics. (To find out more about working with graphics, see Chapter 3.)

Opening an existing movie

If you want to work on a movie you've already created when you first open Flash, choose the movie in the Open a Recent Item section or click Open to find the file. If you've already opened a movie and have the menus available, press Ctrl+O (Windows) or ⌘+O (Mac) or choose File⇨Open; then double-click the movie to open it. The first frame appears on your screen, and you can edit the movie any way that you want.

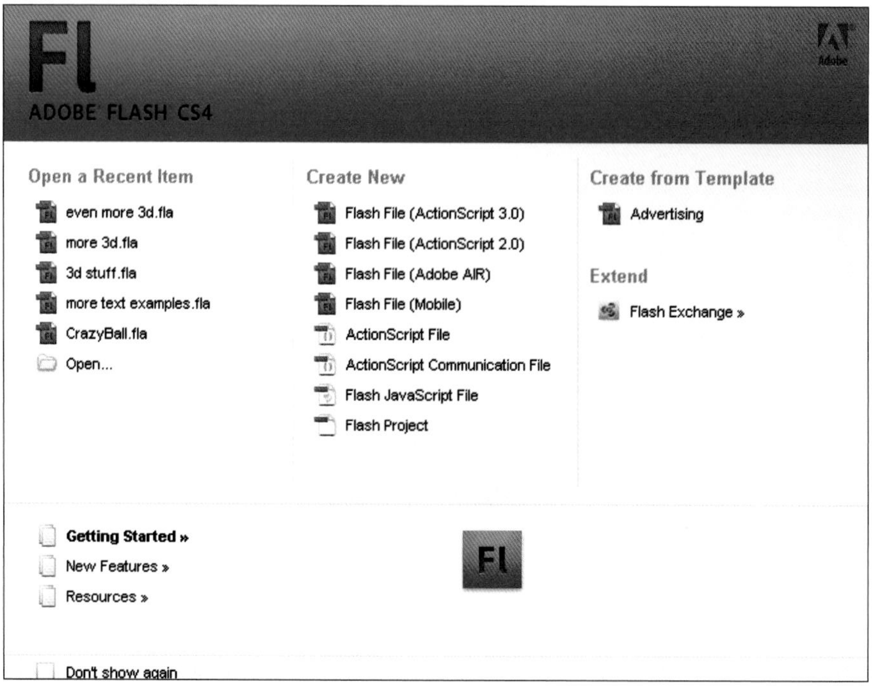

Figure 1-2: The Startup screen.

When you open more than one movie, you see a tab at the top for each movie. You can click the tabs to move from movie to movie. The tabs appear in the order you created or opened the movies.

Taking a Look Around

The Flash screen is different from screens in other programs that you might be used to, so take the time to get to know it. You can also customize the Flash screen. Figure 1-3 shows one possible display.

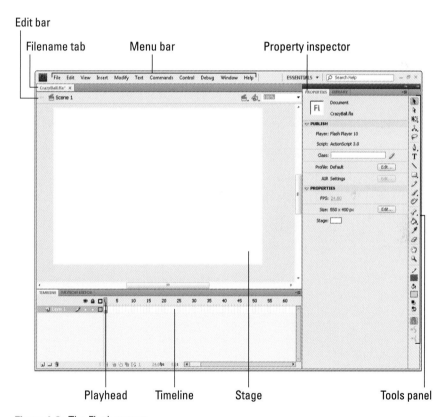

Figure 1-3: The Flash screen.

If your screen opens with several rectangular panels strewn about or docked on various sides, don't worry about them now. We explain how to open and use these panels throughout this book, but you don't need them for this chapter. If they drive you crazy, right-click (Windows) or Control+click (Mac) each panel's title bar and choose Close Group in the menu that appears.

Tooling around the toolbars

Flash contains two toolbars in the Mac version: the Edit bar and the Controller. In Windows, Flash also offers the Main toolbar. To display or hide these toolbars, choose Window⇨Toolbars and click the toolbar that you want to display or hide. Here is a description of the toolbars:

- **Main toolbar (Windows only):** Contains commonly used commands. Many of these are familiar from the Standard toolbar in other Windows programs. By default, Flash does *not* display the Main toolbar.

- **Controller:** Lets you control the playback of movies. For more information, see Chapter 9.

- **Edit bar:** Helps you work with the symbols, scenes, and the user interface. The bar, shown in Figure 1-4, appears below the menu. It includes a button to access symbols (which we cover in Part III), a button for editing scenes, a drop-down list to manage workspaces, and a zoom control. We discuss the workspaces and the Timeline later in the chapter, in the "Following a timeline" section. For detailed information about the Timeline and scenes, see Chapter 9.

Figure 1-4: The Edit bar.

Using panels

Panels give you access to the many Flash tools and settings. You access the panels from the Window menu. We discuss the specific panels throughout this book. In this section, we explain how to keep control over your panels.

Most panels are *dockable,* which means they can sit at the side or bottom of your Flash window without covering up your work and they fit together in a group with other panels. You can also stack undocked panels on top of each other. You control panels by doing the following:

- **Dock a panel.** Drag it by its title bar to the side or bottom of your screen. When you see a blue bar highlight, release the mouse button.

- **Undock a panel.** Drag it by its title bar.

- **Open or close a panel.** Choose it from the Window menu.

- **Close an undocked panel.** Click its Close button.

✔ **Close a docked panel.** Right-click (Windows) or Control+click (Mac) its title bar and choose Close Panel.

 ✔ **Collapse a group of panels to icons.** Click the double right arrow at the top of the group of docked panels.

You can also stack panels. Drag a panel (by its title bar) to another panel to stack it below the first one. You can also collapse or expand panels: A *collapsed* panel displays only its title bar, so it doesn't take up much space. Just click its title bar. Repeat the process to expand the panel again.

The Tools panel contains all the tools you need to draw and edit objects. At the bottom of the Tools panel are options that modify how the tools function. (See Chapters 3 and 4 for a complete description of the Tools panel.)

The Property inspector, shown in Figure 1-5, is another important panel. This panel displays information about selected objects, such as size, name, and location. You can modify objects in the Property inspector as well. It is *context sensitive,* which means that its contents change according to what you're doing. For example, if you select a graphic object, the Property inspector provides settings relating to that object, and you can use the Property inspector to edit that object.

 By default, the Property inspector is grouped with the Library (which we explain in Chapter 2) and the Tools panel.

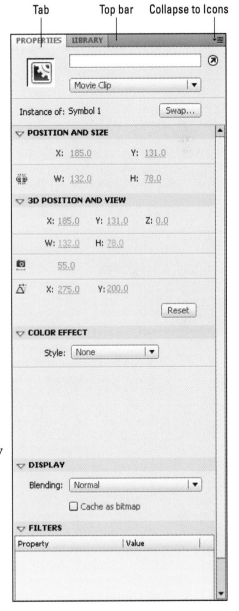

Figure 1-5: The Property inspector.

The Property inspector has several controls for changing its configuration:

- ✓ **Tab:** Double-click the tab to switch between collapsing the Property inspector completely (you see just the tab) and displaying its previous state.

- ✓ **Collapse to Icons button:** Click the small double arrows at the top of the Property inspector to switch between an icon and the open state.

- ✓ **Title bar:** Click the gray bar at the top to minimize or maximize the Property inspector. In the default configuration, the top bar also applies to the Library and the Tools panel.

Discovering the Flash menus

Most drawing functions are available only in the Tools panel. You often use the Timeline for creating animation, as we discuss in the "Following a time-line" section, later in this chapter. Almost every other function in Flash is on a menu somewhere. You just need to find it. In general, we discuss the specific menu functions where appropriate throughout this book. Table 1-1 offers an overview of the menus.

Table 1-1	Flash Menus
Menu	*What It Does*
Flash	(Mac only) Enables you to set preferences, create keyboard short-cuts, and quit Flash.
File	Enables you to open and close files, save files, import and export files, print, publish movies for the Web, send a movie via e-mail, and quit Flash.
Edit	Provides commands that let you undo and redo actions; cut, copy, and paste to and from the Clipboard; delete, duplicate, select, and deselect objects; find and replace; copy and paste entire frames and motions on the Timeline; edit symbols (see Chapter 7 for the story on symbols); set preferences (Windows only); customize the Tools panel; map fonts; and create keyboard shortcuts for commands (Windows only).
View	Helps you get a better view by letting you zoom in and out; show or hide the ruler, grid, and guides; choose a preview mode; and specify snapping preferences for objects for easy placement.
Insert	Enables you to insert symbols (Chapter 7 explains this topic); insert and delete Timeline features, such as frames and keyframes (see Chapter 9 for more); insert layers (check out Chapter 6); and add scenes (see Chapter 9).

Menu	*What It Does*
Modify	Helps you modify symbols, bitmaps, shapes, frames, Timeline features and effects, scenes, or the entire movie (called the *document)*. Offers tools for transforming, aligning, grouping, and ungrouping objects, arranging objects, and breaking objects apart.
Text	Enables you to format text and check spelling.
Commands	Enables you to reuse and manage saved commands. A *command* is any action that you take in Flash, such as drawing or editing an object. You can save commands from the History panel. (See Chapter 4.)
Control	Provides options that let you control the playing of movies, test movies and scenes, engage certain interactive functions, and mute sounds.
Debug	Provides tools for debugging ActionScript code. (See Chapter 10 for more on ActionScript.)
Window	Enables you to open lots of things, including a duplicate window, panels that help you control objects, the Library (more on the Library in Chapter 2), windows for creating interactive controls (which we explain in Chapter 10), workspaces, and the Movie Explorer (to help manage your movie — see Chapter 12).
Help	Comes to the rescue when you need help. You can find a wide variety of resources, including Adobe online forums.

Many menu commands offer keyboard shortcuts. You can also create your own keyboard shortcuts. (See this book's companion Web site for instructions.) The shortcuts are displayed on the menus, next to the command name. Here are some of the most commonly used keyboard shortcuts. (For more shortcuts, see the tear-out Cheat Sheet at the front of this book.)

- **Ctrl+N (Windows) or ⌘+N (Mac):** Open the New Document dialog box so you can start a new movie.

- **Ctrl+O (Windows) or ⌘+O (Mac):** Open an existing movie.

- **Ctrl+S (Windows) or ⌘+S (Mac):** Save your movie. Use this shortcut often!

- **Ctrl+X (Windows) or ⌘+X (Mac):** Cut to the Clipboard. Chapter 4 explains more about using the Clipboard.

- **Ctrl+C (Windows) or ⌘+C (Mac):** Copy to the Clipboard.

- **Ctrl+V (Windows) or ⌘+V (Mac):** Paste from the Clipboard.

✔ **Ctrl+Z (Windows) or ⌘+Z (Mac):** Undo. Would you believe that by default Flash remembers your last 100 actions and can undo them? What a relief! And if you choose Window➪Other Panels➪History, the History panel lists each action so you know what the next Undo will undo. Think of it as a journey into the long-forgotten past. (See Chapter 4 for more on the History panel, and see this book's companion Web site for details on customizing the number of Undos that Flash remembers.)

✔ **Ctrl+Y (Windows) or ⌘+Y (Mac):** Redo. This redoes actions that you undid by using the Undo button. (Got that?) This button remembers just as many actions as the Undo button. If you undo more actions than you want, click Redo (or press Ctrl+Y or ⌘+Y) until you're back where you want to be. Using the Undo and Redo buttons is like traveling through Flash time — and it gives you lots of slack while you're working.

✔ **Ctrl+Q (Windows) or ⌘+Q (Mac):** Exit Flash.

We mention other keyboard shortcuts throughout this book when we discuss their corresponding commands.

You should note, although it's not a shortcut, that you can find the Zoom Control box in the upper-right corner of the Stage — when the Edit bar is open. (Choose Window➪Toolbars➪Edit Bar if necessary.) Click the arrow and choose a zoom factor to zoom in and out. Zooming doesn't change the actual size of objects — it just makes them look bigger or smaller.

You aren't limited to the choices on the Zoom drop-down list. Type a number in the Zoom Control box and press Enter (Windows) or Return (Mac) to set your own zoom factor. For example, type **85** to set the zoom factor to 85 percent.

Customizing the workspace

For the best in customization, you can save any layout of panels you like. Set up the panels and choose Window➪Workspace➪New Workspace. In the New Workspace dialog box that opens, shown in Figure 1-6, give the layout a name and click OK. To restore that layout at any time, choose Window➪Workspace and choose your very own layout. Choose Window➪Workspace➪Manage Workspaces if you need to rename or delete a workspace.

You can access the same workspace features on the right side of the Menu bar. It's easy to choose a new workspace by just clicking the Workspace drop-down list.

Figure 1-6: Make your very own workspace.

Staging your movies

The white box in the center of your screen is the *Stage.* Think of the Stage as a movie screen where you place objects. You can place graphics and text there and then animate them. Flash also plays back movies on the Stage.

Around the edge of the Stage is a gray area called the *Pasteboard.* You can use the Pasteboard to store graphics that you plan to use soon but don't want on the Stage just yet. (For more permanent storage, use the Library, as we explain in Chapter 2.) You can also store data and other nongraphical content on the Pasteboard. Content that you put on the Pasteboard doesn't appear in your Flash movie.

Following a timeline

The Timeline window divides your movie into *frames.* Each frame represents a tiny stretch of time, such as f ¼ of a second. Creating a movie is simply a matter of assembling frames, which are then quickly played in order.

Chapter 9 explains in detail how to make using the Timeline completely painless. For now, you should just understand the essentials. See Figure 1-7 for the basic Timeline.

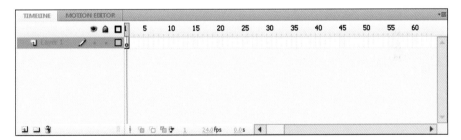

Figure 1-7: The Timeline is your key to managing animation.

On the left side of the Timeline is the layer list. When you open a new movie, you see only one layer, unimaginatively named Layer 1. A *layer* is like a sheet of transparent acetate on which you draw objects. Layers help you keep objects from running into each other, causing unfortunate, messy results. You organize your entire movie by using layers. For example, if you want to keep some text constant throughout the movie but animate a bouncing dot, you would give the dot its own layer and animate it on that layer. The layer list has room for more layers, and you can add as many layers as you want. (Chapter 6 gives you the lowdown on layers.)

You can drag the upper edge of the Timeline to make room for more layers. Hover the mouse cursor over the top of the Timeline's gray title bar until you see the two-headed arrow and drag upward.

To the right of Layer 1, you see a bunch of rectangles, each representing a frame. (Actually, before you start using the Timeline, they're just potential frames, like unexposed frames on a roll of film.) By default, each frame lasts ¹/₂₄ of a second. Each layer has its own row of frames because you can have different animations or objects on each layer.

A *keyframe* is a frame that defines some change in your animation. In some animations, every frame is a keyframe. Other animations need keyframes for only the first and last frames.

The *playhead* indicates the current frame in the animation and consists of a red rectangle as well as a vertical hairline that crosses a frame on all of the layers. Before you create any animation, the playhead is always on Frame 1.

You don't use the Timeline until you're ready to animate. While you work, however, you should organize your objects on separate layers. Don't worry — you can always move an object from one layer to another.

Next to the Timeline's tab is the Motion Editor's tab. We discuss the Motion Editor in Chapter 9. For now, it's good to know that the Motion Editor gives you detailed control over your animations.

Getting Help in a Flash

This book is all that you need to start creating great animations, but we would be remiss if we didn't tell you about the Flash Help system. To use Flash Help, choose Help➪Flash Help.

Help's multiple manuals

Flash Help contains several sections:

- ✐ **Using Flash** is the main Help manual.

- ✐ **ActionScript 3.0 and Components** is a manual on the latest version of ActionScript, Flash's programming language. (See Chapter 10 to find out more.)

   You don't need to program Flash to use it, if you are interested only in graphics and animation.

- ✐ **ActionScript 2.0 and Components** is a user's guide for ActionScript 2.0, Flash's previous programming language. You can still use this language.

- ✔ **Adobe AIR** explains how to use Flash CS4 to create desktop applications.

- ✔ **Flash Lite** explains how to create Flash movies for mobile devices.

- ✔ **Extending Flash** describes how to use JavaScript to create scripts to help automate your work.

To search for a term, click the Search button. Then type the term and click Search. You can then choose from the list of topics.

Finding more help on the Web

Adobe offers support on its Web site. Choose Help➪Flash Support Center, which takes you to www.adobe.com/support/flash. There you can search the knowledge base and tutorials for answers to your questions.

Try It; You'll Like It

Perhaps by now you're getting impatient to try out Flash. Getting started is easy. You collect a few ideas, put together some art, add animation, save your movie, and publish it. Then you view it in a browser either online or offline. That's the gratifying part. In the following sections, you get to try out Flash by working through a basic animation. The rest of the book explains these concepts in more detail.

Conceiving your first animation

Suppose that you want to add an animated logo to a home page that you've already set up. You want the animation to run when the page loads and then stop. Figure 1-8 shows the Rainbow Resources company logo — unanimated, of course — that you can find on this book's Web site, at www.dummies.com/go/flashcs4fd.

Figure 1-8: A company logo that could stand some animation.

Suppose that you want the word *Rainbow* to fly into your page from the right and the word *Resources* to fly in from the left. At the same time, you want the graphic to rotate 180 degrees. The following section shows you how to create this animation.

Creating flashy drawings

You can use Flash to create a company logo, but importing one from this book's Web site is simpler. Often, you import existing graphics (such as a company logo) from a file rather than create them from scratch. (Chapter 3 explains how to import and manipulate graphics.)

If you're going through the steps and make a mistake, choose Edit⇨Undo (or press Ctrl+Z or ⌘+Z) and try again. You can use Undo repeatedly to undo several steps, if necessary.

To import the Rainbow Resources logo into Flash, follow these steps. (The steps might vary if you're importing some other graphic in a different format.)

1. **Start Flash.**

    See the instructions in the section "Starting Flash on a PC" or "Starting Flash on a Mac," earlier in this chapter, if you need help.

2. **In the Create New section of the Startup screen, choose Flash File (ActionScript 3.0).**

    You see a spanking-new movie on your screen.

3. **Go to www.dummies.com/go/flashcs4fd and download the Bonus Content, which contains the rainbow.gif image file.**

    You'll need to unzip the file and extract the image file. Extract this image file to the location where you plan to save your Flash movie.

4. **Choose File⇨Import⇨Import to Stage.**

    The Import dialog box opens.

5. **Browse the dialog box until you find rainbow.gif in the location where you saved it, and then double-click the file to open it.**

    You see the logo on your screen. You need to break the logo into pieces and make it a vector graphic so that you can animate sections of it separately.

6. **Choose Modify⇨Bitmap⇨Trace Bitmap.**

    The Trace Bitmap dialog box appears.

7. **In the Trace Bitmap dialog box, set the color threshold to 100, the minimum area to 1, the curve fit to Pixels, and the corner threshold to Many Corners. Click OK.**

    In our example, we chose to use settings that reproduce the bitmap as faithfully as possible. Flash creates a vector graphic and breaks up the graphic into individual components. The entire graphic, however, is selected.

8. **Click anywhere outside the graphic to deselect it.**

You've got your logo! Now you need to set it up for animation.

Turning your objects into symbols

In the logo that you imported in the preceding section, each letter is a separate object, which can get pretty confusing. Each line in the logo's design is also separate. But you want your words — and the little design — to stay together. So you must combine each word and the logo into a symbol. A _symbol_ helps keep objects together and is required for some kinds of animation. (See Chapter 7 for the scoop on symbols.)

To turn the words and the logo into symbols, follow these steps:

1. **To get a better view of your image, click the Zoom Control drop-down list (at the upper-right corner of the Stage area) and choose 200%.**

   If you don't see the Zoom Control drop-down list, choose Window➪Toolbars➪Edit Bar to display it.

   Use the scroll bar to scroll the words of the logo into view, if necessary.

2. **Click the Selection tool on the Tools panel if it's not already selected.**

3. **Click the upper-right corner of the word _Rainbow_ (just above and to the right of the _w_) and drag to the lower-left corner of the first letter, _R._**

   Dragging from right to left makes it easier to avoid selecting the logo at the same time. The entire word should be selected. If it isn't, click outside the word and try again. Your screen should look like Figure 1-9.

4. **Choose Modify➪Convert to Symbol.**

5. **In the Convert to Symbol dialog box, choose Graphic from the Type drop-down list, enter Rainbow in the Name text box, and then click OK.**

   Figure 1-9: Selecting some text to prepare it for animation.

   When you click OK, Flash places a box around the word so you can see that it's one object.

6. **Repeat the procedure outlined in Steps 3 through 5 with the word _Resources._**

   In this case, you might want to start clicking and dragging from the upper-left area of the word; then choose Modify➪Convert to Symbol again, enter **Resources** in the Name text box, and click OK. Now all the letters of the word _Resources_ are a single object.

7. **Click above and to the left of the logo and drag to the lower right to select the entire logo.**

8. **Hold down the Shift key and click each word to remove both words from the selection.**

   Now the design portion of the logo is selected.

9. **Choose Modify➪Convert to Symbol.**

   The Convert to Symbol dialog box opens.

10. **Enter Lines in the Name text box, and then click OK in the Convert to Symbol dialog box.**

   Flash creates a symbol from the lines of the logo's design.

See Chapter 7 to find out more about what symbols are and how to use them. Symbols are important building blocks in Flash movies.

Putting your graphics on layers

You need to place different pieces on different layers when you're animating. You use layers to organize your movie and keep shapes separate so that they don't interfere with each other. (See Chapter 6 for the complete story on layers.)

To split your three symbols onto three separate layers, you can use a convenient feature of Flash CS4: Distribute to Layers. Follow these steps:

1. **Click the Selection tool on the Tools panel if it's not already selected.**

2. **Drag diagonally across the entire logo, including the two words, to select it.**

   You should see two rectangles inside one bigger rectangle. All three objects in the logo are selected.

3. **Choose Modify➪Timeline➪ Distribute to Layers.**

   You now have three new layers, named Rainbow, Resources, and Lines. The three objects of the logo have been distributed to the three new layers and removed from Layer 1. Your layer list should look like Figure 1-10.

4. **Click the Zoom Control drop-down list (at the upper-right corner of the Stage area) and choose 100%.**

5. **Click outside the Stage to deselect any objects.**

Figure 1-10: In addition to the original Layer 1, you now have three new layers.

6. **To save the file, choose File⇨Save and choose the same location you used for the** `rainbow.gif` **image file.**

   We don't recommend saving the file in the Flash CS4 program folder — it might get lost among your Flash program files.

7. **Give your movie a name, such as *Movie of the Year,* and click Save.**

   Flash creates a file named `Movie of the Year.fla`. Flash adds `.fla` for you because that's the filename extension for Flash movies.

You're now ready for the animation process.

Making graphics move

We explain earlier in this chapter that your goal is to have the word *Rainbow* fly in from the right and the word *Resources* fly in from the left. You also want the graphic to rotate 180 degrees at the same time. What you see now is how the animation should end — the last frame of the movie.

Now go back and create the beginning of your movie. Flash can fill in all the blanks in between. This type of animation is called a *motion tween.* Follow these steps to create the animation:

1. **Right-click (Windows) or Control+click (Mac) the word *Rainbow* and choose Create Motion Tween.**

   Oops! The other two symbols disappear! That's OK. Flash created the motion tween and automatically set the length of the animation to 24 frames, or one second. The playhead is now on Frame 24, but the other two symbols don't exist at the 24th frame yet. Note that the Rainbow row in the Timeline turns blue to indicate that it has a motion tween.

2. **Click Frame 1 on the Timeline.**

   You can click Frame 1 on any layer. Whew! The other two symbols reappear.

3. **Repeat Steps 1 and 2 for the word *Resources* and for the lines.**

   Your Timeline should now look like Figure 1-11. Be sure to click Frame 1 to place the playhead on that frame.

4. **To move the Rainbow symbol to its proper location for Frame 1, press and hold down the Shift key while you drag the word *Rainbow* to the right, just off the Stage into the gray area.**

   You might need to use the horizontal scroll bar or choose a lower zoom percentage in the Zoom drop-down list to see the gray area. Pressing Shift keeps the object from moving up or down while you drag to the right. By clicking the first frame and moving the word, you set its position at the beginning of the animation.

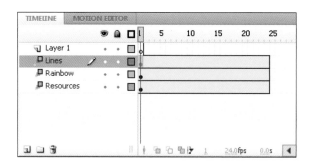

Figure 1-11: The Timeline indicates three motion tweens, each lasting 24 frames.

5. To move the Rainbow symbol to its proper location for Frame 24 (the end of the motion tween animation), click Frame 24 in the Rainbow layer. Then press the Shift key and drag the Rainbow symbol back to its original position.

You now see a dot in Frame 24 on the Rainbow layer. On the Stage, you see a red line indicating the movement of the Rainbow symbol. The motion tween is now complete.

6. Click Frame 1 on the Resources layer.

The playhead is now on Frame 1, and the Resources symbol has a blue selection border.

7. Press the Shift key and drag the Resources symbol to the left just off the Stage.

8. Click in Frame 24 on the Resources layer, press the Shift key, and drag the Resources symbol back to its original location.

You now see a dot in Frame 24 on the Resources layer and a red, horizontal line on the Stage showing the motion of the Resources symbol. The motion tween is now complete.

9. To return to Frame 1 and select the Lines symbol, click in Frame 1 of the Lines layer.

10. Choose Modify⇨Transform⇨Rotate 90° CW to rotate the design 90 degrees clockwise.

11. Repeat the Modify⇨Transform⇨Rotate 90° CW command to rotate the design a total of 180 degrees.

This sets up the desired position of the Lines symbol at Frame 1.

12. Click Frame 24 of the Lines layer.

13. Again choose Modify⇨Transform⇨Rotate 90° CW twice to rotate the Lines symbol a total of 180 degrees.

    Because you only rotated the Lines symbol, but didn't move it, you don't see a red line on the Stage.

14. **If necessary, drag the horizontal scroll box until the Stage is in the center of your screen.** Otherwise, you won't be able to see the entire animation — and you don't want to miss this one!

15. **Click the first frame of any layer.**

    This takes you to the start of your movie. Your screen should look like the one shown in Figure 1-12.

16. **Press Enter (Return) and watch the animation. (Start writing your Academy Award acceptance speech.)**

17. **Save your movie again by choosing File⇨Save.**

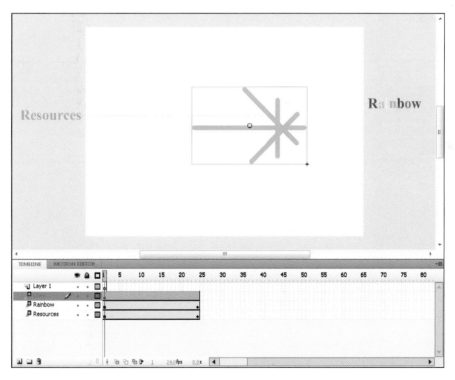

Figure 1-12: Before you run the animation, *Rainbow* appears to the right and *Resources* to the left, and the Lines symbol is rotated.

Publishing your first animation for posterity

You can't watch the animation in a Web browser until you publish your movie and insert it into an HTML document. To do so, follow these steps:

1. **Click an empty area of the Stage to change the display of the Property inspector.**

   If the Property inspector isn't open, choose Window⇨Properties. You may need to click the Property inspector's label to expand it or bring it to the forefront. You should see the Edit button in the Publish section.

2. **Click the Edit button in the Property inspector.**

   The Publish Settings dialog box opens. (We cover publish settings in detail in Chapter 13.)

3. **Click the HTML tab.**

4. **Deselect the Loop check box in the Playback section.**

   We want the animation to play only once.

5. **Click the Publish button, and then click OK to close the dialog box.**

   With scarcely a blip, Flash publishes your movie and creates two files, named `Movie of the Year.swf` (assuming you used that name) and `Movie of the Year.html`. They're in the same folder as your `.fla` movie file. `Movie of the Year.swf` is the file your browser reads to play the animation. `Movie of the Year.html` contains the HTML code required to display your movie on a Web page.

6. **Open your Web browser.**

7. **Choose File⇨Open (or Open File) and find `Movie of the Year.html` (or whatever you named your movie file).**

   You might need to click Browse and navigate to the file.

8. **Double-click the file.**

   Your browser opens the HTML document and reads its instructions to play the Flash movie.

9. **Sit back and watch it roll.**

   Don't blink or you'll miss it. (If you do miss it, click the Refresh or Reload Current Page button in your browser.) You can see the movie in Figure 1-13.

10. **When you finish watching the movie, close your browser.**

You can find the Movie of the Year files (`.fla`, `.html`, and `.swf`) on this book's Web site, `www.dummies.com/go/flashcs4fd`.

Exiting Flash

When you finish creating something in Flash, choose File⇨Exit (Windows) or Flash⇨Quit (Mac).

Figure 1-13: The Movie of the Year animation in detail.

2

Your Basic Flash

*T*his chapter starts with an overview of the process of creating animation in Flash. We then discuss some tools and features that are fundamental to using Flash efficiently.

As you find out in this chapter, you can set the screen size and color, frame rate, and measurement units for the Flash movie as a whole. We also discuss the Library and how it's a storehouse for images, symbols, and sound. Templates enable you to create great movies without much work. Finally, near the end of this chapter, we explain how you can print a Flash movie.

Looking at the Big Picture

When you use Flash to create animation for your Web site, you generally go through several steps of construction. The steps might vary in their order, depending on your situation. After you know the basics, you can start getting creative and make your Web site rock. Here's a typical path to add animation to an existing Web page:

1. **Think about it.** Noodle around, maybe make some doodles on a napkin, collect a few ideas, and choose one or all of them.

2. **Set up your movie.** Flash lets you choose the size and color of the Stage, the speed of animation (number of frames per second), and other general parameters that affect the entire Flash movie. See the next section of this chapter for details.

3. **Add some graphics.** You have to decide whether you want to create graphics in Flash, create them in another graphics software package, or import existing graphics. Your choice partly depends on how artistic you are, whether you have other software available to you, and whether you can find the right graphics elsewhere. You can also use a combination of sources, which is a common practice. (See Chapter 3 for some suggestions on great places to get graphics.)

4. **Lay out your graphics the way you want your animation to start.** Here's where you might want to scale, rotate, or otherwise fiddle with your graphics. (Chapter 4 has more on transforming your graphics.)

5. **Add some text.** Using Flash is a great way to get terrific text onto your Web site. Add text (also called *type*); then reshape it, make it transparent (if you don't want to be too obvious), add other effects, and move it where you want it. (Check out Chapter 5 for typography tips.)

6. **Organize your text and graphics by using layers.** Layers help you keep track of what each graphic and text object does while you organize everything into a powerful, coherent statement. Layers keep your animations from going bump in the night and getting entangled. After you have some objects, create as many layers as you need and transfer your existing graphics and text to those layers. Or create the layers first and then add your graphics and text on those layers. (See Chapter 6 for further details on layers.)

7. **Turn a graphic into a symbol and multiply it all over the Stage.** Converting objects into symbols is a way to keep them from merging with other objects. You also use symbols to keep the file size down, to enable animation, and for interactivity. (Turn to Chapter 7 for more info on symbols.)

8. **Design some buttons.** You know those buttons you click on Web sites all the time? The coolest ones are made in Flash. You can even create animated buttons. (Chapter 8 has more on buttons.)

9. **Animate!** You can create your animation frame by frame or let Flash fill in the animation between your first and last frames, which is called *tweening.* Flash can tween motion, shapes, colors, and transparency, which means that you can create some real magic. (See Chapter 9 for more on animation and the section in Chapter 1 where we step you through your first animation.)

10. **Get interactive.** You want to start a relationship with your Web viewers, so you can create buttons, frames, and symbols that respond to your viewers' actions. This is probably the most complex functionality of Flash, but we make most of it seem easy. (Turn to Chapter 10 for additional info on interactivity.)

11. **Make it louder! Make it move!** Who wants a quiet Web site? Add sound to your movies or your buttons. You can also add video. (Check out Chapter 11 for more on sound and video.)

12. **Publish your magnum opus.** Flash makes getting your movie to your Web site easy by creating both the Flash Player (`.swf`) file and the HyperText Markup Language (HTML) code for your Web page. Flash has other options, too, so you can publish to other formats if you want. (Chapter 12 explains how to put all the elements together, and Chapter 13 shows you how to publish your animation.)

Congratulations! You've completed your first Flash Web animation — in fantasy, at least. The following sections cover some details about how to get started.

Setting the Stage

Before you create graphics and animate them — all that fun stuff — you need to make some decisions about the structure of your entire movie. You should make these decisions before you start because changing midway can create problems.

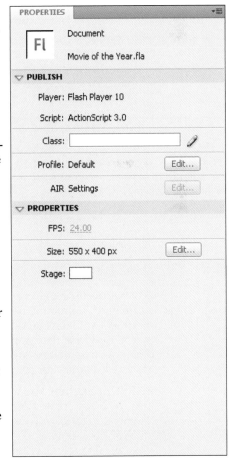

The first step is to decide on the size and color of your Stage and other fundamental settings. Make sure that the Property inspector is open. (Choose Window⇨Properties.) When the Stage is active (just click the Stage), the Property inspector looks like Figure 2-1.

Choosing the Stage color

You can set the color of the Stage to create a colored background for your entire movie. As with other settings, you need to consider the context of the Web page that will contain the Flash movie. For example, you might want to match the color of your Web page's background. If your Flash movie will constitute the entire Web page, set the Stage color to the color you want for the Web page background.

Figure 2-1: You can change movie properties in the Property inspector.

To set the Stage color, click the Stage swatch in the Property inspector. Flash opens the Color palette. Click the color you want.

Specifying the frame rate

Next to the FPS (frames per second) label, click the current value, specify how many frames you want the Flash movie to play each second, and then press Enter (Windows) or Return (Mac). A faster rate allows for smoother animation but might present a performance problem on slower computers. Chapter 9 explains more about this setting. The Flash default is 24 fps, which is a good starting point. Beware that changing the frame rate midstream in the creation process changes the rate of all the animation in your movie, which might not give you the results you want.

Setting the Stage size

The Size label displays the current size of the Stage. By default, Flash uses a Stage size of 550 pixels wide by 400 pixels high. To determine the proper setting, you need to know how your Flash movie will fit into your Web page or site. The default fits on almost everyone's browser screen. However, you might want to fit your movie into a small corner of a Web page — for example, into an animated logo in a top corner of a page. In that case, make the Stage smaller.

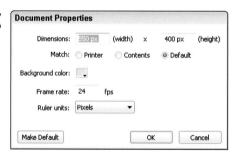

To change the Stage size, click the Edit button in the Properties section to open the Document Properties dialog box, as shown in Figure 2-2. Type the dimensions that you want in the Width and Height text boxes.

Figure 2-2: The Document Properties dialog box sets the movie's overall parameters.

Flash offers two shortcuts for setting the Stage size in the Document Properties dialog box:

- **Match Printer:** Click this option to set the Stage size according to the paper size set in the Page Setup dialog box. (Choose File⇨Page Setup.) For the Mac, the Print Margins dialog box (access by choosing File⇨Print Margins) also affects the paper size. Flash sets the size of the Stage to the maximum possible area of the paper minus the margins. Later in this chapter, in the section "Printing Your Movie," we cover this dialog box in more detail.

> ✔ **Match Contents:** Click this option to set the Stage size to the contents of the Stage. Of course, for this to work, you need some objects on the Stage. Flash creates a Stage size by placing equal space around all sides of the entire contents of the Stage. If you want to create the smallest possible Stage, place your objects in the upper-left corner and then click Match Contents.

To change the units used for measuring the screen and objects, choose a unit in the Ruler Units drop-down list.

Click the Make Default button to make your settings the default for all your new Flash movies. When you've finished setting document properties, click OK to close the dialog box.

Adding Metadata

You can add metadata to your movies. *Metadata* — the information embedded in the movie provides a way to include useful tags for your collaborators.

Flash uses Adobe's eXtensible Metadata Platform (XMP), which enables you to embed the metadata into the file. Programmers can write software that accesses the data to help keep track of workflow, manage rights, and more.

To add metadata, choose File⇨File Info. The dialog box that opens has the name of your movie in its title bar. You can use the various tabs to insert tags and descriptions relating to your movie file. For example, on the Description tab, you can include title, author, and description content. You can even click the stars to give your movie a rating from one to five stars. You can choose whether you want to include your metadata when you publish your movie. For more information, see the section on publishing to SWF in Chapter 13.

Grabbing a Graphic

The next step when creating animation for your Web site is usually to create or import graphics. Before you do that, however, you should know a little about the different kinds of graphics you can use in a Flash movie.

Understanding vectors and bitmaps

If you know enough about graphics to understand the difference between bitmap and vector graphics, feel free to skip this section. (We hope you always feel free.)

Bitmaps are created with lots of dots. Put them all together, and you get a picture. On-screen, they're displayed as *pixels.* As you can imagine, it can take a large file to store the information about all the dots in a bitmap. Another problem with bitmaps is that they don't scale up well. If you try to enlarge a bitmap, it starts to look grainy because you see all those dots (as in the right example shown in Figure 2-3).

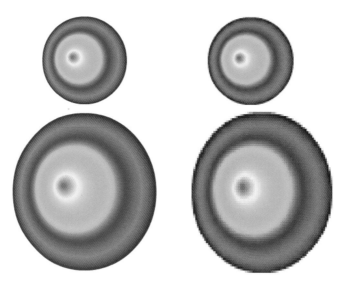

Figure 2-3: Vector graphics remain sharp and clear (left); bitmaps lose focus when enlarged (right).

Vector graphics are defined with equations that specify lines, shapes, and locations. Blank space doesn't have to be recorded, and the equations are particularly efficient at storing information. As a result, file sizes are usually smaller than bitmap file sizes.

Vector graphics are infinitely scalable, either up or down. No matter how big you make your graphic, it always looks perfect, as shown in the left example in Figure 2-3. In fact, your graphic might even look better when it's larger because the curves are smoother.

Flash creates vector-based graphics. The small size of the files means that Flash Player files load and play super-fast on a Web page. As you undoubtedly know, fast file loading means that your Web page viewers don't have to wait a long time to see your effects. That's the advantage of Flash. Nevertheless, you can create great graphics with bitmaps that you can't duplicate with vector graphics; we explain how to import bitmaps in Chapter 3.

Finding graphics

Okay, so you noodled and doodled and played around with some ideas for your Flash animation and perhaps jotted down a few notes or maybe even made a few sketches. You're ready to start building your Flash animation. A logical place to start is to collect some of the graphics that will serve as building blocks in this process.

Where do you get them? You have several choices:

- Create your graphics from scratch (if you feel artistic) by using the Flash drawing tools that we describe in detail in Chapter 3.

- Create graphics in another graphics software package, such as Fireworks, FreeHand, Photoshop, or Illustrator.

- Import graphics from archives of art available on this book's Web site, from other places on the Web, or from digital (or scanned) photographs — perhaps your own.

- Combine any or all of these approaches.

You can also import video files. If you want to add video to your Flash movies, see Chapter 11 for detailed instructions.

Going to the Library

Every graphic that you create in Flash is precious and deserves to be archived in style. Each movie file that you create has a Library. The Library saves the following types of objects so that they never get lost:

- Graphic, movie clip, and button symbols

- Sounds

- Imported bitmap graphics (but not vector graphics that you create in Flash)

- Imported video files

You'll find yourself going to the Library often. Figure 2-4 shows a Library containing symbols, video, a sound, and a bitmap.

To go to the Library of the current movie file, choose Window⇨Library. You can also press Ctrl+L (Windows) or ⌘+L (Mac). When you open the Library, Flash creates a new window or adds the Library panel to the set of panels that are already open.

Collapse to Icons

Pin Library panel | Options menu

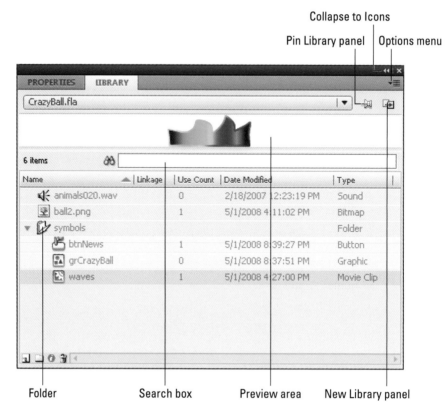

Folder   Search box   Preview area   New Library panel

Figure 2-4: You can store graphics, animation, buttons, sounds, and video files in your current movie file's Library.

To use any object in the Library, follow these steps:

1. **Select the layer on which you want to put the object or create a new layer for the object.**

2. **Click the point on the Timeline where you want the object to start or appear.**

   The point that you click on the Timeline must be a keyframe. Chapter 9 explains keyframes in detail.

3. **Click and drag the object from its listing in the Library to the Stage.**

   You can also drag an object's image from the preview box.

You can drag items to the Pasteboard, the gray area around the edge of the Stage, until you're ready to use them.

Using folders

A Flash movie can contain dozens or even hundreds of symbols, so you need to keep them organized. Flash provides several features to keep you from tearing out your hair.

If you have more than a few symbols, you should organize them into folders. To create a new folder, follow these steps:

1. **Click the New Folder button at the bottom of the Library panel.**

   Flash creates a new folder.

2. **Type a name that describes the type of symbols that you want to put into the folder.**

   For example, you could create a folder named Intro and another one named Conclusion.

3. **Press Enter (Windows) or Return (Mac).**

To put symbols into a folder, drag them to the folder. You can also move symbols from one folder to another — just drag them. Note that folders exist just to help keep you organized. You can move symbols from one folder to another without affecting your movie.

To keep your symbol list from getting unwieldy, you can collapse folders. A collapsed folder doesn't display its contents. As soon as you need to see what's inside, you can expand the folder. Double-click a folder to either collapse or expand it.

To quickly see the structure of your folders, click the Library's Options menu. Choose Collapse All Folders. You can also choose Expand All Folders to see everything in the Library.

More Library housekeeping

By default, Flash alphabetizes items in the Library by name. However, you might have different ideas. You can sort from A–Z (ascending) or from Z–A (descending). You can also sort by any of the columns in the Library. To change the direction of sorting (for any column in the Library), click the heading of the column that you want to sort by. You can click the column heading again to reverse the sort order.

You can re-order the columns in the Library. Just drag a column's name left or right to the desired location. You can resize any column by dragging the column heading's divider to the left or right.

If the Library panel is docked, you can resize it by dragging its left border. If the Library panel isn't docked, you can drag the right border to resize the panel.

To rename any Library item, double-click the item's name, type the new name, and press Enter or Return. Don't worry — the original filenames of imported files remain unchanged at their original locations.

To duplicate an item, select the item. Then right-click (Windows) or Control+click (Mac) and choose Duplicate. To delete an item, select the item and click the Trash can.

If you want to find out which items in the Library you aren't using, look in the third column (Use Count) for items with a zero use count. After you know which items you aren't using, you can delete them.

You can update imported bitmaps and sounds if the original files have changed. Select the file and choose Update in the Options menu of the Library panel.

Using the Libraries of other movies

After you place objects in a file's Library, you can use those objects in any other Flash movie that you create. Just open the movie and display its Library panel, and its Library's contents are available for you to use in your current movie.

Choose File⇨Import⇨Open External Library to open the Library of another Flash movie that isn't open. A new Library panel opens for the other Flash movie.

You can switch among the Libraries of open movies by using a drop-down list at the top of the Library panel.

When you have libraries open from more than one Flash file, you can copy symbols or anything else in a Library from one movie to another by simply dragging them from one Library to another. Choose the Library that you want to use, select an item, and drag it into the other Library. Easy!

To create a new symbol that goes directly into the Library (rather than on the Stage), choose New Symbol in the Library Options menu in the upper-right corner. (Refer to Figure 2-4.) You're transported to symbol-editing mode, where you can create your symbol as you normally would. To return to your main movie, choose Edit➪Edit Document. For more information on creating and editing symbols, see Chapter 7.

Exploring the Flash stock Library

Flash comes with two Libraries that contain an excellent assortment of button symbols and sounds. They are worth looking through. Choose Window➪Common Libraries and choose Buttons or Sounds. (We cover using sounds in Chapter 11.)

Using a Template

To help you create Flash movies more easily, Flash CS4 comes with a few templates for common types of movies. Instructions are included on the templates. To create a Flash movie from a template, choose File➪New and click the Templates tab. In the New from Template dialog box (see Figure 2-5), select one of the templates, and then click OK.

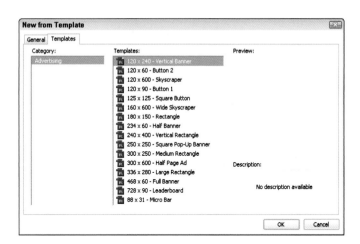

Figure 2-5: Use the New from Template dialog box to create a Flash movie from a template.

The advertising category offers movie sizes suitable for Web-based ads. Here are a few of your options:

- **120 x 240:** Vertical Banner: This is a tower ad, 120 pixels wide x 240 pixels tall.

- **120 x 60:** Button 2: This is a small, vertical rectangular ad.

- **120 x 600:** Skyscraper: This is another tower ad.

✓ **120 x 90:** Button 1: This is another vertical rectangular ad.

✓ **125 x 125:** Square Button: This is a small square ad.

✓ **160 x 600:** Wide Skyscraper: This is another tower ad but wider than the previous ones.

✓ **180 x 150:** Rectangle: This is a horizontal rectangular ad.

✓ **234 x 60:** Half Banner: This is a horizontal banner ad, half the typical full width.

✓ **240 x 400:** Vertical Rectangle: This is a larger, vertical rectangular ad.

When you open a new movie from a template, you should save it as a movie. This way, the template is unchanged, and you are free to make any changes you want.

You can also save movies as templates. If you create a movie that you want to reuse in many variations, choose File➪Save as Template to open the Save as Template dialog box, as shown in Figure 2-6.

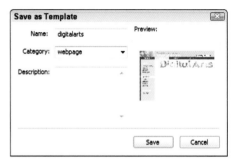

Type a name, choose a category, and enter a description for your template. Then click Save. From now on, you can open your template like any of the templates that come with Flash, just as we describe. Using templates can save you lots of work!

Figure 2-6: The Save as Template dialog box saves your movies as templates.

To create your own category for templates, type a category name in the Category list box instead of choosing one of the existing categories in the list.

Printing Your Movie

Usually, you don't print your movies — you publish them on the Web. But you might want to collaborate on a movie with others who don't have Flash. (How unenlightened of them!) Or you might just want to analyze a movie on paper, tack your animation frames on the wall, and rearrange their sequence. In this type of situation, you can print your animation frame by frame.

To print a movie, follow these steps:

1. **To set page margins, choose File➪Page Setup (Windows) or File➪Print Margins (Mac).**

   The Page Setup (Windows) or Print Margins (Mac) dialog box appears. See Figure 2-7.

2. **In the Margins section, set the margins.**

   You can probably keep the default margin settings.

3. **Select the Center check boxes to center the printing horizontally and vertically on the page.**

4. **(Windows only) In the Paper section, select the size of the paper; define the paper source.**

   Usually, you can leave this section as is because it's based on your printer's default settings.

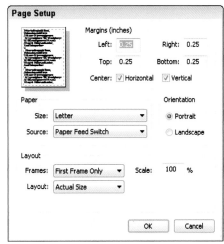

5. **In the Layout section, click the Frames drop-down list and decide whether to print only the first frame or all frames.**

Figure 2-7: Use the Page Setup dialog box to specify how to print your Flash movie.

6. **In the Layout section, click the Layout drop-down list to choose from the following options:**

   - *Actual Size:* Lets you choose a scale. This option prints one frame to a page.

   - *Fit on One Page:* Fits one frame on a page, scaling it to fit the paper.

   - *Storyboard–Boxes:* Places several thumbnail sketches of your movie on a page. You can specify how many frames that you want in a row in the Frames Across text box. You might need to experiment to get the right result. In the Frame Margin text box, enter the space in pixels between the boxes. The Storyboard–Boxes option places each frame in a box.

   - *Storyboard–Grid:* Creates a grid of lines for your storyboard rather than individual boxes around the frames. This option is just a matter of aesthetics — don't get too hung up over these choices.

   - *Storyboard–Blank:* Leaves out the boxes or grid and just prints all your frames in the storyboard. You have the same Frames Across and Frame Margin settings as for the other storyboard options.

7. **(Windows only) If you chose a Storyboard option, select the Label Frames check box to give each frame a number.**

8. (Mac only) When you finish setting your options, click OK; then choose File⇨Page Setup.

   In Windows, you skip this step because you already opened the Page Setup dialog box in Step 1.

9. In the Orientation section, select Portrait (taller rather than wider) or Landscape (wider rather than taller).

10. (Mac only) In the Format section, choose your printer in the drop-down list.

11. (Mac only) In the Paper Size section, select the size of the paper.

12. When you finish setting your options, click OK.

13. To print, choose File⇨Print.

    Alternatively, you can press Ctrl+P (Windows) or ⌘+P (Mac). In Windows, you choose the printer in the Name drop-down list in the Print dialog box.

Figure 2-8 shows an example of the storyboard with the box option. The storyboard shows four frames across with a portrait orientation and includes frame labels. You can find out more about the Flash Player's special printing capabilities in Chapter 13.

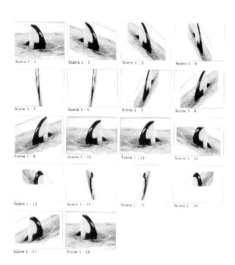

Figure 2-8: You can print a storyboard of your movie that displays a thumbnail sketch of each frame.

Part II
1,000 Pictures and 1,000 Words

The 5th Wave   By Rich Tennant

"I'm not sure—I like the mutual funds with rotating dollar signs, although the dancing stocks and bonds look good, too."

In this part . . .

Graphics are the basis of animation. Before
you can make anything move, you need to
create the graphics that form the building blocks
of your animation. Chapter 3 describes all the
types of graphics that you can use, from basic
shapes created in Flash to sophisticated imported
bitmap graphics. The Flash tools are quite capa-
ble, and you can create exciting effects with gradient fills, softened edges, the spray brush, the Deco
tool, and transparency. The Flash editing features,
as we describe in Chapter 4, offer more opportuni-
ties to create great-looking graphics — including
skewing objects, using the Distort and Envelope
options, and manipulating fills every which way.

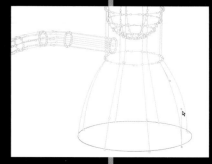

In Chapter 5, you find ways to say great things
with flexible text options and formatting. You can
even break up text and animate it, letter by letter.
To keep all the pieces of your animation from
going completely out of control, in Chapter 6 you
see how to use layers to organize your movie animation. You can use special layers to guide drawing tasks and hide objects behind a mask.
(Peekaboo!)

3

Getting Graphic

*I*n this chapter, you get down to the details of creating your own graphics in Flash. The Flash graphics tools (found on the Tools panel) offer you the capability to easily create interesting and professional-looking shapes. You can also import graphics created in other programs.

After you master all the techniques for drawing and editing, you can create some very cool graphics. If you're new to Flash, take the time to try out all the tools and techniques until you feel comfortable with them. For a handy reference to the Tools panel, which we refer to throughout this chapter, see the Cheat Sheet at the front of this book.

Sharpening Your Pencil

Use the Flash Pencil tool to create freehand shapes. Whenever you want to create a shape not available from other Flash tools (such as the circle and square), you can use the Pencil. But the Pencil tool goes beyond a regular pencil's capabilities by incorporating cool features that smooth or straighten what you draw. The Pencil also includes the *shape-recognition* feature (perfect for those who are less artistic). Draw something that approximates a triangle, and Flash forgivingly perfects it for you.

To start, click the Pencil tool on the Tools panel. To draw without changing the Pencil modifier, move the cursor onto the Stage, click, and draw. After you release the mouse button, Flash modifies the shape according to the active modifier setting, as we explain in the next section.

Setting the Pencil modifier

When you choose the Pencil tool, the Options area below the Tools panel changes to display the drawing mode modifier for the Pencil tool.

The Pencil modifier has three drawing modes:

- ✔ **Straighten:** Straightens lines and converts sloppy squares, rectangles, circles, ellipses, and triangles to perfect ones.

- ✔ **Smooth:** Smoothes out curved lines, eliminating unsightly bumps and lumps. You can specify the amount of smoothing.

- ✔ **Ink:** Slightly smoothes and straightens your curves and lines but leaves them mostly the way you drew them.

In Figure 3-1 on the left, you see a sloppy jagged line. See how Flash modified it by using the Straighten drawing mode.

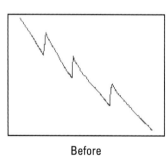 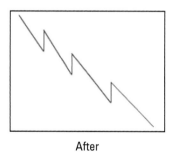

Before   After

Figure 3-1: Use the Straighten mode to draw straight lines.

Suppose that you want to animate some waves on your Web site. You start to draw the outline of the waves. Figure 3-2 shows how the waves look before and after Flash smoothes them out by using Smooth mode. For more complex shapes, Ink mode helps you look good without taking away too much of your own authorship.

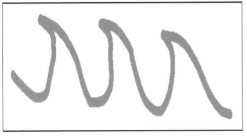

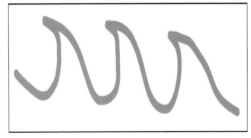

Before   After

Figure 3-2: Smooth mode makes you look like a real smoothie when it comes to drawing curves.

Setting the stroke type

While drawing with the Pencil tool (and any of the other drawing tools), you can also control the type of *stroke* (line style), its *width* (also called *height* or *weight*), its cap (ending), and how it joins with other strokes. To modify stroke settings, follow these steps:

1. **Click the Pencil tool to make it active.**

2. **Open the Property inspector if it's not open by choosing Window⇨Properties.**

   The Property inspector appears, as shown in Figure 3-3. As we explain in Chapter 1, the Property inspector changes depending on which tool is active and which part of the Flash window you're using.

3. **Click the Style drop-down list to display the available line styles and select a new line style.**

   You can choose from seven line styles, including dashed and dotted.

4. **To change the line width, type a new value in the Stroke text box and press Enter or Return, or drag the slider bar.**

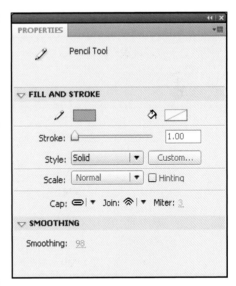

Figure 3-3: Use the Property inspector to control line type and width.

The first available stroke width on the Style drop-down list is Hairline, which creates a hairline-width line. Flash measures *weights* (widths) of

How to set smoothing and shape-recognition preferences

You can tell Flash just how much you want it to smooth or straighten curved lines when you draw with the Pencil tool. Choose Edit⇨Preferences (Windows) or Flash⇨Preferences (Mac) and click the Drawing category. In the Smooth Curves drop-down list, select one of the following options:

✔ **Off:** Flash doesn't smooth or straighten at all.

✔ **Rough:** Flash smoothes or straightens only slightly, honoring your own work as much as possible.

✔ **Normal:** Flash smoothes or straightens a medium amount. Normal is the default setting.

✔ **Smooth:** Flash smoothes and straightens more so that you get fewer bumps and jolts.

In the same way, you can tell Flash how picky you want it to be in recognizing lines, circles, ovals, squares, rectangles, and arcs (90 degrees and 180 degrees). For lines, select Off, Strict, Normal, or Tolerant in the Recognize Lines drop-down list. Normal is the default. Use Tolerant if you're a klutz; use Strict (or even Off) if you don't want Flash fiddling too much (or at all) with your work. For other shapes and arcs, select an option in the Recognize Shapes drop-down list. You have the same Off, Strict, Normal, and Tolerant options.

other line types in points. You can create a line up to 200 points wide. (A point equals ½ of an inch.)

5. **To control the endings of lines, click the Cap drop-down list and select one of the styles:**

   • *None:* The end is square with no added ending.

   • *Round:* A rounded cap is added to the end of the line. The length of the cap is half the line's width.

   • *Square:* A squared cap is added to the end of the line. The length of the cap is half the line's width. See Figure 3-4.

6. **If you want, select the Hinting check box.**

   Stroke hinting makes slight adjustments to avoid blurry horizontal or vertical lines. If your lines don't look as clear as you'd like, try selecting this option.

7. **Click the Join drop-down list and select one of the styles (see Figure 3-5) to control how lines look when they meet:**

   • *Miter:* A pointed corner

Figure 3-4: These lines were all drawn 88 pixels long, but the bottom two lines have round and square caps, so they're longer.

- *Round:* A rounded corner
- *Bevel:* A squared-off (beveled) corner

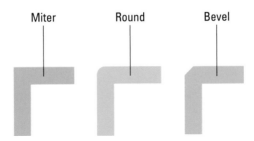

Figure 3-5: You can choose how lines meet. How romantic!

8. **In the Scale drop-down list, select an option to control how lines scale.**

   The Scale options specify how the thickness of strokes scale if you include them in a symbol and then scale the symbol. (We discuss symbols in Chapter 7.)

   - *Normal:* Thickness scales both horizontally and vertically.
   - *Horizontal:* Thickness scales horizontally only. This applies to vertical lines, so that they become thicker as you scale them.
   - *Vertical:* Thickness scales vertically only. This applies to horizontal lines so that they become thicker as you scale them.
   - *None:* Lines don't become thicker as you scale them.

9. **(Optional) In the Miter text box, you can enter a limit to help prevent beveling a miter join.**

   When you draw two lines that meet at a sharp angle with a *miter join* (a sharp point), you might get a bevel instead. If you chose a miter join, you can increase the value in the Miter text box to get a nice sharp point where the two lines meet.

You can create custom line styles, as well. In the Property inspector, click the Custom button. In the Stroke Style dialog box that opens, you can create your own designer line styles.

Setting the color

When using the Pencil tool, you can set the color of the stroke in the Property inspector or in the Colors section of the Tools panel. In either location, click the Stroke Color box to open the color palette and then select a color.

We explain more about using colors in the section "A Rainbow of Colors," later in this chapter.

Creating Shapely Shapes

In the preceding section, we explain that you can draw shapes by using the Pencil tool. You can also draw lines, rectangles, squares, ovals, and circles by using the shape tools. Use these tools when you want more control over your shapes — for example, when you want to draw perfect circles, perfect squares, and straight lines.

Line up

To draw a line, choose the Line tool in the Tools panel. Click the Stage at the desired starting point of the line and drag to the ending point. Then release the mouse button. To keep your lines at multiples of 45 degrees, press Shift while dragging. Flash creates the line at the 45-degree angle closest to your drag line.

When you use the Line tool, you can modify the line weight, style, and color in the same way as for the Pencil tool, as we discuss in the preceding section.

Be square

To draw a rectangle, choose the Rectangle tool in the Tools panel. Click the Stage at one corner of the rectangle and drag to the opposite corner. Then release the mouse button. To create a square, press Shift as you drag.

The Rectangle tool is on a flyout toolbar on the Tools panel. The flyout displays the last tool you used, so you may not see the Rectangle tool. Instead, you may see the Oval tool, the Polystar tool, the Rectangle Primitive tool, or the Oval Primitive tool. Click (with a long click) any one of these to display the flyout, where you can find the Rectangle tool.

When you click the Rectangle tool, you can modify the line weight, style, and color of the rectangle in the same way that you can modify a line when you use the Pencil tool. You can't see the effect of caps when you create a rectangle because it's a closed shape; however, if you later cut out part of the rectangle, the remaining lines take on the cap you specified.

Unlike lines, rectangles contain *two* objects: the *fill* (the area inside the stroke) and the *stroke* (the outline of the rectangle).

Flash provides the following tools for adjusting the settings for rectangles:

 ✔ **Fill Color:** Determines the color that fills the inside of the rectangle. You can click the Fill Color box — either in the Property inspector or in the Colors section of the Tools panel — and select one of the colors in the palette that opens. You can also select from the gradients displayed at the bottom of the palette. (See the section "A Rainbow of Colors," later in this chapter, for details about customizing colors and gradients.)

 ✔ **Stroke Color:** Determines the color of the stroke (the outline) of the rectangle. Click the Stroke Color box — either in the Property inspector or in the Colors section of the Tools panel — and select a color from the palette.

 ✔ **Black and White:** Sets the stroke color to black and the fill color to white. Click the Black and White button in the Colors section of the Tools panel.

 ✔ **No Color:** Sets either the stroke color or the fill color (whichever tool is pressed) to no color. You have to click either the Stroke Color box or the Fill Color box to find the No Color box in the upper-right corner of the palette of colors.

  ✔ **Swap Colors:** Switches the stroke and fill colors.

✔ **Rectangle Corner Radius:** Creates a rectangle with rounded corners. (It's located in the Rectangle Options section of the Property inspector.) By default, the Lock Corner Radius icon allows you to set one radius for all four corners. However, you can click the icon to unlock the setting, enabling you to separately enter a different value for each of the rectangle's corners in the Rectangle Corner Radius text box. The rectangle that you draw has nicely rounded corners, as you specified. Use a value of zero for a sharp corner. You can create cute cutout corners by using a negative number for the radius, as shown in Figure 3-6.

 You can specify the dimensions of the rectangle in advance. Select the Rectangle tool, press Alt (Windows) or Option (Mac), and then click the Stage. The Rectangle Settings dialog box opens, with Width and Height text boxes that you can use to get exactly the size rectangle you want. You can also set a corner radius

Figure 3-6: Where did my corner go?

here. When you click OK, the rectangle appears immediately. You can then move it to the location you want.

The Rectangle Primitive tool also creates rectangles. For more information, see "Getting primitive" later in this chapter.

Be an egg

To draw an oval, choose the Oval tool in the Tools panel. Click the Stage at one corner of the oval and drag to the opposite corner. (Ovals don't really have corners, but you'll get the idea after you try one or two.) Then release the mouse button. To create a perfect circle, press and hold Shift while you drag.

The Oval tool is on a flyout toolbar on the Tools panel. The flyout displays the last tool you used, so you may not see the Oval tool. Instead, you may see the Rectangle tool, the Polystar tool, the Rectangle Primitive tool, or the Oval Primitive tool. Click (with a long click) any one of these to display the flyout, where you can find the Oval tool.

After you click the Oval tool, you can change the line color, type, and weight in the same way as we describe for the Pencil tool, in the "Setting the stroke type" section earlier in this chapter. You can set the colors as we describe in the preceding section on drawing rectangles.

You can specify the exact width and height of the oval. Select the Oval tool, press Alt (Windows) or Option (Mac), and then click the Stage. The Oval Settings dialog box opens. Use the Width and Height text boxes to specify the size you want, and then click OK to create the oval.

Go for the stars

The Polystar tool is on the same flyout as the Rectangle and Oval tools. This tool creates stars and polygons. Follow these steps:

1. **Display the Property inspector.**

   Choose Window➪Properties to display the inspector if it's not already open.

2. **In the Tools panel's Rectangle tool flyout, choose the Polystar tool.**

3. **In the Property inspector, click the Options button to open the Tool Settings dialog box.**

4. **In the Style drop-down list, choose Polygon or Star.**

5. **In the Number of Sides text box, enter a number.**

The maximum number is 32, which is probably plenty.

6. **In the Star Point Size text box, enter a value between 0 and 1 to indicate the depth of the points.**

A lower value, such as 0.1, creates deeper points, making your star spiky looking. A higher value, such as 0.8, creates shorter points. See Figure 3-7. This setting is irrelevant for polygons.

7. **Drag on the screen to create the star or polygon.**

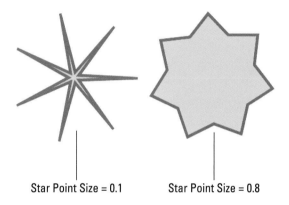

Star Point Size = 0.1   Star Point Size = 0.8

Figure 3-7: You can create a wide variety of stars.

Mixing and Matching Shapes

After you create shapes on the Stage, you need to understand what happens when two objects touch. It's a little weird, but you soon see how flexible the Flash drawing tools are. Two basic rules exist about objects that touch.

Cutting up shapes

The first rule is that when you use the Pencil or Line tool to draw a line that intersects any other shape or line, the line acts like a knife to cut the other shape or line. The line you draw is also cut into segments. You don't see the effect until you try to select or move one of the objects. Suppose that you want to draw a broken heart. You can draw the breaking line by using the Pencil tool. You now have several objects, and you can easily move apart the two halves of the heart. In the right-hand heart (see Figure 3-8), we erased the line and separated the halves of the heart.

Placing objects on top of each other

The second rule about objects that touch is that when you place one shape on top of another, the top shape replaces whatever is beneath it. Again, you can see the results only when you try to select or move the shapes. But now it gets a little complicated:

- ✔ If the two shapes are the same color, they merge into one combined shape.

- ✔ If the two shapes are different colors, they remain separate.

Figure 3-9 shows a circle and a triangle on the left. They are the same color. On the right, you can see the result after moving the circle down over the triangle. Presto! It's a chocolate scoop of ice cream on a sugar cone. If you try to select the shape, it's now one object.

When you combine shapes of different colors, you create cutouts. Rather than adding the shapes together, the top shape just replaces the area beneath it. Figure 3-10 shows how you can create a cutout. We display the grid on the Stage (find more about that in Chapter 4) so that you can see that the image on the right is a cutout.

To create a cutout effect, follow these steps:

Figure 3-8: Intersect any shape with a line, and the line splits the shape and is itself segmented.

Figure 3-9: Build complex shapes by combining basic shapes of the same color.

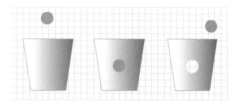

Figure 3-10: A cutout. There's a hole in the bucket!

1. Create two separate shapes of different colors.

2. Move one shape on top of another shape.

3. Deselect the shape that you moved by clicking anywhere off the shape.

4. Select the top shape again, and either drag it away from the bottom shape to create the cutout or delete it.

See Chapter 4 for details on selecting and moving objects.

Keeping Objects Safe and Secure

What do you do if you want to put objects next to or on top of each other while maintaining their integrity? Two methods of drawing keep your objects safe from cutups, replacements, and cutouts. We discuss these in this section.

Using the object-drawing model

You can use the *object-drawing model* to keep your objects whole, no matter what else they touch. When you draw using this model, objects maintain their integrity — no dishonest objects here! Other objects on top of or beneath these objects do not cut up, cut out, or merge with them.

To draw any object with the object-drawing model, follow these steps:

1. **Choose any drawing tool in the Tools panel.**

2. **Click the Object Drawing modifier in the Options section so that the button darkens.**

   You click the modifier again to turn off the Object Drawing modifier. You can also press the J key to turn the object-drawing model on and off.

3. **Draw your object.**

   Your object now has a blue rectangular bounding box around it. This bounding box is similar to the one you see when you turn objects into a symbol (as we explain in Chapter 7) or group objects. (See Chapter 4 for more information.)

If you change your mind and don't want your object to stay separate from touching objects, select the object and choose Modify⇨Break Apart. You can convert existing objects to object-drawing model shapes. Just select the shape, and choose Modify⇨Combine Objects⇨Union.

Getting primitive

A special type of shape, called a *primitive,* does not merge with other objects. These objects act like objects that you draw using the object-drawing model. Two primitives are available: a rectangle and an oval. These primitives allow you to specify certain properties, called *parameters,* that define their shape.

Creating a rectangle primitive

When you draw a rectangle primitive, you can create a rounded rectangle by specifying a radius for the corners. Use the Rectangle Corner Radius text box or slider bar in the Property inspector to specify a value. But you can do the same with the regular Rectangle tool, as we describe earlier in this chapter, so what's the point? The difference is how you can edit the radius of the corners, after you create the rectangle. When you select a rectangle primitive, you see markers at the corners. You can drag these markers to change the corner radii, as shown in Figure 3-11, or you can use the Rectangle Options section of the Property inspector.

Figure 3-11: Change the radius of a rectangle primitive's corners.

The other difference between a normal rectangle and a rectangle primitive is that the primitive acts like objects that you draw using the object-drawing model. You can't merge it or cut it out. Similarly, when you select it, you see a bounding box around the entire shape.

 To draw a rectangle primitive, select the Rectangle Primitive tool in the Tools panel. Display the Property inspector (choose Window➪Properties) and specify one or more corner radii in the Rectangle Options section, as explained in the discussion of the Rectangle tool earlier in this chapter. Then click the Stage at one corner of the rectangle and drag to the opposite corner. The rectangle is selected, so you can immediately drag the corners to adjust them if you want.

 The Rectangle Primitive tool is on a flyout toolbar on the Tools panel. The flyout displays the last tool you used, so you may not see the Rectangle Primitive tool. Instead, you may see the Rectangle tool, the Oval tool, the Polystar tool, or the Oval Primitive tool. Click (with a long click) any one of these to display the flyout, where you can find the Rectangle Primitive tool.

Creating an oval primitive

To draw an oval primitive, select the Oval Primitive tool in the Tools panel. Display the Property inspector (choose Window➪Properties) and specify the Start Angle, End Angle, Inner Radius, and whether the path should be closed, as explained next. Then click the Stage at one corner of the oval and drag to the opposite corner.

The Oval Primitive tool is on a flyout toolbar on the Tools panel. The flyout displays the last tool you used, so you may not see the Oval Primitive tool. Instead, you may see the Rectangle tool, the Polystar tool, the Oval tool, or the Rectangle Primitive tool. Click (with a long click) any one of these to display the flyout, where you can find the Oval Primitive tool.

When you draw an oval primitive, you can specify the following parameters in the Property inspector:

↙ **Start and End Angle:** By separately specifying a start angle and an end angle, you can create part of an oval (or circle), as shown in Figure 3-12. When specifying angles, note that 0 degrees is to the right and that degrees increase in a clockwise direction. In the Property inspector, enter values in the Start Angle and End Angle text boxes, or drag the sliders.

↙ **Inner Radius:** By specifying a value from 1 to 99, you can indicate the percentage of the oval's fill that you want to remove, thereby creating a donut (yum)! See Figure 3-12 for an example. Enter a value in the Inner Radius text box, or drag the slider.

Figure 3-12: I had a donut. A little creature came and ate a bite. Then it went on to eat the rest, leaving only the outline!

↙ **Close Path:** Select this check box to include a fill as well as an outline around the entire shape. (The Close Path check box is selected by default.) Deselect the Close Path check box to omit the fill and draw an outline only. If you used the Start Angle and End Angle controls to create part of an oval or a circle, you get an unfilled shape when you deselect the Close Path check box, as shown in Figure 3-12.

When you deselect the Close Path check box to create an open oval, you draw only the outline. What happens if you defined the oval without a fill? The entire object disappears! To get it back, choose Edit↪Undo and add an outline. For detailed instructions, see the discussion of the Rectangle tool earlier in this chapter.

Figure 3-12 shows oval primitives with the following parameters from left to right: an inner radius; no inner radius, but start and end angles; a closed path with an inner radius and start and end angles; and finally, an open path with an inner radius and start and end angles. You can see that opening the path removes the fill.

When you select an oval primitive, you see two markers, one at the inner radius (or center, if the inner radius is 0) and one at the outer radius. You can drag the inner radius to change it. Drag the outer radius marker to change the start and end angles.

Creating Curves with the Pen

The Pen tool lets you draw *Bezier* curves, also called splines. Bezier curves are named after the French mathematician Pierre Bézier, who first described them. By using the Pen tool, you can create smooth curves that flow into each other. You can also create straight lines.

You can set preferences for the Pen tool by choosing Edit⇨Preferences (Windows) or Flash⇨Preferences (Mac) and clicking the Drawing category. We suggest enabling the Show Pen Preview option to display a preview of the line or curve while you draw. This setting helps you get a better idea of what the result will be. Click OK when you finish setting your preferences.

 To create a line or curve, choose the Pen tool in the Tools panel. What you do next depends on whether you want to draw a straight line or a curve. The following sections show you how to draw both.

Drawing straight lines

To draw a straight line with the Pen tool, follow these steps:

1. **To create a line segment, click the start point and then click the end point.**

2. **Continue to add line segments by clicking additional points.**

3. **Double-click to complete the process.**

   Flash previews segments in a color that depends on the layer you're working on — see the color of the square next to the current layer as shown on the Timeline. (Chapter 6 explains layers in full.) When you choose another tool or press the Esc key, Flash displays Beziers in the current stroke color.

Close a figure by pointing near the start point. You see a small circle at the cursor. Click the start point, and Flash closes the figure.

Drawing curves

Drawing curves with the Pen tool involves a couple of steps, depending on the complexity of the curve that you want to create. The main principle to understand is that you define the curve by specifying the location of anchor points. Each *anchor point* controls a bend in the curve. To draw a curve with the Pen tool, follow these steps:

1. **Click where you want to start and drag the mouse in the desired direction. About one-half of the way to the next anchor point (the end of the curve), release the mouse button, as shown in Figure 3-13(a).**

   You see *tangent lines* that define both the direction and length of each part of the curve, as shown in Figure 3-13(b).

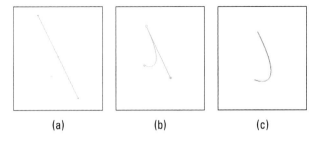

(a)   (b)   (c)

Figure 3-13: Drawing a curve with the Pen tool: 1, 2, 3, and you have a big nose!

2. **To create one curve, move the mouse cursor to the desired end of the curve; then double-click to end the curve, as shown in Figure 3-13(c).**

   If you set preferences to show a preview of the curve (as we explain earlier in the section "Creating Curves with the Pen"), you also see a stretchy line attached to your mouse cursor that previews the shape.

3. **To continue to draw curves, again click and drag in the desired direction, release the mouse button, and move the mouse cursor to wherever you want the end of the next curve to be. Double-click to end the curve.**

If you drag in an opposing direction to the first curve, you create a simple curve, sometimes called a *C curve*. If you drag in a similar direction to the first curve, the curve doubles back on itself, which is sometimes called an *S curve*. For both lines and curves, you can press and hold Shift to constrain the lines or curves (the tangent lines) to 45-degree angles. Drawing curves with the Pen tool takes practice, but you'll soon get the hang of it.

Getting Artistic with the Brush

The Brush tool lets you create artistic effects that look like painting. You can adjust the size and shape of the brush, and if you have a pressure-sensitive pen and tablet, you can adjust the width of the stroke by changing the pressure on the pen.

To paint with the Brush tool, select it on the Tools panel and then click and drag anywhere on the Stage. Press and hold Shift while you brush to keep your strokes either horizontal or vertical. The brush doesn't have a stroke (line) color. The brush creates only fills. Use the Fill Color drop-down list in the Property inspector or in the Colors section of the Tools panel to select a fill color.

The Brush tool is on a flyout toolbar on the Tools panel. The flyout displays the last tool you used, so you may not see the Brush tool. Instead, you may see the Spray Brush tool. Click (with a long click) any one of these to display the flyout, where you can find the Brush tool.

When you choose the Brush tool, the Brush modifiers appear in the Options section of the Tools panel, as shown in Figure 3-14.

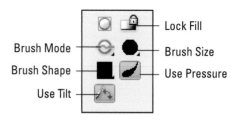

Figure 3-14: The Brush modifiers control how the brush functions.

Brush Mode modifier

The Brush Mode modifier determines how the brush relates to existing objects on the Stage. Here are your choices for Brush Mode. (Figure 3-15 shows some examples.)

 ✏ **Paint Normal:** You just paint away, oblivious to anything else. Use this setting when you don't need to worry about other objects.

 ✏ **Paint Fills:** You paint fills and empty areas of the Stage. The paint doesn't cover lines. Note that your lines seem to be covered while you paint, but they reappear when you release the mouse button.

 ✏ **Paint Behind:** You paint behind and around existing objects, but only in blank areas of the Stage. While you paint, the brush seems to cover everything, but your existing objects reappear when you release the mouse button. You can messily paint over your objects, knowing that they won't be affected.

 ✏ **Paint Selection:** You paint only a filled-in area that you previously selected. While you paint, your existing objects are covered, but they reappear when you release the mouse button. You don't need to worry about painting within the lines because Flash fills only the selected area.

 ✏ **Paint Inside:** You paint inside lines. Only the fill where you start brushing is painted. Paint Inside also paints an empty area on the Stage if that's where you start brushing. Again, at first the paint seems to cover up everything, but when you release the mouse button, Flash keeps your paint nice and neat, inside the lines — like every little kid discovers in kindergarten.

Original corn

Corn with worms -
Paint Normal

Corn with
bad kernels -
Paint Fills

Corn with
background -
Paint Behind

Sheath with
gray gradient -
Paint Selection

Corn with
bad kernels -
Paint Inside

Figure 3-15: Set the Brush mode when using the Brush tool to get the effect you want.

Brush Size drop-down list

Click the Brush Size drop-down list and select a size in the list of circles. This list defines the width of the brush. If you use a Brush mode that helps you draw neatly, such as Paint Selection, you don't need to be too concerned with the size of the brush. On the other hand, if you're creating an artistic effect by using Paint Normal mode, the width of the brush is important.

Brush Shape drop-down list

Flash offers several brush shapes you can choose from. Click the Brush Shape drop-down list and select one of the shapes. Each shape produces a different effect, especially when you paint at an angle — you just need to try them out to see what works best. Figure 3-16 shows a honey jar drawn with various brush shapes.

Figure 3-16: Each brush shape creates a different effect — especially at the ends of the stroke.

Pressure and Tilt modifiers

If you have a pressure-sensitive pen and tablet, Flash also displays a Pressure modifier so that you can vary the width of your strokes according to the pressure you put on your pen while you draw. Click the Use Pressure tool (refer to Figure 3-14) to turn on this feature.

Flash fully supports pressure-sensitive pens and adds the ability to use the opposite end of the pen to erase — just like a real pencil. Figure 3-17 shows this type of pen and tablet.

A pressure-sensitive pen works together with a tablet to help you draw in Flash. The tablet tracks the movement and pressure of the pen while you draw. You can also use the pen as a mouse to choose menu and dialog box items. In other words, if you want, you can use the pen for all of your Flash work. Alternatively, you can use the pen and tablet just for drawing and use the mouse when you want to work with menus and dialog boxes.

The Tilt modifier varies the angle of your brush stroke when you vary the angle of the stylus on the tablet. For example, holding the stylus straight up and down produces a different shape of brush stroke than the one you get if you hold the stylus at a 45-degree angle to the tablet.

Photo courtesy of Douglas Little of Wacom

Figure 3-17: This Wacom pen and tablet set is easier to draw with than a mouse and enables you to easily vary the brush width as you draw.

Use the Tilt modifier for fine control over your brush strokes. Click the Use Tilt tool in the Options section of the Tools panel to turn on this feature. You see the effect most clearly with a large brush size and one of the narrow brush shapes. When you start to draw, change the angle of the stylus to the tablet. Watch the cursor shape turn, giving you a hint as to the shape of the brush stroke. Try brushing at a few angles to see how this works.

See the "A Rainbow of Colors" section, later in this chapter, for an explanation of the Lock Fill modifier, one of the brush tool's modifiers.

Brush smoothing

Smoothing brush strokes is similar to smoothing pencil strokes. You can finely adjust how much your brush strokes are smoothed after you finish drawing them. You can set smoothing anywhere from 0 to 100.

To set brush smoothing, follow these steps:

1. **Click the Brush tool.**

2. **Open the Property inspector if it's not open. (Choose Window⇨ Properties.)**

3. **In the Smoothing section, enter a new Smoothing value or drag upward or downward to set a new value.**

   The lower values change your strokes less. Therefore, if you set Smoothing to 0, the brush stroke is closest to what you actually drew. Lower values create more vectors, resulting in a larger file size for your movie. The higher values smooth and simplify your strokes more.

Creating Graffiti with the Spray Brush

You can create the effect of spray paint, or *stippling* (filling an area with dots), by using the Spray Brush tool.

The Spray Brush tool is new for Flash CS4. This tool allows you to quickly fill up an area with polka dots of any color. You can substitute a graphic or movie clip symbol in the Library for the dots. (We discuss symbols in Chapter 7.) Figure 3-18 shows a flower that uses the Spray Brush tool in several places.

To create a spray of dots using the default settings, click the Spray Brush tool on the Tools panel and drag anywhere on the Stage to place the dots. The Spray Brush tool uses the current fill color for the dots.

Figure 3-18: The Spray Brush tool easily adds a fine level of decoration to your artwork.

The Spray Brush tool is on a flyout toolbar on the Tools panel. The flyout displays the last tool you used, so you may not see the Spray Brush tool. Instead, you may see the Brush tool. Click (with a long click) either of these to display the flyout, where you can find the Spray Brush tool.

Setting symbol properties

You can specify your own symbol to use in place of the dots. Because you can't control the spacing between the dots, simple symbols work best. To use your own symbol, follow these steps:

1. Create a symbol, or import one into the Library. (We explain all about symbols in Chapter 7.)

2. Click the Spray Brush tool in the Tools panel.

3. Open the Property inspector (Window⇨Properties) if it is not already open. In the Symbol section, click the Edit button.

   The Swap Symbol dialog box opens.

4. Choose the symbol you want to use and click OK.

5. If desired, enter new values for Scale Width and Scale Height in the Property inspector.

   Scaling enables you to use large symbols in your spray. For example, you can scale the width and height to 15%. You can also scale upward by using values of more than 100%.

6. To create a variety of sizes, select the Random Scaling check box.

7. To rotate the symbol around your cursor as you drag, select the Rotate Symbol check box.

8. To randomly rotate the symbol, select the Random Rotation check box.

9. Drag on the Screen to place the spray.

   Figure 3-19 shows a raindrop symbol using random scaling.

The Spray Brush tool makes it easy to quickly add hundreds of dots or instances of your symbol to your movie. This can make the movie balloon in size quickly. Check your movie size before and after, and don't go overboard!

Figure 3-19: It's raining, it's pouring.

Setting brush properties

You have control over the width, height, and angle of the brush, whether you use the default dots or your own symbol. To set brush properties, follow these steps:

1. Click the Spray Brush tool in the Tools panel.

2. Open the Property inspector (Window⇨Properties) if it is not already open.

3. In the Brush section, enter a value for the Width.

   The width is the horizontal dimension. If you drag vertically when you place the spray, the resulting shape is the width that you specified.

4. **Enter a value for the Height.**

   The height is the vertical dimension. If you drag horizontally when you place the spray, the resulting shape is the height that you specified.

5. **To specify an angle, enter a Brush Angle value.**

6. **Drag on the Stage to place the spray.**

Working with Spray Brush dots

It could get very difficult to delete some of those dots if they were all individual objects! Luckily, when you create a spray, they're grouped together as one object. (We discuss groups in Chapter 4.) Click inside a group of dots and you'll see a blue border. You can press the Del key to delete them, or you can drag them to move them. If you really do want individual objects, select them and choose Modify⇨Break Apart. For more information on editing objects, see Chapter 4.

Pouring on the Paint

The Paint Bucket creates fills that fill shapes with color. You might want to fill an enclosed area that you created with the Line or Pencil tool. You can also fill enclosed shapes created with the Pen or Brush tool, which we discuss earlier in this chapter.

The Paint Bucket is also handy for changing existing fills. You can change the color as well as fiddle around with gradient and bitmap fills. (See Chapter 4 for more on editing fills.)

 To use the Paint Bucket, choose it in the Tools panel. Set the color by clicking the Fill Color tool and selecting a color. Alternatively, you can use the Fill Color drop-down list in the Property inspector.

 The Paint Bucket is on a flyout toolbar on the Tools panel. The flyout displays the last tool you used, so you may not see the Paint Bucket tool. Instead, you may see the Ink Bottle tool. Click (with a long click) either of these to display the flyout, where you can find the Paint Bucket tool.

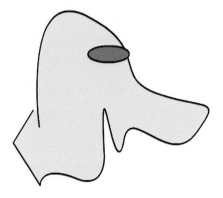

Figure 3-20: Fill areas that aren't completely closed by using the Gap Size modifier.

Flash can fill areas that aren't completely closed. The Gap Size modifier (in the Options section of the Tools panel) determines how large of a gap Flash will overlook to fill in an almost enclosed area. Choices range from Don't Close Gaps to Close Large Gaps. Because *small* and *large* are relative terms, you might have to experiment to get the result you want. After you choose an option from the Gap Size modifier, click any enclosed or almost enclosed area to fill it, as shown in Figure 3-20.

After you use the Paint Bucket to fill a shape created with another tool, you can delete the outline of the shape and keep just the fill.

Strokes, Ink

You use the Ink Bottle tool to create an outline on an existing shape. You can use the Ink Bottle tool also to change an existing line, or *stroke.*

 To use the Ink Bottle tool, click it on the Tools panel. Click the Stroke Color tool to select a color. Use the Property inspector, as we explain earlier in this chapter (in the discussion of the Pencil tool) to select a line thickness and line style. Then click anywhere on the shape. If the shape has no existing line, Flash adds the line. If the shape has a line, Flash changes its color, width, or style to the settings you specified in the Property inspector.

 The Ink Bottle tool is on a flyout toolbar on the Tools panel. The flyout displays the last tool you used, so you may not see the Ink Bottle tool. Instead, you may see the Paint Bucket Ink Bottle tool. Click (with a long click) either of these to display the flyout, where you can find the Ink Bottle tool.

A Rainbow of Colors

Flash offers you lots of color options. By default, Flash uses a palette of 216 colors that are Web safe, which means they look good on all Web browsers and monitors. Or, in these days when most computers can displays millions of colors, you can create your own colors.

Solid citizens

When you choose either the Stroke Color or Fill Color tool, Flash opens the *current color palette,* which is the active set of colors that Flash uses.

Creating new colors or editing existing colors

Flash provides two ways for you to specify your own colors:

✔ Choose the Stroke Color or Fill Color tool in the Tools panel and click the Colors Window button in the upper-right corner of the palette to open the Color dialog box.

✔ Choose Window⇨Color to open the Color panel.

These two methods duplicate each other; here, we explain how to use the Color panel, which is shown in Figure 3-21.

If you select an object before you use the Color panel, the object's color changes immediately when you change the color in the panel.

To create a new color or edit an existing color, follow these steps:

1. **Click the Options menu icon in the upper-right corner of the Color panel to open the pop-up menu, and then choose the color mode.**

   RGB specifies a color according to red, green, and blue components; HSB specifies a color by hue, saturation, and brightness. You can also define a color by using *hexadecimal notation,* which is the color system used on the Web: Just type the hexadecimal code in the Hex box of the Color panel.

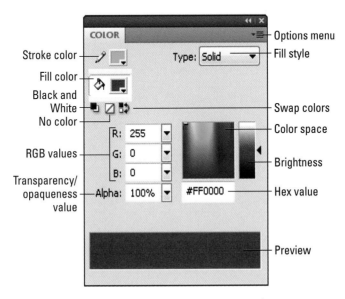

Figure 3-21: Use the Color panel to create your own colors.

2. **Click the Stroke Color or Fill Color icon to specify which color you want to change — stroke or fill.**

   Click the icon to the left of the Stroke Color or Fill Color box — not the box itself. (If you click the box, you open the color palette.)

3. **Type the color specs in the text boxes, use the sliders (click the down arrow) to drag to the desired color, or find a color in the color space that's close to the one that you want. Then click that color.**

4. **Set the level of opacity/transparency (also called *alpha*) by using the Alpha slider or by typing a number in the Alpha box.**

   A setting of 0% is completely transparent and 100% is opaque.

5. **If you want to create a new color swatch, click the Options menu icon and choose Add Swatch.**

   Flash adds the new color to the color palette so that you can access it from the Stroke Color or Fill Color boxes on the Tools panel, the Property inspector, and the Swatches panel.

Managing colors

If you've added or changed colors, you can save this new palette. (A *palette* is a set of colors.) You can then save the palette for use in other Flash movies or import a color palette from another Flash movie (so that you don't have to bother creating the colors again). Color palettes are saved as `.clr` files and are called *Flash color set* files. To save a color palette, choose Save Colors in the Swatches option menu. (Choose Window⇨Swatches to open the Swatches panel and click the Options menu icon in the upper-right corner of the panel to display the menu.) In the Export Swatch dialog box, choose a location for the file, name it, and click Save.

Adobe Fireworks and Photoshop use Color Table files (`.act` files), and Flash can save and import these as well. To save your color palette as an `.act` file, choose Color Table (*.act) in the Save as Type drop-down list in the Export Swatch dialog box.

To import a color palette that you've saved, use the Options menu of the Swatches panel. Choose Add Colors if you want to append this imported palette to an existing palette. Choose Replace Colors if you want the imported palette to replace an existing palette. You can use the same Swatches panel Options menu to manage your color palettes. Choose from the following options:

- ✔ **Duplicate Swatch:** Creates a duplicate of a swatch. Do this when you want to create your own color and use an existing color as a basis.

- ✔ **Delete Swatch:** Deletes a color.

- ✔ **Load Default Colors:** Replaces the active color palette with the Flash default palette.

- ✔ **Save as Default:** Saves the active color palette as the default palette for any new Flash movies that you create.
- ✔ **Clear Colors:** Clears all colors except black and white — for when you really want to start from scratch.
- ✔ **Web 216:** Loads the Web-safe, 216-color palette.
- ✔ **Sort by Color:** Sorts the display of colors by luminosity.

Using color themes

If you would like some help gathering a palette of compatible colors for a project, a new feature can come to the rescue — *kuler* colors. Kuler is an Adobe-supported online collection of color themes, available independently at `http://kuler.adobe.com`. Kuler is also a community, so you can upload your themes to share with others. From within Flash, choose Window⇨ Extensions⇨Kuler to open the Kuler panel. Figure 3-22 shows the Browse and Create tabs.

Use the Browse tab to find color themes that you like. From the Choose Which Themes You Wish to Display drop-down list, you can display themes by Highest Rated, Most Popular, Newest, Random, Saved (by you), and Custom (saved custom searches).

When you find a theme that you like, choose it and click the Add Selected Theme to Swatches button to add the colors to your Swatches panel. To edit a theme so that it's more to your liking, choose the theme and click the Edit Theme in Create Tab button. You can also find these options by clicking the arrow on the right side of any theme, after you choose the theme.

The Create tab is where you get creative, of course. Start by selecting one of the *harmony* rules. A harmony rule is a principle that governs how the colors in the theme relate to each other. For example, the Shades harmony rule results in colors that are all lighter and darker versions of the same color. If you want free rein, choose Custom.

You can double-click a theme on the Browse tab to open it on the Create tab.

To edit a color theme, choose a color swatch in the kuler panel to highlight that color's position in the color wheel. Then drag the position marker around to change the color, or inward/outward to make it lighter or darker. Alternatively, you can enter RGB values, use the RGB sliders, or enter a hexa-decimal value in the Hexadecimal Code text box.

Click a color in the theme and click the Bull's-Eye button to make that color the base color. The base color is important when you choose a harmony rule other than Custom because all of the other colors relate to the base color according to the rule that you have chosen.

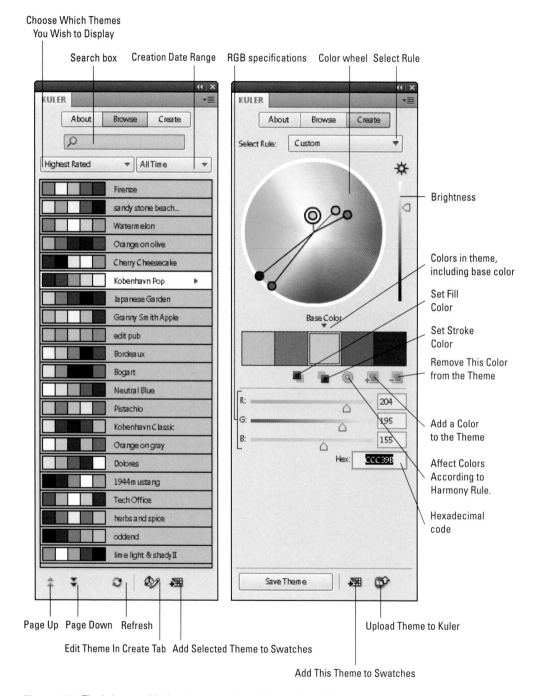

Choose Which Themes You Wish to Display

Search box   Creation Date Range   RGB specifications   Color wheel   Select Rule

Brightness

Colors in theme, including base color

Set Fill Color

Set Stroke Color

Remove This Color from the Theme

Add a Color to the Theme

Affect Colors According to Harmony Rule.

Hexadecimal code

Page Up   Page Down   Refresh

Edit Theme In Create Tab   Add Selected Theme to Swatches

Upload Theme to Kuler

Add This Theme to Swatches

Figure 3-22: The kuler panel is the place to go for mixing and matching colors.

When you're done creating a beautiful color theme, don't forget to click the Save Theme button to name and save your theme. You can then find that theme by clicking the Browse tab and choosing Saved from the Choose Which Themes You Wish to Display drop-down list.

You can also quickly add the colors to the Swatches panel by clicking the Add This Theme to Swatches button. Finally, be a good community member and share with others — click the Share This Theme button to upload the theme to the kuler Web site so that others can use it.

Gradient colors

So you're bored with solid colors and want something more interesting. *Gradients* are combinations of two or more colors that gradually blend from one to another. Flash can create gradients of as many as 16 colors — quite a feat. The gradient can be linear or *radial* (concentric), as shown in Figure 3-23.

Flash offers a few standard gradients that you can find at the bottom of the color palette. But you often need a more customized look, and Flash has the tools to create just about any gradient you want.

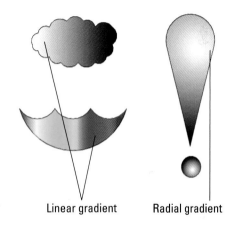

Linear gradient   Radial gradient

Figure 3-23: Linear and radial gradients make your graphics more interesting than plain solid colors.

Radial gradients look best on curved objects. A circle can suddenly look like a sphere when you fill it with a radial gradient. If you put white at the center of a radial gradient, it gives the impression of light highlights. Linear gradients look best on straight objects.

To create your own gradient, follow these steps:

1. **Choose Window⇨Color to open the Color panel. (Refer to Figure 3-21.) Then choose Linear or Radial in the Fill Style drop-down list.**

   You see a gradient bar with color pointers that specify the colors of the gradient and where the gradient changes from one color to the next.

   If you select a fill before you use the Color panel, the object's fill color changes immediately when you change the gradient in the Color panel.

2. **To use an existing gradient as a starting point, click the Fill Color box on the Tools panel and choose a gradient from the bottom of the color palette.**

You can also choose Window➪Swatches to open the Swatches panel and choose a gradient from the bottom of the color palette there.

3. **To specify the color for each color pointer, click and hold the pointer and then release the mouse button. (This is like a long mouse click.) When the color swatches appear, select a color.**

   You can click the Fill Color box and select an existing color from the color palette or specify a new color by using the methods we describe in the earlier section, "Creating new colors or editing existing colors."

   Note that when you click a pointer, its point turns black to indicate that it's the active pointer. The square beneath the point displays the color pointer's current color.

4. **To change the number of colors in the gradient, add or delete color pointers.**

   To add a color pointer, click where you want the pointer to appear, just below the gradient bar. To delete a color pointer, drag it off the gradient bar.

5. **To adjust where the color changes, drag a color pointer to the left or right.**

6. **To add control over how colors are applied to a selected shape beyond the gradient, select one of the following overflow modes in the Overflow drop-down list:**

   • *Extend:* Extends the last or outermost gradient color past the end of the gradient

   • *Reflect:* Fills the shape by mirroring the gradient pattern

   • *Repeat:* Repeats the gradient from beginning to end

   To use these effects, fill a shape with a gradient and then use the Gradient Transform tool to reduce the size of the gradient so that it no longer completely fills the shape. (We discuss the Gradient Transform tool in Chapter 4.) Then try out the three overflow modes to see the results.

   Select the Linear RGB check box to create a gradient that complies with Scalable Vector Graphics (SVG) standards. SVG is an XML language for describing 2-D graphics.

7. **To save the gradient, click the Options menu icon in the upper-right corner of the Color panel and choose Add Swatch.**

The new gradient now appears in the color palette of the Fill Color box on the Tools panel and in the Swatches panel. Go ahead and fill something with it! You can also move a gradient's center and focal points, change its width and height, rotate it, scale it, skew it, and tile it. See Chapter 4 for more on editing gradients.

Bitmap fills

You can create the coolest, weirdest fills by importing a bitmap graphic and using the bitmap to fill any shape. For a hypothetical Web site protesting genetically engineered foods, for example, we could find a bitmap of a bug (representing the Bt bacteria genetically engineered into corn) and use it to fill a graphic of corn. Figure 3-24 shows the result.

To use a bitmap graphic to fill a shape, follow these steps:

1. **Create the object or shape that you want to fill.**

2. **Select the fill.**

3. **If you haven't already imported the bitmap, choose File⇨Import⇨Import to Library, choose the bitmap you want, and then click Open/Import.**

   We explain more about importing graphics in the section "The Import Business — Using Outside Graphics," at the end of this chapter.

4. **In the Color panel, chose Bitmap from the Type drop-down list and choose your bitmap from the swatches that appear at the bottom of the panel.**

   Flash applies the bitmap to the selected fill. You may need to scale the bitmap. See the section on transforming fills in Chapter 4 for details.

Figure 3-24: You can fill any shape with a bitmap, repeated over and over and over.

For either method of choosing a bitmap, you can choose the Brush tool (instead of using the Paint Bucket tool) and then brush with the bitmap. Use a brush size that's thick enough to clearly show the bitmap.

Locking a fill

Flash has another trick up its sleeve for gradient or bitmap fills. A *locked fill* looks as though the fill is behind your objects and the objects are just uncovering the fill. As a result, if you use the same fill for several objects, Flash locks the position of the fill across the entire drawing surface instead of fixing the fill individually for each object. Figure 3-25 shows an example of a locked fill. In this figure, you see some windows and portholes filled with a locked bitmap of the sky. Doesn't it look as though the sky is really outside the windows?

 To lock a fill, choose the Brush tool or the Paint Bucket tool with a gradient or bitmap fill, as we explain in the two preceding sections. Then click the

Lock Fill modifier in the Options section of the Tools panel. Start painting where you want to place the center of the fill and continue to other areas.

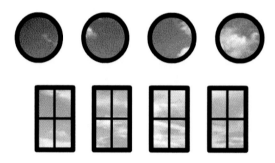

Figure 3-25: When you lock a fill, the fill's pattern continues across the Stage but appears only where you use it.

Pattern fills

If you like a decorative look, you can use the Deco tool to create three pattern effects:

- A Vine fill that reminds us of Victorian wallpaper
- A Grid that creates a rectangular grid
- A Symmetry Brush that creates symmetrical patterns

Each type of pattern offers you lots of flexibility, so you can really let your creative juices flow!

The Deco tool creates lots of objects! Luckily, they're grouped so that you can click any one to select them all and then delete or move them. (We discuss groups in Chapter 4.) To use the Deco tool, click the Deco tool on the Tools panel. Then choose the pattern effect you want from the Drawing Effect section of the Property inspector. (Choose Window⇨Properties.) These effects are described in the following three sections.

Vine fill

The Vine fill creates a vine of flowers and leaves. To create a vine, choose the Deco tool on the Tools panel and then choose Vine Fill from the Drawing Effect drop-down list in the Property inspector. Click once anywhere on the Stage, or click inside a closed shape to fill that shape. Figure 3-26 shows the vine with pink flowers and green leaves.

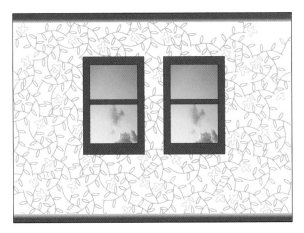

Figure 3-26: One click covered the entire wall. If only putting up wallpaper were so easy!

In the Property inspector, you can vary the vine in the following ways:

- **Leaf:** Click the color swatch to choose another color. Instead, you can click the Edit button to choose a graphic or movie clip symbol from the Library to replace the leaf. (We explain how to create symbols in Chapter 7.)

- **Flower:** Click the color swatch to choose another color. Instead, you can click the Edit button to choose a graphic or movie clip symbol from the Library to replace the flower.

- **Branch Angle:** Specify a new angle to change the angle of the branches. This is like rotating the pattern.

- **Branch Color:** Click the color swatch to change the color of the branches

- **Pattern Scale:** Enter a value to scale the entire pattern. You can scale both up (more than 100%) for a less busy look and down (less than 100%).

- **Segment Length:** Enter a value to set the length between the leaf and flower nodes.

- **Animate Pattern:** Select the Animate Pattern check box to automatically animate the drawing of the vine so that each section goes to a new keyframe in the Timeline. Instant animation! (We explain animation in Chapter 9.)

- **Frame Step:** Enter a value to specify how many frames you want to include for each second of the animation.

Grid fill

The Grid fill creates a simple, rectangular array. By default, it uses a black square as the arrayed object. In the Property inspector (Window➪ Properties), you can vary the pattern as follows:

- ✔ **Fill Symbol:** Click the Color swatch to change the color or click the Edit button to choose a graphic or movie clip symbol from the Library to replace the square.

- ✔ **Horizontal Spacing:** Enter a value to set the horizontal spacing.

- ✔ **Vertical Spacing:** Enter a value to set the vertical spacing.

Figure 3-27: Droplets in a drop.

- ✔ **Pattern Scale:** Enter a percent to scale the object that you're arraying and, therefore, the entire pattern.

Figure 3-27 shows a grid pattern. We thought the black square was pretty boring, so we filled a big drop with little droplets.

Symmetry brush

The Symmetry brush creates four types of symmetrical designs. To choose one, click the Deco tool on the Tools panel and display the Property inspector (Window➪Properties). You can use the default black square or click the color swatch to choose another color. Alternatively, click the Edit button to choose a graphic or movie clip symbol. (We explain symbols in Chapter 7.) Then choose one of the following in the Advanced Options drop-down list:

- ✔ **Reflect Across Line:** Displays a vertical green line with a rotation handle at one end and a moving handle at the other. Drag the rotation handle to rotate the line. Drag the moving handle to move the line. Click on one side of the line to place the specified object, and you automatically get a mirror image on the other side of the line.

- ✔ **Reflect Across Point:** Displays a green circle. Click on one side of the circle to place the specified object, and you automatically get a mirror image on the other side of the point.

- ✔ **Rotate Around Point:** Displays two green lines. One line is like the line for the Reflect Across Line symmetry; the other appears at an angle that determines the number of objects placed around the point. You can drag the end of the second line to change the angle. Click on one side of the vertical line, and you get a radial pattern around the central point. You can continue to place more objects, as shown in Figure 3-28.

- ✔ **Grid Translation:** Displays a horizontal and a vertical axis with handles near the axes' origin that let you change the distance and angle of the grid. Click to create a grid pattern.

TIP

After creating a pattern, but before deselecting it, you can adjust the green line, or circle, and change the pattern of the objects you've added. You can even choose a different pattern type from the Advanced Options drop-down list. But once you move on to another tool, you have to delete the group of objects and start over to change the pattern.

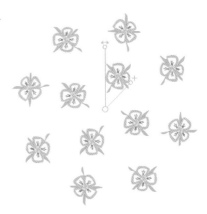

Figure 3-28: With two clicks, we created this radial pattern of flowers.

Drawing Precisely

If drawing in Flash seems too loosey-goosey to you, you need to know about a few features that can help you draw more precisely. Other programs do offer more precise tools, but Flash might have the tools you need.

The ruler rules

To help you get your bearings, you can choose View➪Rulers to display the Flash ruler along the top and left side of the Stage, as shown in Figure 3-29.

Figure 3-29: Display the ruler to help you draw more precisely; for more control, drag guides onto the Stage.

To give yourself more room to work while you create drawing objects on the Stage, you can hide the Timeline by choosing Window⇨Timeline. Do the same to display the Timeline again when you need to work with layers or start animating your work.

By default, the ruler is measured in *pixels.* Computer screens are measured by how many pixels they display horizontally and vertically. Pixels are useful for Web site work because Web browsers work with only this unit. A pixel, however, is not a fixed physical size because it depends on the resolution capacity and settings of your screen. You might find it easier to think in inches or millimeters.

You can set the ruler to the unit of measurement that is most helpful to you. Choose Modify⇨Document to open the Document Properties dialog box. In the Ruler Units drop-down list, choose one of the units (pixels, inches, points, centimeters, or millimeters) and then click OK.

When the ruler is displayed, lines appear on the top and side rulers whenever you drag an object — either while creating it or editing it. For example, when you drag to create a rectangle, you see a line on each ruler telling you where you started and where you ended up. If you're moving the rectangle, Flash displays two lines on each ruler indicating the outside dimensions of the rectangle. You can easily move the rectangle 1 inch — or 50 pixels — to the left by looking at the lines on the top ruler.

Using guides

Guides help you lay out the Stage more precisely. *Guides* (refer to Figure 3-29) are horizontal and vertical lines that you can use as drawing aids while you work. Don't worry — guides never appear in the published Flash Player file. To use the guides, you must display the rulers, as we describe in the preceding section.

To display the guides, you need to drag them from the rulers. Drag from the left ruler to create a vertical guide, and drag from the top ruler to create a horizontal guide. (If you still don't see the guides, choose View⇨Guides⇨Show Guides and make sure that there's a check next to the Show Guides menu item.)

To customize the guides, choose View⇨Guides⇨Edit Guides to open the Guides dialog box, where you can choose the guide color or clear all the guides. To force objects to *snap* (attach) to the guides, select the Snap to Guides check box in the Guides dialog box. You can use the Snap Accuracy drop-down list in the Guides dialog box to choose how precisely Flash snaps to the guides. To lock the guides so that they don't move while you work, choose View⇨Guides⇨Lock Guides. To remove an individual guide, drag it back to its vertical or horizontal ruler.

Working with the grid

You can display a grid on the Stage to help you draw more accurately and gauge distances. The grid exists only to guide you — it never appears when the movie is printed or published on a Web site. Simply displaying the grid doesn't constrain your objects to points on the grid. Use the grid by itself when you want a visual guide for drawing, sizing, moving, and laying out the Stage.

To display the grid, choose View➪Grid➪Show Grid. Use the same command to hide the grid again. You can set the size of the grid squares and change the color of the grid lines in the Grid dialog box. To open the dialog box, choose View➪Grid➪Edit Grid. You can change the units of measurement used for the grid by choosing Modify➪Document. In the Modify Document dialog box, select the unit that you want in the Ruler Units drop-down list and click OK.

Snapping turtle

When you want even more precision, you can turn on snapping. *Snapping* tells Flash to snap objects to the intersections on the grid or to other objects. Usually, you want the grid on when you use snapping so that you can see the snap points.

 To turn on snapping, choose the Selection tool and click the Snap modifier in the Options section of the Tools panel or Choose View➪Snapping➪Snap to Objects. To snap to the grid, choose View➪Snapping➪Snap to Grid. Use the same method to turn snapping off again. Snapping pulls your cursor to the grid points and to existing objects while you work. You can take advantage of snapping both while drawing new objects and editing existing objects. When you have snapping on and select an object, Flash displays a small, black circle and snaps the circle to the grid points.

Setting snap-to-grid preferences

 You can get downright picky about how Flash snaps to grid points. Do you want the end of a line (for example) to always snap, or should it snap only if it's close to a grid point or an existing object? To set your preferences, choose View➪Grid➪Edit Grid. In the Snap Accuracy drop-down list, select one of the options, which range from Must Be Close to Always Snap.

Setting snap-to-objects preferences

Because snapping applies to objects as well as grid points, you can separately set how Flash snaps to objects. Choose Edit➪Preferences (Windows) or Flash➪Preferences (Mac) and then click the Drawing category. In the Connect Lines drop-down list, select Must Be Close, Normal, or Can Be Distant. Although Flash calls this the Connect Lines setting, it affects rectangles and ovals as well as the lines you draw with the Line and Pencil tools.

This setting also affects how Flash recognizes horizontal and vertical lines and makes them perfectly horizontal or vertical. For example, the Can Be Distant setting adjusts a more angled line than the Must Be Close setting.

Pixel, pixel on the wall

If the grid isn't precise enough, you can snap to pixels. Choose View⇨Snapping⇨Snap to Pixels to toggle snapping to pixels on and off. If Snap to Pixels is on, Flash automatically displays the pixel grid when you zoom in to 400% or higher. With Snap to Pixels on, you can snap all objects that you create or move to the pixel grid.

When Snap to Pixels is on, you can press the C key to temporarily turn off pixel snapping. In the same situation, you can hold down the X key to temporarily hide the pixel grid (but not while you're in the process of drawing). You can also precisely align existing objects. For more information, see Chapter 4.

The Import Business — Using Outside Graphics

So maybe you're the lazy type — or totally without artistic talent — and you really need help. Flash hasn't given up on you completely. Rather than create your own graphics, you can use the work of others. Although Flash creates vector-based graphics, it can import both bitmap and vector graphic files.

When using others' artwork, be careful about copyright issues. For example, some graphics available on the Web can be used for personal, but not commercial, purposes. Most Web sites that offer graphics for downloading offer a policy explaining how you can use their graphics.

Importing graphics

To import a graphic file, follow these steps:

1. **Choose File⇨Import⇨Import to Stage.**

   The Import dialog box opens.

2. **In the dialog box, locate and choose the file that you want.**

3. **Click Open/Import to open the file.**

   The file appears on the Stage. If the file is a bitmap, it also goes into the Library. To import a graphic file directly into the Library without displaying it on the Stage, choose File⇨Import⇨Import to Library.

A cool feature of Flash is its capability to recognize and import sequences of images. If the image file that you choose in the Import dialog box ends with a number — and other files in the same folder have the same name but end with consecutive numbers (for example, animal1, animal2, and so on) — Flash asks whether you want to import the entire sequence of files. Click Yes to import the sequence. Flash imports the images as successive frames on the active layer so that you can use them as the basis for animation. (Chapter 9 explains more about frames and animation.) Table 3-1 provides a list of the types of files you can import into Flash.

Table 3-1	Files That Flash Can Import	
File Type	**Windows**	**Mac**
Adobe Illustrator (.ai) through version 10	X	X
AutoCAD DXF (.dxf); 2D only	X	X
Bitmap (.bmp)	X	X*
Enhanced Metafile (.emf)	X	
Flash Player 6/7 (.swf)	X	X
FreeHand (.fh*); versions 7 to 11	X	X
FutureSplash Player (.spl)	X	X
GIF/animated GIF (.gif)	X	X
JPEG (.jpg)	X	X
MacPaint (.pntg)*	X	X
Photoshop (.psd)	X	X
PICT (.pct, .pic)*		X
PNG (.png)	X	X
QuickTime image (.qtif)*	X	X
Silicon Graphics Image (.sgi)*	X	X
Targa (.tga)*	X	X
TIFF (.tif)*	X	X
Windows Metafile (.wmf)	X	

*Only if QuickTime 4 or later is installed

You can also simply copy and paste graphics. From the other application, copy the graphic to the Clipboard; then return to Flash and choose Edit⇨ Paste. However, in some cases, you might lose transparency when using this method. See Chapter 13 for details on exporting objects.

Flash CS4 offers special controls for importing Photoshop and Illustrator files. For Photoshop files, you can import the layers intact. When you import the file, a dialog box opens where you can specify which layers you want to keep. You can convert layers to Flash layers or to keyframes. For each layer, you decide whether to import the layer with editable layer styles or as a flattened (simple) image. For Illustrator files, you can maintain the ability to edit text and paths in Flash. These and other controls give you a huge amount of power over the result of the import. Choose Edit➪Preferences and choose PSD File Importer or AI File Importer to set default settings when you import these files. You can change these settings whenever you import a file.

Using imported graphics

Vector graphics from any drawing program become a grouped object that you can use like any other Flash object. The `.wmf` format, which is a Windows vector graphics format, also imports in this way. These formats work especially well when imported into Flash. You can sometimes find `.wmf` graphics in clip art collections and on the Web. Import text from a text editor, and Flash turns it into a Flash text object so that you can edit and format in Flash. See Chapter 5 for more on text.

When you import a bitmap graphic, you often need to take some steps before you can use the graphic in your Flash file. You can manipulate your graphics in several ways to make them more Flash friendly:

- **Delete the background.** Some files may include a rectangular background you don't want. To get rid of that background, deselect the imported object, select just the rectangular background, and press Delete. If that doesn't work, read on.

- **Ungroup the graphic.** Ungrouping separates grouped elements into individual elements. Ungrouping retains most of the features of your graphic. Select the graphic and choose Modify➪Ungroup. If you find that you still can't work with your graphic properly, read the next item.

- **Break apart the graphic.** Break imported graphics to separate them into ungrouped, editable elements. Breaking apart is useful for reducing the file size of graphics that you import. Breaking apart converts bitmaps to fills, converts text to letters and outlines, and breaks the link between an OLE (Object Linking and Embedding) object and its source application. In other words, the Break Apart command is a powerful tool. Select the graphic and choose Modify➪Break Apart. You may have to repeat the process to break the graphic completely apart.

- **Trace the bitmap.** Flash can work magic. If you want total control within Flash, convert a bitmap to a vector graphic.

To trace a bitmap, follow these steps:

1. Import the bitmap — don't deselect it or perform any other action on it.

2. Choose Modify⇨Bitmap⇨Trace Bitmap.

   The Trace Bitmap dialog box opens.

3. In the Color Threshold text box, type a number to represent the threshold.

   The higher the number, the fewer the colors you get in the final vector graphic. For close results, try a value of 10.

4. In the Minimum Area box, type a number to represent the number of nearby pixels that Flash considers when assigning a color to a pixel.

   For greatest fidelity, try a value of 1.

5. In the Curve Fit drop-down list, select an option to represent how smoothly Flash draws the outlines.

   For the most exact results, select Pixels.

6. In the Corner Threshold drop-down list, select an option to represent how Flash reproduces sharp edges.

   For sharpest results, choose Many Corners.

7. Click OK to close the Trace Bitmap dialog box, and then deselect the graphic to see the result.

Figure 3-30 shows the result on our hummingbird photograph.

Figure 3-30: Convert complex bitmaps to vector drawings.

When you import a bitmap graphic, Flash places it in the current movie's Library. For best results, don't delete the original graphic from the Library, even if you have modified it. Flash continues to refer to the graphic after you have converted it to a symbol. (Chapter 2 explains all about the Library. See Chapter 7 for our total wisdom on symbols.)

Whether you created your graphics in Flash or imported them, you probably need to edit them. Chapter 4 explains the details of editing objects.

4

You Are the Object Editor

*T*his chapter tells you all you need to know about editing objects. You can manipulate objects in a zillion ways to suit your artistic fancy. The Flash editing tools can give you precisely the results that you want. Sometimes you need to edit because you made a mistake (rarely, of course), but often, editing is just part of the creation process. You might also find that you have to alter imported graphics so that they fit into the scheme of things.

Selecting Objects

Before you can edit any object on the Stage, you need to select it. Flash offers many ways to select objects. After you get the hang of using the Flash selection tools, you'll find them efficient and easy to use.

Selecting with the Selection tool

To select an object, click the Selection tool (the dark-colored arrow in the Tools panel) and click the object. That sounds pretty basic. But just when you thought it was safe to skip the rest of this section, we add some ifs and buts, so read on.

What defines an object? A shape that includes an outline (also called a *line* or a *stroke*) and a fill (such as a filled-in circle) has two objects — the outline and the fill.

Most of these selection guidelines don't work when you use the object-drawing model for creating objects. When you use the object-drawing model to draw an object (such as a rectangle), both the stroke and the fill are considered one object, so you can't select the stroke or the fill individually. (We explain the object-drawing model in Chapter 3.) The same holds true for symbols, which we cover in Chapter 7.

Here are some pointers for selecting objects:

- ✔ **If the object doesn't have an outline and is just a fill,** you're home free. Click the object with the Selection tool, and it's selected.

- ✔ **If the object has an outline and a fill,** clicking the fill selects only the fill. The outline remains deselected. To select both the fill and the outline, double-click the object.

- ✔ **To select the entire object,** you can use the Selection tool to create a selection box. Click at one corner and drag to an opposite corner, making sure that the bounding box completely encloses the object or objects that you want to select, as shown in Figure 4-1.

- ✔ **To select just an outline,** click the outline with the Selection tool. Still, you never know when an outline is really several objects, like the one in Figure 4-1, which is made up of several curves. To select the entire outline, double-click it.

- ✔ **To select several unconnected objects,** select one object, press and hold the Shift key, and select additional objects. When you press Shift, you can add to already selected objects and select as many objects as you want.

Figure 4-1: Create a bounding box with the Selection tool.

To deselect selected objects, click any blank area.

So you're happily drawing away, using the various drawing tools. Then you want to select one of the objects, but you forget to change to the Selection tool. Oops! You draw another object by accident. Immediately choose Edit➪Undo. Then use one of the Flash shortcuts:

- Press the V key to switch to the Selection tool.

- To temporarily switch to the Selection tool while you're using another tool, hold Ctrl (Windows) or ⌘ (Mac) while you select an object or objects.

Lassoing your objects

For you rodeo types, you can lasso your objects so that they can't escape. The Lasso tool creates a customized selection area and selects everything inside. Use the Lasso tool when you want to select a number of objects that are near other objects that you want to remain free.

 To lasso objects, click the Lasso tool on the Tools panel.

To lasso freehand, make sure that the Polygon Mode modifier (in the Options section of the Tools panel) is not selected. Click anywhere on the Stage and drag around the objects that you want to select. Flash creates a selection area while you drag. Release the mouse button close to where you started it to close the lasso's loop, as shown in Figure 4-2.

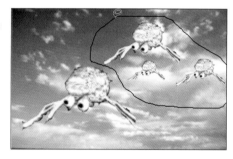

You might find that freehand lassoing is hard to control. If you tend to inadvertently cut across objects rather than glide around them, use the Polygon Mode modifier to draw polygons instead — like a lasso with a very stiff rope.

Figure 4-2: Lasso freehand to select only the objects you want.

To lasso by using straight lines, follow these steps:

1. **Click to choose the Lasso tool.**

 2. **Click the Polygon Mode modifier in the Options section of the Tools panel.**

3. **Click where you want the first line of the polygon to start.**

4. **Click again where you want the first line to end.**

5. **Continue to click, creating line segments as you go.**

6. **Double-click when you finish lassoing the objects.**

Selecting everything in one fell swoop

Suppose that you want to select or deselect all objects at one time. Flash has some handy shortcuts to help you do that:

- **To select everything:** Press Ctrl+A (Windows) or ⌘+A (Mac). Or choose Edit➪Select All. The Select All command selects all objects on all layers except for objects on locked or hidden layers. (See Chapter 6 for an explanation of layers.)

- **To select everything on one layer:** Click the layer name.

- **To deselect everything:** The easiest method is to click off the Stage or on any blank area of the Stage. Alternatively, you can press Ctrl+Shift+A (Windows) or ⌘+Shift+A (Mac). Or choose Edit➪Deselect All. The Deselect All command deselects all objects on all layers.

To lock a group or symbol so that it can't be selected or edited, select the group or symbol and choose Modify➪Arrange➪Lock. To unlock a group or symbol, choose Modify➪Arrange➪Unlock All. (See the section "Getting Grouped," later in this chapter, to find out about groups. Chapter 7 is all about symbols.)

Moving, Copying, Deleting, and Erasing

The most common changes that you make to objects are to move, copy, delete, and erase them. Usually, these are straightforward tasks — but Flash has a few tricks up its sleeve, so keep on truckin'.

Movin' on down the road

Before you can move an object, you have to select it. After you select your object or objects, place the mouse cursor over any selected object until your cursor displays the dreaded four-headed arrow. (Okay, most people don't dread it at all.) Then click and drag to wherever you're going. Press Shift while you drag to constrain the movement to a 45-degree angle.

Moving precisely with Snap Align

When you drag an object, you see vertical and horizontal dashed lines when your object approaches existing objects. This Snap Align feature displays temporary dashed lines when you move objects to show you when the edges of objects are aligned, both vertically and horizontally, with existing objects.

Snap alignment is great for quickly aligning two objects without using the Align panel. While you drag a selected object, the dashed lines appear when you move an object in alignment with an existing object, as shown in Figure 4-3. You also see the lines when you drag an object close to any edge of the Stage.

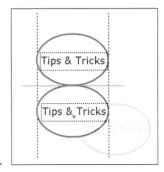

To turn on snap alignment (although it is on by default), choose View➪Snapping➪Snap Align. You see a check mark next to the Snap Align item. Repeat the process to turn off snap alignment.

Figure 4-3: Snap alignment displays alignment between objects while you move them.

You can customize your snap alignment settings. Choose View➪Snapping➪Edit Snapping to open the Edit Snapping dialog box. Then click the Advanced button to expand the dialog box, as shown in Figure 4-4.

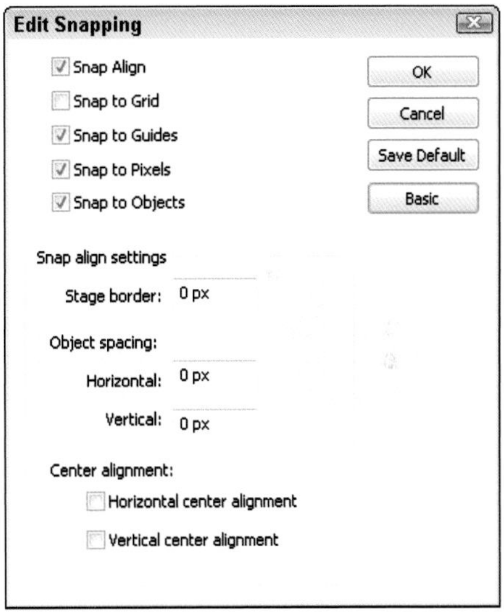

In the Edit Snapping dialog box, you can also turn on snap alignment for the centers of objects — for easy centering of objects — by selecting both check boxes in the Center Alignment section.

Flash assumes that a border exists around the edge of the Stage. To change the border width, type a different number in the Stage Border box. To change the precision for alignment between objects, type a number in the Horizontal and Vertical boxes in the Object Spacing section of the dialog box. Click OK when you're finished to close the dialog box.

Figure 4-4: Make your snap alignments snap to your orders.

You can also use the grid and turn on the snapping feature for moving and copying objects. (See Chapter 3 to find out about the grid and snapping.) For example, you can attach one object to another by moving your first object until it snaps to the second, using the small black circle at the cursor as a guide.

The snap align feature aligns objects by their edges. Object snapping aligns objects by their transformation point. See the "Changing the Transformation Point" section, later in this chapter, for more information.

You can also use the four arrow keys on your keyboard to move a selected object or objects. Each press of an arrow key moves the selection one screen pixel in the direction of the arrow. Press Shift plus an arrow key to move the selection by 10 screen pixels.

Moving with the Clipboard

You can move an object by cutting to the Clipboard and pasting if you want to move the object to another layer, scene, file, or application. After you select the object or objects, choose Edit➪Cut. Alternatively, press Ctrl+X (Windows) or ⌘+X (Mac). Choose another layer or scene or open another file and do one of the following:

- ✔ **To paste the selection in the center of the display:** Choose Edit➪Paste, or press Ctrl+V (Windows) or ⌘+V (Mac).

- ✔ **To paste the selection in the same position relative to the Stage:** Choose Edit➪Paste in Place, or press Ctrl+Shift+V (Windows) or ⌘+Shift+V (Mac).

Moving with the Property inspector

If you want to place objects precisely, use the Property inspector. After you select an object or objects, choose Window➪Properties, as shown in Figure 4-5.

Use the X and Y values to specify the location. The X setting specifies horizontal distance and the Y setting specifies vertical distance — and both are measured from the top-left corner of the Stage. To change a value, click it, type a new one, and then press Enter; or, drag the value up or down.

Figure 4-5: Use the Property inspector to place objects precisely.

Moving with the Info panel

You can also use the Info panel to specify the X and Y positions of objects. Choose Window➪Info to open the panel, as shown in Figure 4-6. You can use the grid next to the X and Y text boxes to specify if you're measuring either from the upper-left corner or the center of the selection. Just click the grid to toggle between the two options. Flash uses the units you specify in the Document Properties dialog box. (See the section

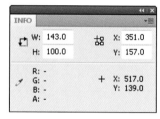

Figure 4-6: The Info panel.

in Chapter 3 on drawing precisely for information on setting the units.) Then enter the desired X and Y location in the X and Y text boxes.

Remember that moving an object onto another existing object on the same layer does one of the following:

- ✔ Joins it, if the objects are the same color

- ✔ Cuts it out, if the objects are different colors — unless you drew the object in object-drawing mode or you used a primitive shape (oval or rectangle)

See the section in Chapter 3 on mixing and matching shapes for more information.

Aligning objects with the Align panel

The Snap Align feature, as we explain in the "Moving precisely with Snap Align" section, earlier in this chapter, is the quick way to align objects. However, for more options and precision, use the Align panel. The Align panel gives you the tools to line up two or more objects vertically or horizontally and also lets you put equal space between three or more objects. Align and space objects to make your Flash movie look professional, as opposed to something that you might create at 3 a.m. when your vision is too blurry for you to see straight.

To align objects, select the objects and choose Window➪Align to open the Align panel, as shown in Figure 4-7.

Figure 4-7: Use the Align panel to line up and evenly distribute objects.

In the panel, choose the option that you want for aligning or distributing objects. For example, you can align objects along their tops, their left sides, or any other direction. You can match the size of objects (resize them) by using the Match Size buttons, or you can make the spaces between objects the same with the Space buttons. Experiment with the options in this panel until you get the results that you want.

To perfectly center one object on the Stage

1. **Select it and open the Align panel.**

2. **Click the To Stage button.**

3. **Click both the Align Vertical Center and the Align Horizontal Center buttons.**

    Flash centers the object on the Stage.

A quicker way is to cut and paste the object because Flash automatically pastes objects at the center of the display (which is at the middle of the Stage if you haven't panned or scrolled the display).

If you use the To Stage button, be sure to deselect it when you're finished because it can cause unexpected results the next time you use it.

Copying objects

After you spend loads of time creating a cool graphic, you might want to copy it all over the place. The easiest way is to clone it directly by dragging. Just select the object and press Ctrl (Windows) or Option (Mac) while you drag. Flash makes a copy and moves it wherever you drag.

You can also copy objects to the Clipboard. Select an object or objects and then choose Edit⇔Copy or press Ctrl+C (Windows) or ⌘+C (Mac). You can paste the selection on the same layer or move it to another layer, scene, or file by using one of these techniques:

- ✔ **To paste the selection in the center of the display:** Choose Edit⇔Paste, or press Ctrl+V (Windows) or ⌘+V (Mac).

- ✔ **To paste the selection in the same position relative to the Stage:** Choose Edit⇔Paste in Place. If you're on the same layer, scene, and file, you now have two copies, one on top of the other. The new object is selected, so you can immediately drag it to a new location.

Because Flash pastes objects from the Clipboard to the exact center of the display, cutting and pasting is a great technique for centering objects on top of each other. For example, if you want to create two concentric circles, one on top of the other, create the circles in separate locations. Cut and paste the larger circle first and the smaller circle second. You now have perfect concentric circles, as shown in Figure 4-8, and you can move them together to the desired location. This technique works only if the Stage is at the center of your display — that is, if you haven't scrolled the display.

Figure 4-8: Perfectly concentric circles create a bulls-eye!

When you paste a new object, be sure to move the new object right away if it covers an existing object on the same layer. If you deselect the new object, it either joins the existing object (if the objects are the same color) or cuts it out (if they're different colors). Of course, that might be your intention. See the section in Chapter 3 on mixing and matching shapes for more information, including how to avoid this joining and cutout behavior.

Makin' objects go away

Making objects go away is easy. Just select them and press Delete or Backspace (Clear on the Mac).

Erasing objects

Erasing objects is like using a blackboard eraser (remember those?) or pencil eraser. Flash erases, pixel by pixel, where you erase. Luckily, Flash offers some tools that help you control the process.

 To erase objects, choose the Eraser tool on the Tools panel. Click and drag across any object to erase where you drag. The eraser erases objects drawn with or without object-drawing model on. However, it does not erase grouped objects, symbols, or text. (We cover grouping later in this chapter. We cover text in Chapter 5 and symbols in Chapter 7.)

 To erase all the objects on the Stage — and even objects off the Stage — double-click the Eraser tool. All gone!

 You can control how the eraser works. You can set the size and shape of the eraser. For example, if you need to get into a small spot, make the eraser smaller. To set the size, click the Eraser Shape button in the Options section of the Tools panel. In the drop-down list that appears, you can choose a circle or square shape, and both shapes come in several sizes.

 You can specify several eraser modes to fine-tune your results. To set the Eraser Mode modifier, click the Eraser Mode button to display the following options:

- ✔ **Erase Normal:** Dragging erases strokes and fills wherever you drag.
- ✔ **Erase Fills:** You can erase only fills, so you can messily drag over strokes without harming them. The strokes look like they're erased as you drag, but they magically reappear when you release your mouse button.
- ✔ **Erase Lines:** You can erase only strokes, so you can messily drag over fills without harming them. The fills look like they're erased as you drag, but they magically reappear when you release your mouse button.
- ✔ **Erase Selected Fills:** Select fills before you start. Then, dragging erases only the fills you selected and nothing else.
- ✔ **Erase Inside:** If you start dragging on a fill, you erase only that fill. All other fills are immune. If you start dragging in an empty area, nothing happens at all. This mode does not affect strokes.

 The Faucet modifier is like using the Delete key for fills and strokes. Choose the Eraser tool, click the Faucet modifier, and click any fill or stroke to instantly delete it. You don't even have to select the object first.

Making Shapes More Shapely

Suppose that you created an object and now you want to tweak it a bit. Flash has many techniques to help you perfect your artwork, and you can modify both lines and fills.

Reshaping shapes and outlines

The Selection tool can do more than select objects. It can also reshape them as long as you didn't create them by using the object-drawing model or a primitive shape. When you reshape with the Selection tool, you do *not* select the object.

To reshape an outline or a fill, choose the Selection tool and place the mouse cursor near the object or on the edge of the object:

- **If you see a corner next to the cursor,** you can move, lengthen, or shorten an end point, as shown on the left side of Figure 4-9.

- **If you see a curve next to the cursor,** you can reshape a curve, as shown on the right side of Figure 4-9.

Figure 4-9: The Selection tool modifies end points and curves.

Click and drag in the desired direction. Flash temporarily displays a black drag line to show you what the result will look like when you release the mouse button. If you don't like the result, choose Edit⟳Undo — or press Ctrl+Z (Windows) or ⌘+Z (Mac) — and try again.

Like with drawing, you might find it helpful to increase the zoom factor. Try editing at 200 or 400 percent.

Using the Subselect tool

You can use the Subselect tool to reshape individual strokes or fills created by using the Pen, Pencil, Brush, Line, Oval, or Rectangle tools. When you use the Subselect tool, you move *anchor points,* which are small circles that appear on the object. To use Subselect, follow these steps:

1. **Choose the Subselect tool (the light-colored arrow in the Tools panel).**

2. **Click the stroke (outline) or fill to display the anchor points.**

3. Drag the anchor points to modify the shape.

4. To change the direction of a curve, click any anchor point to display tangent lines and drag the tangent line handles (the little dots at the ends of the tangent lines), as shown in Figure 4-10.

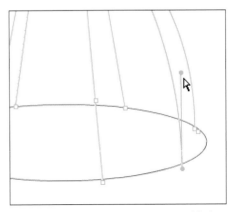

The tangent lines indicate the direction of the curve. See the section in Chapter 3 on drawing curves with the Pen tool for information on anchor points and tangent lines.

Figure 4-10: Subtle changes are easy with the Subselect tool.

If you use the Subselect tool to click a graphic and points aren't displayed on its edges, you might have grouped the graphic (as we describe later in this chapter), or you might have created it with the object-drawing model, or maybe you didn't create it with the Pen, Pencil, Brush, Line, Oval, or Rectangle tool. Try choosing Modify⇨Ungroup or Modify⇨Break Apart and then using the Subselect tool.

You can also delete anchor points. Flash reshapes the shape without that anchor point. Select the object with the Subselect tool, select an anchor point, and then press Backspace or Delete.

When you use the Subselect tool on an oval or rectangle primitive, you can change only its parametric properties. For example, you can change the corner radius of a primitive rectangle. For a primitive oval, you can change the inner radius, start angle, and end angle.

Adjusting curves with the Pen tool

You can make adjustments to objects that you drew with the Pen tool. Click the Pen tool and then click the object. You now see anchor points along the curves and lines. Here's what you can do:

- ✔ **Add an anchor point.** Hover the cursor over any place that doesn't already have one. You see a little plus sign. Just click wherever you want to add the point. Alternatively, click and hold the Pen tool to display the flyout and choose the Add Anchor Point tool.

- ✔ **Delete an anchor point.** Hover the cursor over any anchor point. You see a little minus sign. Click the anchor point. Alternatively, click and hold the Pen tool to display the flyout and choose the Delete Anchor Point tool.

✔ **Convert an anchor point.** Anchor points can be curve points or corner points. To convert from one to the other, click and hold the Pen tool to display the flyout and choose the Convert Anchor Point tool. Then click any object you created with the Pen tool and click an anchor point. If you're converting to a curve point, immediately drag to position the tangent line handles.

Freely transforming and distorting shapes

For way-cool distortions and reshapings, use the Free Transform tool, with its Distort & Envelope options. The Free Transform tool can work its magic on objects, groups, instances, or text blocks. In addition to its special ability to create distortions, it's flexible enough to move, rotate, scale, and skew objects. Flash has other tools that rotate, scale, and skew — we cover them later in this chapter.

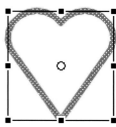

Figure 4-11: We love the Free Transform tool!

 To use the Free Transform tool, select an object, symbol instance, group, or text block. (See Chapter 7 for more about symbols. We discuss groups later in this chapter.) Click the Free Transform tool in the Tools panel. The object displays a bounding box with handles and a *transformation point,* shown as a circle at the center of the bounding box, as shown in Figure 4-11.

You can perform the following transformations on the selected object:

✢ ✔ **Move.** Place the cursor on the object itself; when you see the four-headed arrow, click and drag to move the selected object.

❏ ✔ **Set the center for rotation and scaling.** Place the cursor on the transformation point; when you see the small circle, you can drag the circle at the center of the bounding box to move the transformation point. The *transformation point* is the base point used for the current rotation or scaling operation.

↷ ✔ **Rotate.** Place the cursor just outside any corner handle; when you see the circular arrow, drag the object to rotate it around the transformation point.

 Press Shift while you drag to constrain the rotation to 45-degree increments. Press Alt (Windows) or Option (Mac) while you drag to rotate around the diagonally opposite corner from your cursor.

- **Scale both dimensions.** Place the cursor on any corner handle; when you see the broken, two-headed arrow, drag inward or outward. Press Shift while you drag to ensure that the object is scaled proportionally without being distorted.

You can select as many objects as you want, and Flash scales them all. When you select more than one object, Flash places the handles around an imaginary bounding box that encompasses all the objects. Sometimes you might not get exactly the result you want with this method, so check carefully.

- **Scale one dimension.** Place the cursor on any side handle; when you see the two-headed arrow, drag inward or outward to scale in the direction that you're dragging.

- **Skew.** Place the cursor anywhere on the bounding box except the handles; when you see the parallel lines, drag in any direction. (We cover skewing in more detail in the "Getting skewy" section, later in this chapter.)

In the following sections, you find out about the more exciting transformations that you can create with the Free Transform tool.

Tapering objects

You can turn a square into a trapezoid by tapering. When you *taper,* you use the Free Transform tool to drag a corner handle. While you drag, the adjoining corner moves an equal distance in the opposite direction, as shown in Figure 4-12. You can taper any shape except rectangle and oval primitives.

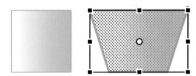

Figure 4-12: Tapering turns a square into a trapezoid.

To taper, press Ctrl+Shift (Windows) or ⌘+Shift (Mac) while you drag on a corner handle of the bounding box. You can also use the Distort option of the Free Transform tool: Click the Distort button in the Options section of the Tools panel and press Shift while you drag any corner handle. (This technique is ideal for people who have trouble pressing both Shift and Ctrl or ⌘ at the same time.)

Distorting objects

For even weirder effects, you can *distort* shapes (objects) — but not primitives, symbols, symbol instances, text, or groups. When you distort an object, you change the shape of the bounding box, and the shape is stretched in the same amount and direction as the bounding box, as shown in Figure 4-13.

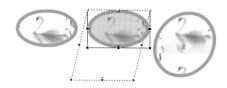

To distort shapes with the Free Transform tool, press Ctrl (Windows) or ⌘ (Mac) and drag either a corner or a side handle on the bounding box. To use the menu, choose Modify⇨Transform⇨Distort.

Figure 4-13: Drag the bounding box into a new shape; the object follows suit.

Stretching the envelope

You can make even more-refined changes in the shape of the bounding box by using the Envelope command. With this option, the bounding box takes on editing points like you see when you use the Pen tool. As you drag the points, tangent lines appear, as shown in Figure 4-14.

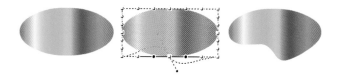

Figure 4-14: The oval is like taffy when you push the envelope.

To use the Envelope command, select an object — a shape — but not a symbol, instance, text, or group. Click the Free Transform button on the Tools palette and then click the Envelope button in the Options area. (To use the menu, choose Modify⇨Transform⇨Envelope.) Drag any of the points in or out and then drag the end of any of the tangent lines to change the direction of the curve.

To end a free transformation, click anywhere off the selected object.

Straightening lines and curving curves

Just like you can straighten and smooth strokes by using the Straighten and Smooth modifiers of the Pencil tool, respectively, you can straighten and smooth strokes and fills of existing objects. (See Chapter 3 for more about the Pencil tool.)

You can activate the Straighten and Smooth modifiers repeatedly and watch while Flash slightly reshapes your strokes or fills each time. Eventually, Flash reaches a point where it can't smooth or straighten anymore.

Choose Edit⇨Preferences and then choose the Drawing category to adjust how Flash calculates the straightening and smoothing. Change the Smooth Curves and Recognize Shapes settings.

To straighten a stroke, follow these steps:

1. **Select the object.**

   It's often useful to select several connected strokes.

2. **Choose Modify⇨Shape⇨Straighten.**

3. **In the Straighten dialog box that appears, select the Preview check box to see whether you like the result before closing the dialog box.**

4. **Click the arrow to the right of the Straighten Strength text box and then drag the slider upward. Release the mouse button to see the results.**

5. **Continue to try various strengths until you find the one that works for you.**

   Flash straightens out curves and recognizes shapes, if appropriate.

6. **Click OK to close the Straighten dialog box.**

 A simpler way to straighten an object is to select it with the Selection tool active and repeatedly click the Straighten modifier button in the Options section of the Tools panel.

 Smooth softens curves and reduces the number of segments that create a curve. To smooth a curve, follow these steps:

1. **Select the object.**

   It's often useful to select several connected strokes.

2. **Choose Modify⇨Shape⇨ Smooth.**

   The Smooth dialog box appears, as shown in Figure 4-15.

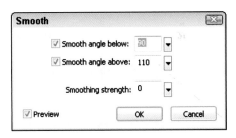

Figure 4-15: Use the Smooth dialog box to be a smooth operator.

3. **Select the Preview check box to see whether you like the result before closing the dialog box.**

4. **Click the arrow to the right of the Smoothing Strength text box and then drag the slider upward. Release the mouse button to see the results.**

5. **If you want, adjust the angles, above and below which the smoothing applies by entering angle values in the Smooth Angle Below and Smooth Angle Above text boxes.**

   You can clear one of the check boxes (but not both) to restrict smoothing to only below or only above a certain angle.

6. Continue to try various strengths until you find the one that works for you.

7. Click OK to close the Smooth text box.

A simpler way to smooth an object is to select it with the Selection tool active and repeatedly click the Smooth modifier button in the Options section of the Tools panel.

Modifying line endings

You can use *line caps* to customize the ends of lines that you draw. (See the section on setting the stroke type in Chapter 3 for details on caps.) You can change existing line caps. You can also choose a join style for the meeting point of two lines. Select a line and display the Property inspector. (Choose Window⇨Properties⇨Properties.) Select a new option in the Cap or Join drop-down list. You'll notice the effect more on wide lines.

Optimizing curves

Flash offers a technique for curves called optimizing. *Optimizing* reduces the number of individual elements in a curve, thus reducing the size of your file and resulting in faster download times on your Web site. You can optimize repeatedly, just as you can with smoothing and straightening. Optimizing works best for complex art created with many lines and curves. The visual result is somewhat like smoothing but might be subtler.

To optimize, select the object or objects and choose Modify⇨Shape⇨Optimize. Flash opens the Optimize Curves dialog box, as shown in Figure 4-16.

Figure 4-16: Optimize to reduce the number of curves.

As you can see in the dialog box, you can specify an Optimization Strength to determine how much Flash optimizes curves. Select the Preview check box to see the result without dismissing the dialog box. If you mangle your work too much on the first try, undo it and try again with a different setting. You can select the Show Totals Message check box to see how many curves Flash cut out and the percentage of optimization that number represents. Click OK to close the dialog box.

Be careful to check the results after optimizing. Flash sometimes eliminates small objects that you may want to retain. If you don't like the results of optimizing, choose Edit⇨Undo.

Expanding and contracting fills

You can expand and contract shapes. Expanding and contracting works best on shapes with no stroke (outline) because Flash deletes the outline when executing the command. If you want to expand or contract a shape with a stroke, scale it. We explain scaling later in this chapter in the "Scaling, scaling . . ." section. The advantage of expanding and contracting is that you can specify a change in size in terms of pixels.

To expand or contract a shape, select it and choose Modify➪Shape➪Expand Fill. The Expand Fill dialog box appears, as shown in Figure 4-17. Type a number in the Distance box, using the units that you have set for the entire movie. By default, movies are measured in pixels. (See the section in Chapter 3 on drawing precisely for the details on setting movie units.)

Figure 4-17: The Expand Fill dialog box.

To expand a shape, select the Expand option. To contract a shape, select the Inset option. Then click OK.

Softening edges

Softening edges is another shape-modification tool. You can soften edges of a shape to get a graphic to look like you created it in a bitmap image editor, such as Adobe Photoshop. Figure 4-18 shows some text before and after its edges are softened. Note that adding softened edges can increase your file size.

Figure 4-18: Soften the edges of objects to create cool effects.

You can create this effect by breaking apart the text twice before softening the edges. We discuss breaking apart objects later in this chapter; Chapter 5 explains more specifically about breaking apart text into editable shapes.

To soften edges, select the object or objects and choose Modify⇨Shape⇨Soften Fill Edges. Flash opens the Soften Fill Edges dialog box, as shown in Figure 4-19.

To soften edges, follow these steps:

1. **Set the distance, which is the width of the softened edge.**

   The distance is measured in pixels unless you have changed the document units. (See the section in Chapter 3 on drawing precisely for information on setting the units in the Document Properties dialog box.)

   Figure 4-19: Soften up your boss . . . uh, graphics.

2. **Select the number of steps, which means the number of curves that Flash uses to create the softened edge.**

   Try the Flash default first and change it if you don't like the result. You can increase the number to get a smoother effect.

3. **Select the Expand option to create the softened edge outside the shape or the Inset option to create the softened edge within the shape.**

4. **Click OK to create the softened edge.**

   Your shape is still selected, so click anywhere outside it to see the result. If you don't like it, press Ctrl+Z (Windows) or ⌘+Z (Mac) and try again using different options.

You can create soft edges also by using gradients that blend into the Stage color or with partially transparent colors. Chapter 3 explains more about using colors. Flash also has a blur filter that you can use on text, movie clip symbols, and buttons. Chapter 7 describes filters.

Converting lines to fills

Flash offers lots of great ways to fill a shape — for example, with gradients and bitmap images. But what about those boring strokes or outlines? You can convert lines to fills and make them fun, fun, fun. (See Chapter 3 for an explanation of fills, including gradients and bitmap images.)

Mind you, there's not much point in converting a line to a fill if it's so thin that no one would ever see a fill in it. Figure 4-20 shows some waves we created by using the Pencil tool and a 10-point-wide line. We converted the line to a fill and then used the Paint Bucket tool to fill the line with a gradient.

Figure 4-20: Change the line to a fill and use the Paint Bucket tool to change the fill.

To convert a line to a fill, select the line and choose Modify⇨Shape⇨Convert Lines to Fills. You don't see any visible difference when you deselect the line, but now you can change the fill to anything you want.

Transforming Fills

The Gradient Transform tool offers a unique way to edit gradient and bitmap fills. You can perform the following changes to a fill:

- ✐ Move its center point.
- ✐ Change its width or height.
- ✐ Rotate it.
- ✐ Scale it.
- ✐ Tile it.
- ✐ Change the radius of a radial gradient.
- ✐ Move the focus of a radial gradient.
- ✐ Skew (slant) it.

From this list, you can see that there's no point in fiddling with solid fills. They would look the same no matter what direction, size, or scale they were. (See the section in Chapter 3 on colors for colorful coverage of gradient and bitmap fills.)

 To edit a fill, choose the Gradient Transform tool. This tool is well hidden; you'll find it by clicking the Free Transform tool on the Tools toolbar to open a submenu. Click any gradient or bitmap fill. Flash places an editing boundary and editing handles around the fill. The editing boundary varies with the type of fill — bitmap, linear gradient, or radial gradient, as shown in Figure 4-21.

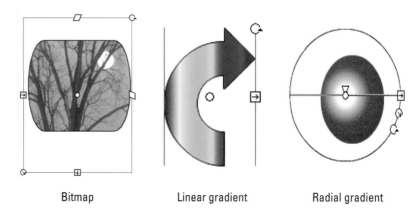

Bitmap   Linear gradient   Radial gradient

Figure 4-21: The Gradient Transform tool places an editing boundary around the fill.

After you have a fill with an editing boundary, you're ready to go ahead and fiddle with the fills. Here's how to make changes:

- **Move the center of a fill.** Drag the center point, marked by a small circle at the center of the fill. You can move a center fill to move the center of a radial gradient, move the stripes of a linear gradient, or place a bitmap off center.

- **Move the focal point of a fill.** Drag the focal point, marked by a triangle along the center line of a radial gradient. For example, moving the focal point makes the apparent direction of light move from side to side in a radial gradient with a lightly colored center.

- **Change the width of a fill.** Drag the square handle on one side of the editing boundary. To change the height of a fill, drag the handle on the bottom of the editing boundary. If a fill doesn't have one of these handles, you can't edit the fill that way. Changing the width of a linear fill that's perpendicular to the direction of its stripes is the same as scaling the fill — the stripes get wider (or narrower).

- **Rotate a fill.** Drag the rotation handle, which is a small circle just outside the corner of the editing boundary. On a radial gradient, use the bottom of the three handles on the circumference of the boundary.

  When rotating a fill, you can press and hold the Shift key while you drag to constrain the rotation of the fill to multiples of 45 degrees.

- **Scale a bitmap fill.** Drag the square handle at the corner of the editing boundary — inward to scale down and outward to scale up. To scale a circular gradient, drag the middle circular handle on the editing boundary. Figure 4-22 shows a bitmap gradient at its original size and scaled down. Flash tiles the bitmap if you scale down significantly.

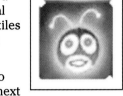 

If you scale down a bitmap so that you see many tiles, the next time that you want to edit the bitmap, Flash places an editing boundary around each tile so that you have to edit each one individually. That could take a long time! If you want to edit a bitmap in several ways, save scaling down for last.

Figure 4-22: Scale a bitmap fill to make it larger or smaller.

✔ **Skew (slant) a fill.** Drag one of the rhombus-shaped handles on the top or side of the editing boundary. You can skew only if the fill is a bitmap. Skewing is different from rotating because the bitmap is distorted. Figure 4-23 shows an example of a skewed bitmap.

Later in this chapter, we explain how to rotate, scale, and skew entire objects.

Figure 4-23: Skew a bitmap fill for really weird results.

Transferring Properties

You can use the Eyedropper tool to copy outline and fill properties from one object to another. (See the section on bitmap fills in Chapter 3 for instructions on using the Eyedropper tool to create bitmap fills.)

To transfer properties, follow these steps:

   1. **Click the Eyedropper tool.**

2. **Click an outline or a fill.**

   If you click an outline, Flash activates the Ink Bottle tool. If you select a fill, Flash activates the Paint Bucket tool and turns on the Lock Fill modifier. (For more information on the Lock Fill modifier, see the section in Chapter 3 that discusses locking a fill.) If you don't want a locked fill, click the Lock Fill modifier in the Options section of the Tools panel to deselect it.

3. **Click another outline or fill.**

   Flash transfers the properties of the original outline or fill to the new object.

Finding and Replacing Objects

One way to change an object is to change its properties. You can find graphics objects by color or bitmap and then replace the color or bitmap. For example, you can easily change every blue fill or stroke to red if your Web color scheme changes.

You can find and replace according to color, bitmap, text, and font (Chapter 5); sound; or video (Chapter 11). You can also find and replace symbols (Chapter 7).

To find and replace objects, choose Edit⇨Find and Replace to open the Find and Replace dialog box, as shown in Figure 4-24.

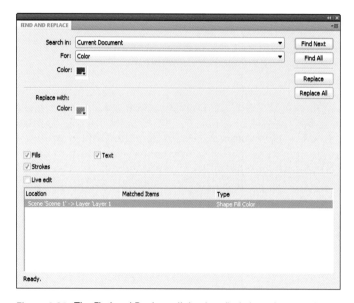

Figure 4-24: The Find and Replace dialog box finds lost sheep and can change their color.

In the Search In drop-down list, choose to search in the entire Flash movie document or only in the current scene. (See Chapter 9 for a full explanation of scenes.)

In the For drop-down list, select what you want to find: text, font, color, symbol, sound, video, or bitmap. The dialog box changes according to the choice you make. For example, to find and replace a color, follow these steps:

1. Click the top Color button and select a color that exists in your document.

2. Click the Replace with Color button and select the replacement color that you want.

3. Mark one or more of the three check boxes — Fills, Strokes, and Text — to define what type of objects you want to find.

4. Click Find Next to find the next occurrence of the color or click Find All to find every object with that color.

5. Click Replace to replace the color of the currently selected object or click Replace All to replace the color of every object.

6. Click the Close button of the dialog box to return to your movie.

Find and Replace is an efficient way to make mass changes of color, text, symbols, sound, video, or bitmaps.

Transforming Objects

Earlier in this chapter, in the "Freely transforming and distorting shapes" section, we explain how you can use the Free Transform tool to reshape objects. You can do many of the same tasks by using the Transform command.

To scale, rotate, and flip objects, choose Modify⇨Transform and then choose one of the submenu commands. When you scale, rotate, or skew an object, Flash kindly remembers the object's qualities so that you can return the object to the state it was in before you fiddled around with it.

Scaling, scaling . . .

Most of the time, scaling by using the Free Transform tool (as we describe earlier in this chapter) is the easiest, fastest way to go. When you want more precision, however, scale the selected object in the Property inspector. (Choose Window⇨Properties. Change the value in the W (width) box, the H (height) box, or both.

To make sure that the proportions of the object stay the same, click the padlock next to the W and H values so that it looks locked. When you change either the W or the H value, the other box adjusts proportionally.

For yet more scaling options, select an object and choose Window➪Transform to open the Transform panel, as shown in Figure 4-25.

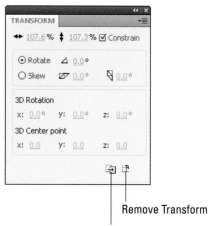

Remove Transform

Duplicate Selection and Transform

The controls in the Transform panel work only if an object is selected. If you forgot to select an object, you don't need to close the panel; just select an object.

To scale the selected object or objects, click the Width (left) value and type a scale value between 1 and 1000, or drag the number up or down to change its value. Any value less than 100 reduces the size of the object, so a value of 10 creates a new object at 10 percent of the original object, and a value of 1000 multiplies the object's size by a factor of 10. Then press Enter or Return. By default, the Constrain check box is selected, so changing the width also changes the height.

Figure 4-25: Use the Transform panel to scale, rotate, and skew objects with great precision.

To make a copy of an object at a scaled size, click the Duplicate Selection and Transform button (the left button in the lower-right corner of the panel) instead of pressing Enter or Return. The copy appears on top of the original object but is selected so that you can move it immediately if you want. Figure 4-26 shows an example of how you can use scaling and copying together to create the impression of objects at varying distances. After you make the copy, just move it to a new location. When you're finished, click the Close button of the Transform panel to close it.

Figure 4-26: The brain creatures are attacking!

To return the object to its original properties before transformation, click the Remove Transform button at the lower-right corner of the Transform panel.

'Round and 'round and 'round we rotate

Most of the time, you can probably use the Free Transform tool to rotate objects, as we explain earlier in this chapter. If you want to rotate something by an exact number of degrees, such as 20 degrees, use the Transform panel.

Select the object and choose Window⇨Transform to open the Transform panel. (Refer to Figure 4-25.)

To rotate the selected object or objects clockwise, type a value between 1 and 359, or drag the number up or down to change its value. To rotate counterclockwise, specify a value between –1 and –359. Then press Enter or Return.

If you don't like the results, click the Remove Transform button (in the lower-right corner of the panel) and try again.

To make a copy of an object at a different rotation, click Duplicate Selection and Transform (the left button in the lower-right corner of the panel) before specifying the rotation. The copy appears on top of the original object but is selected so that you can immediately move it.

If you want to rotate a section by 90 degrees by using the menu, do the following:

- **To rotate right (clockwise):** Choose Modify⇨Transform⇨Rotate 90° CW.

- **To rotate left (counterclockwise):** Choose Modify⇨Transform⇨ Rotate 90° CCW.

When you rotate, Flash rotates the object around its center. To rotate around a different point on the object, you can convert the object to a group or symbol and change its *registration point,* the point on an object that Flash references when rotating. See the section later in this chapter on changing the transformation point, which also discusses registration points.

You can create groovy circular patterns by using the rotate and copy functions, as shown in Figure 4-27. Unless the object you're working with is completely symmetrical, you need to change the registration point.

Figure 4-27: Rotate and copy an object at the same time to add flower power to your site.

Getting skewy

Skewing is a variation of rotating. Rather than rotate an entire object, you slant it horizontally, vertically, or both. Skewing a square creates a rhombus (diamond). In Figure 4-28, you see a simple arrow before and after skewing.

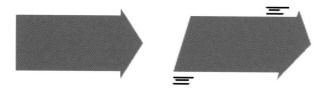

Figure 4-28: A skewed arrow looks like it's in a hurry.

The easiest way to skew objects is by using the Free Transform tool. Just select an object, choose the Free Transform tool, and drag along one of the sides of the boundary.

Usually, you can eyeball the skewing process. If you want precision or to combine skewing with scaling, use the Transform panel. Select the object and choose Window⇨Transform to open the Transform panel. To skew the selected object or objects, click the Skew option.

Use the left box to skew horizontally. To skew clockwise, click the current value and then either type a value between 1 and 89 or drag up. To skew counterclockwise, click the current value and then either type a value between –1 and –89 or drag down. Then press Enter or Return.

To skew vertically, click the current value and then either type a value in the right box or drag up or down. Positive values skew clockwise, and negative values skew counterclockwise. If that sounds confusing, just try something out and see whether you like it. If you don't, click Remove Transform (the button in the lower-right corner of the panel) and try again.

To make a copy of an object at a skewed angle, click the Duplicate Selection and Transform button (the left button in the lower-right corner of the panel) before starting the skewing operation. The copy appears on top of the original object but is selected so that you can move it immediately.

Flippety, floppety

Flipping reverses an object so that you have a mirror image of your original object. You can flip both horizontally (left to right or vice versa) and vertically (up to down or vice versa). Flash flips objects about their center so that they stay in their original position on the Stage.

Figure 4-29 shows a curlicue design in its original form, flipped horizontally and flipped vertically. If you flip an object horizontally and then vertically, you end up with an object that has been mirrored in both directions.

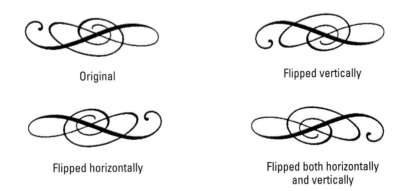

Original

Flipped vertically

Flipped horizontally

Flipped both horizontally and vertically

Figure 4-29: You can flip objects vertically, horizontally, or both.

To flip an object, select it and choose Modify➪Transform➪Flip Vertical or Flip Horizontal. To flip an object in both directions, flip it in one direction and then in the other.

To create symmetrical objects, you need to change the object's registration point from the center to one side or corner. Later in this chapter, in the "Changing the Transformation Point" section, we explain how to use flipping to create symmetrical objects.

Combining Objects

You can combine objects in various ways to create new and more interesting shapes. You can perform the following actions:

✔ **Union:** Combines two objects into one object. The effect is similar to grouping objects, which we cover in the next section of this chapter. (In fact, you can use the Ungroup command to separate the objects again.) Combining two objects puts a boundary around them, like the boundary you see when you use the object-drawing model. To combine objects, select them and choose Modify➪Combine Objects➪Union.

See the section on keeping objects safe and secure in Chapter 3 for more information on how to use the object-drawing model.

✓ **Intersect:** Creates a shape that is the intersection of two overlapping shapes; the shape that remains is from the top object, as shown in Figure 4-30. However, this works only with objects that you create by using the object-drawing model. (We explain the object-drawing model in Chapter 3.) To combine objects, select them and choose Modify➪Combine Objects➪ Intersect.

Figure 4-30: A quarter-circle is all that's left after using the Intersect feature.

✓ **Punch:** Removes the object on top from an object beneath it. This operation requires two objects that you drew by using the object-drawing model. If you put a smaller circle on top of a larger circle, the Punch feature is like punching a hole in the larger circle (but it doesn't hurt). Select two overlapping objects and choose Modify➪Combine Objects➪Punch.

✓ **Crop:** Creates a shape that is the intersection of two partially over-lapping shapes that you created by using the object-drawing model; removes any part of the bottom object that extends beyond the shape of the top object. Select two overlapping objects and choose Modify➪ Combine Objects➪Crop.

Getting Grouped

When you know how to create objects, you can get carried away and create so many objects on the Stage that they're hard to manage. You might want to move a number of objects at once. Although you can select them all and move them, that technique might not be enough. For example, you might inadvertently leave behind one piece and discover that it's hard to move that piece in the same way that you moved the rest. That's why Flash provides *grouping*. You select multiple objects and group them once. From then on, you can select them with one click. If you move one of the grouped objects, the rest come along for the ride.

In Flash, grouping has an additional advantage: If you put objects on top of each other, they merge if they're the same color, or they create cutouts if they're different colors, unless you draw them using the object-drawing model or a primitive shape. One way that you can avoid such friendly behav-ior and keep the integrity of objects is to group them. (You can also put them on different layers, as we explain in Chapter 6, or you can turn them into sym-bols, as we explain in Chapter 7.)

Grouping objects is easy. Select them and choose Modify⇨Group. You short-cut types can press Ctrl+G (Windows) or ⌘+G (Mac). When you group objects and select them, all the objects are surrounded by one blue selection border.

After you group objects, you can ungroup them at any time. Select the group and choose Modify⇨Ungroup. You can also break apart a group. See the discussion later in this chapter on breaking apart objects.

If you want to edit an element of the group without ungrouping first, Flash lets you do so. To edit without ungrouping, follow these steps:

1. **Using the Selection tool, double-click any object in the group.**

 Flash dims other objects on the Stage and displays the Group symbol above the Stage.

2. **Edit any of the group components.**

3. **Return to regular editing mode.**

   Double-click any blank area on the Stage with the Selection tool, click the current Scene symbol to the left of the Group symbol, or click the Back arrow to the left of the scene symbol.

Changing the Transformation Point

When Flash rotates or scales an object, it uses a *transformation point* as a reference. This point is generally the center of the object. For positioning and certain transformations of lines and shapes, Flash uses the upper-left corner. You might find that the point Flash uses isn't suitable for your needs. For example, you might want to rotate an object around its lower-left corner. For a single rotation or scaling of a simple graphic object, use the Free Transform tool and drag the transformation point — the little circle — to the desired location. If you deselect and reselect the object, you see that the circle has returned to its original central position.

Changing the transformation point is useful when you want to create symmetrical objects by flipping. To use flipping to create symmetrical objects, follow these steps:

1. **Select the object.**

 2. **Click the Free Transform tool and drag the transformation point to one edge of the object, from where you want to mirror the object.**

3. Choose Edit⇨Copy to copy the object to the Clipboard.

4. Choose Edit⇨Paste in Place to paste the copy on top of the original.

5. Choose Modify⇨Transform⇨Flip Vertical or Flip Horizontal.

   You see your original and the copy. The copy has been flipped so that it's a mirror image of its original.

6. (Optional) To create a four-way symmetrical object, group the original and mirrored objects (as we explain in the previous section) and change the transformation point to one side of the combined group. Then repeat Steps 3, 4, and 5, this time flipping in the other direction.

Figure 4-31 shows a weird creature created by copying, changing the transformation point, and then flipping. The straight lines assist in placing the transformation point accurately.

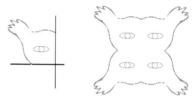

Figure 4-31: Create scary, symmetrical creatures by manipulating the transformation point.

Groups, symbol instances, text, and bitmaps have a *registration point,* which Flash uses to animate and transform these objects. When you use the Free Transform tool to move the circle on these objects, the circle keeps its position even after you deselect and reselect it. To move an object's registration point, follow these steps:

1. Select a group, symbol instance, text object, or bitmap.

2. Click the Free Transform tool.

   Flash displays a small circle at the transformation point.

3. Drag the circle to the desired location.

4. Click anywhere else on the Stage to hide the registration point.

To return the registration point to its original position, double-click it.

Breaking Apart Objects

With the Break Apart command, you can break apart text, groups, instances of symbols, and bitmaps into separate objects that you can edit individually. To break apart one of these types of objects, select it and choose Modify⇨ Break Apart.

What happens to your objects when you break them apart? Do they splatter all over the Stage? Here's what happens when you break apart the following objects:

- **Text:** Flash divides the words into individual letters, each one a separate object. If you use the Break Apart command a second time on one of the letters, the letter becomes a shape that you can modify like any other shape.

  Break apart blocks of text and then use the Distribute to Layers command to animate individual letters. See Chapter 5 for more information about text and Chapter 6 for more on layers.

- **Shapes created in the object-drawing model:** The shape loses its object-drawing model status, as if you had drawn it without using the object-drawing model.

- **Groups:** Flash breaks up the group into its component parts. The result is the same as ungrouping.

- **Instances of symbols:** The symbol becomes a shape. (Symbols are covered fully in Chapter 7.)

- **Bitmaps:** Flash converts the bitmap to a fill. You can then erase parts of it.

Establishing Order on the Stage

Flash stacks objects in the order in which you create them. If you draw a circle and then an overlapping square, the square looks like it's on top of the circle because you created it more recently.

If you place an object on top of another object, the two objects become one if they're the same color. If they're different colors, the top object cuts out the underlying object.

One exception is if you use the object-drawing model to draw the objects. Oval and rectangle primitives are another exception. A different way to keep the integrity of objects is by grouping them or turning them into symbols. (Symbols are covered in Chapter 7.) Groups, object-drawing model shapes, primitives, and symbols are always stacked on top of regular objects. Therefore, to move objects above existing groups or symbols, you need to group them or convert them to a symbol. You might also need to turn some imported graphics into a symbol or group before you can move them in the stack.

TIP

If you draw an object and it immediately disappears beneath another object, it's often because you tried to draw the object on top of a group, primitive, or symbol. Group the object or change it to a symbol if it must be on top.

Another way to reorder objects is to put them on different layers. You can then reorder the objects by reordering their layers. (See Chapter 6 for the details.)

As long as you have objects that can maintain their integrity, you can change their stacking order. You can move them up or down in the stack or from the top or bottom of the stack — all within the same layer. To change the stacking order of an object, select the object and choose Modify⇨Arrange. Then choose one of these options:

- ✔ **Bring to Front:** Brings the selected object to the tippy-top of the stack.

- ✔ **Bring Forward:** Brings the selected object up one level.

- ✔ **Send Backward:** Moves the selected object down one level.

- ✔ **Send to Back:** Sends the selected object down, down, down to the bottom of the stack.

Figure 4-32 shows an example of two objects stacked in different ways: the big, old-fashioned bitmap star and the small, up-and-coming vector star vying to be in front.

Figure 4-32: The big, old-fashioned bitmap star and the small, up-and-coming vector star vying to be in front.

Undoing, Redoing, and Reusing

Sometimes you do something in Flash and decide that it's a mistake. Oops! For this situation, you can undo actions. You can even redo the actions that you undid. Finally, if you're environmentally conscious, you can reuse earlier actions to avoid wasting any more of your energy.

Undoing actions

To undo your last action, choose Edit⇨Undo or press Ctrl+Z (Windows) or ⌘+Z (Mac). You can continue this process for a very long time. This is the familiar — and default — type of undo, and Flash calls it *document-level undo.*

To set the number of undo steps that Flash remembers, follow these steps:

1. **Choose Edit⇨Preferences (Windows) or Flash⇨Preferences (Mac).**
2. **In the Preferences dialog box that appears, click the General category.**
3. **From the Undo drop-down list, select Document-Level Undo.**
4. **In the text box just below the Undo drop-down list, enter the number of undo actions you want Flash to track.**

   The default is 100, and the allowable range is from 2–300.

Later in this chapter, in the "Reusing actions with the History panel" section, we explain another way to undo actions.

Redoing actions

Maybe you were right the first time. After you undo an action, suppose that you want to redo it. You can do that, too. To redo actions, choose Edit⇨Redo or press Ctrl+Y (Windows) or ⌘+Y (Mac).

If you haven't undone anything, you can use the same command (and keyboard shortcut) to repeat your last action, in which case it's called the Repeat command.

Using object-level undo and redo

Generally, undos and redos apply to every action you take in Flash. But sometimes you might find object-level undo and redo more helpful.

Object-level undo applies only to editing symbols, which we cover in Chapter 7. When you use object-level undo and redo, Flash remembers actions by symbol. Therefore, when you're editing a symbol, using the Undo command applies only to changes that you made to that symbol, even though you have made other changes to your movie in the meantime. If you use a lot of symbols, object-level undo offers you more flexibility. Object-level redo works in the same way.

You can use only one type of undo and redo at a time. To use object-level undo and redo, choose Edit⇨Preferences (Windows) or Flash⇨Preferences (Mac). Select the General category. In the Undo drop-down list, select Object-level Undo. You see a message explaining that switching from one type of undo to another will delete your current undo history. Flash can keep track of only one stream at a time. Click OK to close the message and click OK again to close the Preferences dialog box.

Deleting your current history is not generally a problem. But if you are in the middle of a long, complicated experiment and might need to undo many steps, choose another time to switch.

Reusing actions with the History panel

If you make several changes to an object and would like to make the same changes to other objects, you can save time and increase accuracy by saving and reusing the steps for the operations that you perform. Flash tracks the steps in the History panel.

The History panel lists every command that you perform in Flash during one session. When you save and close the file, the history list isn't saved for the next time. Choose Window⇨Other Panels⇨History, and the History panel appears, as shown in Figure 4-33. The shortcut is Ctrl+F10 (Windows) or ⌘+F10 (Mac).

Figure 4-33: The History panel keeps track of everything you do.

You can use the History panel to troubleshoot recent steps, repeat steps, undo steps, or save steps as commands for future use.

By default, Flash records up to 100 steps in the History panel. You can change the number of steps recorded by choosing Edit⇨Preferences (Windows) or Flash⇨Preferences (Mac) to open the Preferences dialog box. On the General tab, change the value for Undo levels. If you want to be able to go back and save earlier steps as commands, you probably need to record more than the default 100 steps.

Undoing steps

One of the simplest things that you can do in the History panel is to undo one or more operations. You can also undo operations by choosing Edit⇨Undo, but you can see more specific descriptions of the operation. For example, the Move operation appears in the History panel as Move {x:0, y:−103.6}. To view the specifics, right-click (Windows) or Control+click (Mac) any history item and choose View⇨Arguments in Panel. With these details, you can more easily predict the result of undoing an operation.

You undo steps by using the slider on the left side of the History panel:

 ✐ **Undo the last operation that you performed.** Drag the slider up one step.

 ✐ **Undo several steps.** Drag the slider to the step above the first step that you want to undo. For example, if you want to undo three steps, drag the slider up three steps — it's now next to the step previous to the one that you undid. This is the last step that has still been executed. You can also click to the left of a step, along the slider. The slider scrolls up to that step and undoes all the later steps.

When you undo a step, the step appears dimmed in the History panel.

Replaying a step

You can repeat any command from any time during a Flash session. For example, if you filled an object with a specific color, you can fill another object with the same color, even if you have performed other operations in the meantime.

To replay a step, click the step itself (not the left side of the step along the slider) in the History panel. Then click the Replay button. If you want to replay the step on a different object, first select that object, and then click the Replay button.

Copying steps

 You might want to keep a list of certain steps or use them in a different movie. Select one or more steps in the History panel and click the Copy Selected Steps to the Clipboard button.

To use these steps in another Flash movie, open the movie and choose Edit⇨Paste. To apply the steps to an object, select the object first.

 Flash copies the step or steps as JavaScript code. Therefore, when you paste the step or steps into a word processor or text editor, you see the JavaScript code, which looks more complex than the step listed in the History panel. Usually, you can figure out what it means, even if you don't know JavaScript. For example, `Fill Color: '#0000ff'` appears as `fl.getDocumentDOM().setFillColor('#0000ff');`.

Saving commands

If you want to save a step or set of steps to use the next time that you open the movie, save a command. Saving a command is even useful if you want to re-execute some steps several times later in the same session because scrolling back to find the exact steps that you want to reuse can be time consuming.

To save a command, follow these steps:

1. **In the History panel, select the steps that you want to save.**

   You can drag along the step names (not along the left side, where the slider is). You can also use the usual methods of selecting multiple objects in a list. Click the first object, press Shift and click the last, or press and hold Ctrl (Windows) or ⌘ (Mac) and click each step that you want to select.

    To see more details about the commands, click the Options menu button (in the upper-right corner of the panel), and choose View⇨Arguments in Panel.

2. **Click the Save Selected Steps as a Command button.**

   This button is in the lower-right corner of the History panel. The Save As Command dialog box opens.

3. **Enter a name for the command.**

   You can simply summarize the steps. For example, you might name a command `fill blue, rotate 90`.

4. **Click OK to close the dialog box.**

When you save a command, it appears on the Commands menu. The menu in Figure 4-34 shows the command `fill blue, rotate 90`, which fills any selected shape with blue and rotates the shape 90 degrees. To use that command, you simply select a shape and then choose Commands⇨Fill Blue, Rotate 90. Presto! It's all finished. As you can imagine, you can combine complex commands and save them to automate the authoring process of creating Flash movies.

> Manage Saved Commands...
> Get More Commands...
> Run Command...
>
> Copy Motion as XML
> Export Motion XML
> fill blue; rotate 90
> Fill green 66ff00
> Import Motion XML

Figure 4-34: Saved commands appear on the Commands menu.

Clearing the History panel

If you don't want the History panel to record everything that you do — perhaps it makes you feel as if you don't have any privacy left anymore — you can clear the history list. Clearing the history list doesn't undo any steps. To clear the History panel, click the Options menu button at the upper-right corner of the panel and choose Clear History. Then click Yes.

For good Commands menu housekeeping, choose Commands⇨Manage Saved Commands to open the Manage Saved Commands dialog box. In this dialog box, you can delete or rename a command. When you're finished, click OK to close the Manage Saved Commands dialog box.

mysteries!

Grow your brain   *Cra... ...les an... ...r our*   **mJ**   **Gro**   **5**   **rain**   *Cra... ...les an... ...r our*   *mysteries!*

Grow your brain

What's Your Type?

*W*e assume that occasionally you want to say something on your Web site, so this chapter covers text in all its forms and formats. You can use Flash to create the text for your Web pages if you want (although you don't have to). But if you want flashy text effects, Flash is definitely the way to go.

Typography is the art or process of arranging text on a page, and basically that's what this chapter is all about. Many graphics programs call text *type*. We use the words interchangeably here — we don't care what you call it.

Presenting Your Text

The majority of text on most Web sites is formatted by using HyperText Markup Language (HTML) coding that sets the font, size, and color of the text. Using HTML code is ideal for larger amounts of text because the HTML is simple to code and loads quickly.

For smaller amounts of text that you want to have special formatting or effects, Flash offers more options than HTML. Of course, if you want to animate your text, you can use Flash. For example, an animated logo usually includes not only the graphic art but also the name of the organization, which is, of course, text.

Grapple with enigmas and master our mysteries!

Grow your brain with our brain teasers!
 Unravel baffling riddles, and cut your teeth on curious conundrums!

Here are some innovative things you can do with text:

✔ Rotate, scale, skew, or flip text without losing the ability to edit the text.

✔ Turn text into shapes and modify them any way you want. However, after you turn text into shapes, you can't edit the text characters by simply typing. Figure 5-1 shows some text that was modified in this way.

Figure 5-1: You can turn text into a shape and modify it to your heart's content.

✔ Create transparent type.

✔ Create hyperlinked text that sends the user's browser to another Web page when the user clicks the text.

✔ Enable viewers to control some aspect of the movie by entering text in a text box

✔ Load text, such as sports scores or current weather, dynamically from a server.

Creating text

Creating text in Flash using the default settings is simple. Follow these steps:

1. Click the Text tool on the Tools panel.

2. Specify the text starting point on the Stage.

- To specify the width of the text, click the Stage in the left edge where you want your text to start and drag to the right until you have the width that you want. Flash places a square block handle in the upper-right corner of the text block.

- To create a text block that expands while you type, just click the Stage at the desired starting point. Flash places a round block handle in the upper-right corner of the text block.

3. Start typing.

To force a return to the left margin after you type one or more lines, press Enter or Return. Otherwise, if you specified a width, the text wraps to the next line when it fills up that width.

4. After you finish typing, click anywhere off the Stage to deselect the text.

Congratulations — you've just said something! We hope it was worthwhile.

Editing text

After you type text, it never fails that you want to change it. Editing text is easy in Flash, but first you have to select the text. Here are the selection techniques:

- ✒ **To edit an entire text block:** Click the Selection tool and then click the text. Flash places a selection border around the text. You can move, rotate, and scale all the text in a text block this way, just as you would with any other object. For example, you can use the Free Transform tool to scale the text.

- ✒ **To edit the content of the text itself:** Double-click the text with the Selection tool active. (Or click the Text tool and then click the text.) Flash switches to the Text tool automatically and places the text cursor where you clicked or double-clicked the text, more or less.

- ✒ **To select a character or characters individually:** Click the Text tool and drag across one or more characters. Do this when you want to edit only those characters.

- ✒ **To select a word:** Click the Text tool and double-click any word to select it.

- ✒ **To select a string of words or block of text:** Click the Text tool, click at the beginning of the text you want to select, and then Shift+click at the end of the desired selection.

- ✒ **To select all the text in a text block:** Click the Text tool, click in a text block, and then press Ctrl+A (Windows) or ⌘+A (Mac).

To change the content of the text, select the characters or words that you want to change, as we explain in the preceding list. Type to replace the selected text. Other text-editing techniques are the same as in your word processor. For example, you can press the Delete key to delete characters to the right of the text cursor or press the Backspace key (Windows) or Delete key (Mac) to delete characters to the left of the cursor.

Checking spelling

Spell checking works like the spell checker in your word processor, so you'll probably find it easy to use. This feature shows Adobe's commitment to reducing typos on the Web!

The first step is to set up the parameters for spell checking. Choose Text⇨ Spelling Setup to open the Spelling Setup dialog box, as shown in Figure 5-2. If the Check Spelling item isn't available on the Text menu, you need to open this dialog box and close it again.

The Spelling Setup dialog box has three sections:

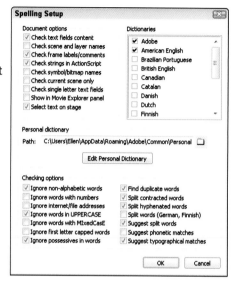

Figure 5-2: Use the Spelling Setup dialog box to specify how spell checking works.

✏ **Document Options:** Choose which parts of a movie you want to check. For example, you may not want to spell-check symbol and bitmap names.

✏ **Personal Dictionary:** You can change the location of the file that holds words that you add to the dictionary. Click the Edit Personal Dictionary button to add words directly. Otherwise, you add words when you are checking the spelling of specific text.

✏ **Checking Options:** Set options that define how spell checking works. For example, you can choose to ignore words in uppercase or with numbers.

You can also choose which dictionaries you want to use in the Dictionaries list (in the upper-right corner of the Spelling Setup dialog box).

When you're finished, click OK to return to your movie. You're now ready to check spelling.

To check spelling, you can select text if you want to check just that text or leave all the text deselected to check the entire movie. Choose Text⇨Check Spelling to open the Check Spelling dialog box, as shown in Figure 5-3.

Figure 5-3: The Check Spelling dialog box.

If you selected text, Flash checks that text first and then asks whether you want to check the rest of the document. Click Yes to continue or No to end the spell check. For each misspelled word, you can do one of the following:

✏ Choose one of the suggestions and click Change to change that instance of the word.

✏ Choose one of the suggestions and click Change All to change all instances of the word.

✏ Click Ignore to go to the next misspelled word.

✏ Click Ignore All to ignore all instances of that word and go to the next misspelled word.

✏ Click Delete to delete the word.

✏ Click Add to Personal to add the word to the Personal Dictionary so that it won't appear as misspelled in the future.

To finish spell checking, click Close. You may see a message asking whether you want to start from the beginning of the document. Click Yes to do so. When spell checking is complete, you see a Spelling Check Completed message. Click OK to return to your movie.

Finding and replacing text

If you need to change all instances of the word *big* to *large,* for example, you're in luck. The Find and Replace feature comes to the rescue. In Chapter 4, we discuss how to find and replace color. Here we explain the steps (which are similar) for finding and replacing text:

1. **Choose Edit⇨Find and Replace.**

   The Find and Replace dialog box appears.

2. **In the For drop-down list, choose Text.**

3. **In the Text box, enter the text that you want to find.**

4. **In the Replace with Text box, enter the replacement text.**

5. **(Optional) Enable one or more of the three check boxes on the left to define what type of text you want to find: Whole Word, Match Case, and Regular Expressions.**

   Regular expressions are formulas you use to locate specific text patterns in a text string. Regular expressions are beyond the scope of this book, but you can find a good tutorial at `www.regular-expressions.info/tutorial.html`.

6. **(Optional) Select one or more of the check boxes on the right to define where you want Flash to look for text.**

   • *Text Field Contents* searches text objects.

   • *Frames/Layers/Parameters* looks for frame labels and scene names (see Chapter 9), layer names (see Chapter 6), and component parameters (see Chapter 10).

   • *Strings in ActionScript* looks for text in ActionScript.

   • *ActionScript* looks for all ActionScript code.

7. **To edit each object on the Stage, select the Live Edit check box.**

8. **Click the appropriate button as needed:**

- Click *Find Next* to find the next occurrence of the text.
- Click *Find All* to find all occurrences of the text.
- Click *Replace* to replace the currently selected object.
- Click *Replace All* to replace all instances of that text.

When Flash finds the specified text, the box at the bottom of the Find and Replace dialog box displays its location and type along with the entire text so that you can see the context of the text you're replacing. You can resize the Find and Replace dialog box as well as the columns in the list of found items. When you're finished, click the Close button in the Find and Replace dialog box to return to your movie.

Setting character attributes

Of course, you don't always want to use the Flash default font and size for your Web site. Boring! You can set the attributes before you start typing or edit the attributes of existing text. To edit existing text, double-click the text block and then select the characters or words you want to format. To either set or edit attributes of text, display the Property inspector (Window➪Properties).

Figure 5-4 shows the Property inspector when some static text is selected. (*Static text* is normal text that just sits there and looks pretty.) The Property inspector changes slightly depending on which type of text you select. See "Creating input and dynamic text," later in this chapter, for more information about the various types of text.

Setting the font, font size, and font style

Usually, the first step in formatting text is selecting a font. To choose a font for selected text, choose one in the Font drop-down list in the Property inspector, which helpfully provides a sample of the font. Flash changes the font of the selected text.

You can change the font characteristics that control specific properties of the font, such as size and style:

- **To select a font size:** Type a font size in the text box or drag the slider to the desired value.
- **To select a font style:** Click an option, such as Bold, from the drop-down list. The available options vary by font.

Render as HTML

Selectable   Font Size

Width and Height   Show Border around Text

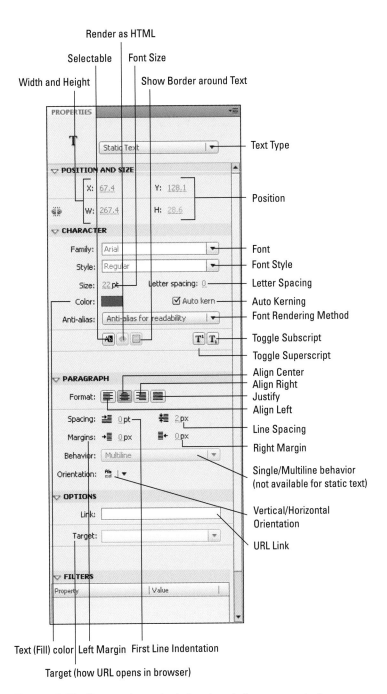

Text Type

Position

Font

Font Style

Letter Spacing

Auto Kerning

Font Rendering Method

Toggle Subscript

Toggle Superscript

Align Center
Align Right
Justify
Align Left

Line Spacing

Right Margin

Single/Multiline behavior
(not available for static text)

Vertical/Horizontal
Orientation

URL Link

Text (Fill) color   Left Margin   First Line Indentation

Target (how URL opens in browser)

Figure 5-4: The Property inspector is the place to liven up your text.

You can also select fonts, font sizes, and font styles directly from the Text menu. This menu is devoted entirely to helping you format your text.

You can create vertical text, where letters flow downward rather than across. Okay, so the purpose is mostly for languages that are often written vertically, such as Chinese. Vertical text must be static and can go from either left to right or right to left. (We explain static, input, and dynamic text later in this chapter.) Figure 5-5 shows some vertical text.

To create vertical text, follow the instructions for creating normal text, but before clicking the Stage to place the text, select the Vertical, Left to Right or the Vertical, Right to Left option from the Orientation button on the Property inspector. (Refer to Figure 5-4).

**D
o
w
n
w
e
g
o
!**

Figure 5-5: Try vertical text for a change of direction.

Specifying text color

Black is the Flash default color, but you have lots of additional options. The first concern is that the text is legible against its background. For example, yellow text looks great in front of a black background, but it's almost invisible against white. Also consider that text is often unreadable in front of complex graphic images, no matter what the color.

To set text color, select the text that you want to change if you've already created the text. In the Property inspector, click the Text Color button (refer to Figure 5-4) to open the color palette, and select a color. (For more information on colors, see Chapter 3.) If you haven't created the text yet, choose the Text tool, select the color, and then create the text. Click anywhere else to deselect the text so that you can see the new color.

To create transparent (or semitransparent) text, select the text and choose Window⇨Color to open the Color panel. In the Alpha text box, type a new Alpha percentage and press Enter or Return. A 100% alpha setting results in opaque text. Text with a 0% alpha setting is completely transparent. A setting of 50% is semi-transparent. You can also set the transparency after you choose the Text tool but before you type anything.

Adjusting kerning and tracking

Kerning reduces the spacing between certain letters, such as *V* and *A*. Because of the diagonal line on the *A* and *V*, without kerning, the letters might look too far apart. Figure 5-6 shows an example of text with and without kerning.

By default, Flash uses a font's kerning information, which is embedded in the font definition. Sometimes with smaller font sizes, kerning can make text hard to read, so you can turn it off. Without kerning, text takes up slightly more space. To turn off kerning, select the characters that you want to adjust and clear the Auto Kern check box in the Property inspector.

VACATION
VACATION

Figure 5-6: The first line uses kerning; the second line doesn't.

You can adjust the spacing between all the letters, a process called *tracking*. Perhaps you need the text to fit into a tight space or you want to stretch it out without changing the font size. Figure 5-7 shows some text with various tracking settings. To change tracking in the Property inspector, type a value in the Letter Spacing text box or drag the slider bar to the desired value.

Split the scene   Split the scene
and leave it clean   and leave it clean

Split the scene and   Split the scene and
leave it clean   leave it clean

Figure 5-7: Stretched and condensed text.

Making text selectable

Do you want users of your Web site to be able to select text and copy it to the Clipboard? If so, you should make the text selectable. To do so, select the text (naturally), and click the Selectable button in the Property inspector. Deselect this button to prevent users from selecting text.

Hyperlinking text

You can create text that acts as a link to other Web pages. Flash underlines linked text, following the global convention on Web sites. To create text with a hyperlink, follow these steps:

1. **Select the text.**

2. **Choose Window⇨Properties to open the Property inspector.**

3. **Expand the Options section of the Property inspector, if necessary.**

4. **In the Link text box, type the URL (Uniform Resource Locator, or Web address) of the Web page that you want to use.**

   When you complete the URL, a dotted line appears around the text to indicate that it's a hyperlink. When your Flash movie appears on a Web site (or even when you test the movie on your own computer), clicking the hyperlinked text sends the user the URL you specified.

   The dotted line around the text doesn't appear when you test or publish the movie.

5. **In the Target drop-down list, choose one of the window targets for the URL.**

   The two most commonly used are _blank, which opens the URL in a new browser window, and _self, opens the URL in the same window and is the default.

Getting the best text appearance

Flash usually stores outlines of the text in your movie when you publish or export it, so your audience will see your fonts in your movie even if they're not installed on your audience's computer. However, not all fonts displayed in Flash can be stored as outlines when you publish or export your movie.

To test whether Flash can export a font with a movie, choose View➪Preview Mode➪Antialias Text. If the text appears jagged, Flash cannot export the text with the movie.

Anti-aliasing is a method of making text look smoother — reducing the jaggies that sometimes create stair-like lines on text. Anti-aliasing is especially helpful for smaller font sizes. If you're worried about the jaggies, try choosing the Anti-Alias for Readability option in the Font Rendering Method drop-down list in the Property inspector.

The way that your type looks on the Stage is only an approximation of how it will look when you publish or export your movie. To see a more accurate rendering of how your type will look when you publish or export it, view your movie by choosing Control➪Test Movie.

If you want to use type in a font that Flash can't export, you can break apart the type into shapes, as we describe at the end of this chapter. However, this option increases the size of your movie file and makes the text no longer editable.

If you'd like a space-saving alternative to storing your text as outlines in your Flash movie, you can use Flash's three *device fonts* that the Flash Player always converts to the closest available font on the local computer:

- ✔ _sans: A sans serif font similar to Arial (Windows) and Helvetica (Mac).

- ✔ _serif: A serif font similar to Times New Roman (Windows) and Times (Mac).

- ✔ _typewriter: A font that looks like it has been typed on a typewriter. (Are you old enough to remember what that is?) It's similar to Courier New (Windows) and Courier (Mac).

When you use device fonts, your resulting published movies are smaller, so download time is shorter. With device fonts, your text also might be more legible in text sizes below 10 points. To use device fonts, specify one of the device fonts from the top of the Family drop-down list in the Property inspector, and then deselect the text. Then select Use Device Fonts in the Anti-Alias drop-down list in the Property inspector. (This setting applies only to horizontal static text.) When you publish your movie, select the Device Font check box on the HTML tab (Windows only) of the Publish Settings dialog box. Chapter 13 tells you more about publishing settings.

Setting up paragraph formats

You can set paragraph attributes such as alignment, margins, indents, and line spacing. Use these settings whenever you type more than one line of text. (You are getting long winded, aren't you!)

Setting text alignment

You can align text along the left margin or right margin of the text block. You can also center text. You can create an even edge along both margins, called *full justification* or *justified text*. By default, text is left aligned.

To align text, select it and display the Property inspector. (Choose Window➪ Properties to open the Property inspector or click its title bar if its collapsed.) In the Paragraph section, click the Align Left, Align Center, Align Right, or Justify button.

Setting margins and indents

The *margin* is the space between the text block border and your text. By default, the margin is 0 pixels. You can increase the margin to guarantee some space around the text. You can set only the left and right margins (not the top or bottom ones).

To set the left margin, select the paragraph and type a value for the Left Margin item or click the value and drag up or down to specify a value. Then press Tab or Enter (Windows) or Return (Mac) to see the result right away. To set the right margin, use the Right Margin item.

Indentation creates an indented first line. It's equivalent to placing a tab at the beginning of a paragraph. (Remember your sixth-grade teacher who told you to always start each paragraph with an indent?) To indent the first line, select the paragraph and type a value for the Spacing (Indentation) item or click the value and drag up or down.

Specifying line spacing

Line spacing determines the space between lines. Flash measures line spacing in points ($\frac{1}{72}$ of an inch) because font size is measured in points. For example, if your text is 18 points high and you want to double-space the lines, use a line spacing of 18 points so that a space exactly one line high exists between lines of text. To set the line spacing, select the paragraph and type a value for the Line Spacing item or click and drag up or down. Press

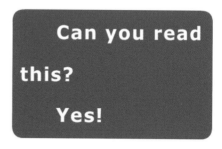

Figure 5-8: You can add indents and expand line spacing for easier reading.

Tab or Enter (Windows) or Return (Mac). Figure 5-8 shows some text with both an indent and expanded line spacing.

Flash remembers paragraph properties from movie to movie. When you change paragraph properties for one movie, the properties rear their ugly heads in your next movie. If your text automatically indents at the beginning of paragraphs or comes out double-spaced, check the Paragraph section of the Property inspector.

Creating input and dynamic text

You can create three kinds of text in Flash:

- ✔ **Static text:** Regular text that doesn't change or do anything, although you can animate it.

- ✔ **Input text:** Text that viewers can enter, as in a text box. You can use input text, for example, for forms and surveys or to interactively create values that affect the movie.

- ✔ **Dynamic text:** Text that changes based on data coming from an external source (such as a Web server), an internal source (such as ActionScript), or input text in the movie. Dynamic text is often used for data such as sports scores, current weather, and stock prices.

To choose the type of text, use the Text Type drop-down list in the Property inspector. (It's a good thing the Flash creators didn't call it the Type Type drop-down list.)

Several text settings in the Property inspector apply only to input or dynamic text (and therefore don't appear if you use static text):

- **Instance Name:** This text box appears above the Text Type drop-down list when you select input or dynamic text. An instance name identifies the text object so that you can refer to the text in ActionScript. (See Chapter 10 for the scoop on ActionScript.) Instance names are handy because with input or dynamic text, the contents of the text field can change while your Flash movie is playing; but if you give your text field an instance name, you can always refer to it in your ActionScript, even though you don't know the contents of the text field ahead of time.

- **Line Type:** Defines how text is displayed.

    - *Multiline* displays the text in multiple lines.

    - *Single Line* displays the text as one line.

    - *Multiline No Wrap* displays text in multiple lines that break only if the last character is a breaking character, such as Enter (Windows) or Return (Mac).

    - *Password* displays asterisks.

- **Render Text as HTML:** Preserves formatting, such as fonts and hyperlinks, with certain HTML tags. You need to create the formatting by using ActionScript.

- **Show Border Around Text:** Displays a black border and white background for the text field. This border helps users know where to enter text in an input text block.

- **Maximum Characters:** Specifies the maximum allowable characters that users can input in a text box. For example, you could limit a zip code to five digits. This setting is in the Options section.

- **Embed:** Opens the Character Embedding dialog box, where you can select options for embedding font outlines. Choose one or more of the options (such as Uppercase and Lowercase). You can press Ctrl (Windows) or ⌘ (Mac) and click several options. Or click the Don't Embed button if you don't want to embed font outlines. When you're finished, click OK. The font outlines you chose are exported when you publish the movie to ensure a smooth appearance. Limiting the font outlines you export helps to make the file size smaller.

Creating Cool Text Effects

Flash wouldn't be worth its salt if you couldn't create some flashy effects with text. You can manipulate text in several ways:

- **Transform text just like other objects.** In other words, you can scale, rotate, skew, and flip type. Figure 5-9 shows an example of skewed text.

✔ **Convert type to shapes by breaking it apart.** Select the text and choose Modify➪Break Apart. The first time that you use the Break Apart command, words are broken up into individual letters. Use this command again, and letters are turned into shapes so that you can then edit the text in the same way that you edit shapes. However, you can no longer edit the text as text, so check your words before converting them! (Refer to Figure 5-1 for an example of text turned into shapes.)

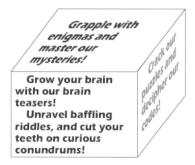

Figure 5-9: This text is skewed to match the angles of the skewed rectangles.

✔ **Apply special graphic effects to text, called *filters*.** Select the text and expand the Filters section of the Property inspector. Click the Add Filter button at the bottom and choose one (or more) of the following filters: Drop Shadow, Blur, Glow, Bevel, Gradient Glow, Gradient Bevel, or Adjust Color. Each filter has a number of settings that you can adjust to get just the right effect. Figure 5-10 shows these effects in the order listed here.

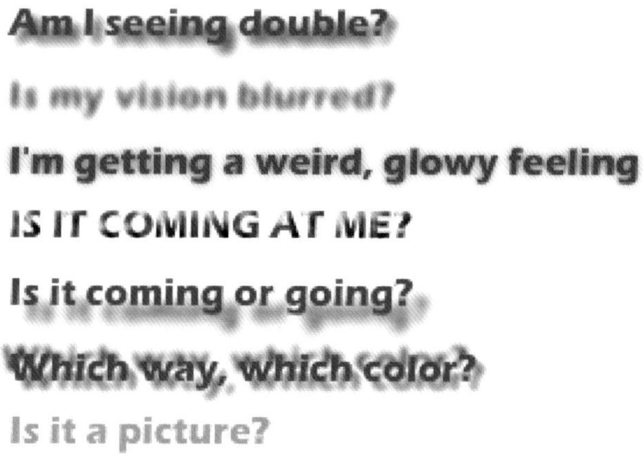

Am I seeing double?

Is my vision blurred?

I'm getting a weird, glowy feeling

IS IT COMING AT ME?

Is it coming or going?

Which way, which color?

Is it a picture?

Figure 5-10: Filters are shortcuts to cool looking (but not necessarily legible) text.

You can animate text to your heart's content. To animate text, you usually break it apart so that you can move letters individually. You can then use the Modify➪Timeline➪Distribute to Layers command to put each letter on a separate layer. After that, you can animate each letter. (See Chapter 9 for the details on animation.)

Layering It On

*F*lash lets you organize objects on the Stage in layers. *Layers* keep objects separated from each other. Flash either combines or creates cutouts when two objects overlap if you don't use the object-drawing model (as we explain in Chapter 3). By placing the two objects on different layers, though, you avoid this behavior yet retain the appearance of overlapping objects. In addition, by rearranging your layers, you can easily rearrange the order of your objects — that is, which objects appear to be on top and which appear to be on the bottom.

Layers are also necessary for error-free animation. To move one object across the Stage in front of other objects, such as a background, you need to put the object on its own layer. If you want to animate several objects across the Stage, put each object on a separate layer.

You can hide layers. Flash doesn't display objects on hidden layers. Hidden layers are great for hiding some objects temporarily while you figure out what to do with all the rest of the stuff on the Stage.

Finally, you use layers as a storage place for sounds and ActionScript code. For example, you can name a layer Music and put your music there. Then you can easily find the music if you want to change it. Layers provide a great way to keep the various components of your movie organized. (See Chapter 10 to find out more about ActionScript.) In this chapter, you get all the information you need to use layers effectively.

Creating Layers

Flash lists layers at the left side of the Timeline. New movies start out with one layer, named Layer 1. You can, and should, change the name of this layer and new layers to something more descriptive, as shown in Figure 6-1.

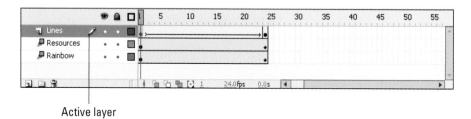

Active layer

Figure 6-1: Flash keeps you organized by listing all your layers.

If you're the organized type, think about your animation in advance and decide which layers you need. However, animations often don't work out the way you plan, and you might find yourself creating layers after you create objects. Either way, your method for creating layers is the same.

 To create a layer, click the Insert Layer button at the bottom of the layer list (or choose Insert⇨ Timeline⇨Layer). Flash displays the new layer above the active layer and makes the new layer active, as shown in Figure 6-2. To name the layer, double-click its name, type something meaningful, and then press Enter (Windows) or Return (Mac).

Figure 6-2: A new layer.

Using layers

Any object that you create goes on the active layer. You can tell which layer is active because it's highlighted and has a pencil icon next to its name. (Refer to the Lines layer in Figure 6-1.) To change the active layer, just click any inactive layer's name. You can also click anywhere in the layer's row on the Timeline.

To help make your work easier, Flash automatically changes the active layer to match any object that you select. So, if you're working on a layer named Text and then select a shape on a layer named Shapes, Flash automatically activates the Shapes layer. Any new objects that you create are now on the Shapes layer. Of course, if that's not the layer you want, switch to any other layer at any time by clicking its name.

When you click a layer to make it active, Flash selects all the objects on that layer that exist in the current frame. (Even if a layer is already active, you can click its name to select all its objects.) This feature is helpful for working with all the objects on a layer and discovering which objects a layer contains. If you don't want the objects selected, click anywhere that there's not an object.

Because in many cases, each animated object needs to be on its own layer, you often need to distribute objects to their own layers. Select the objects and choose Modify⇨Timeline⇨Distribute to Layers. This command saves lots of work!

Changing layer states

Besides being active or inactive, layers have three states that determine how objects on that layer function or look; you can

- ✔ Show or hide a layer.
- ✔ Lock or unlock it.
- ✔ Display objects on a layer as outlines.

Use these states to help you organize how you work. The more objects and more layers that you have, the more you need to use these layer states.

Above the layer list, on the right side, you see an eye, a lock, and a box. These aren't mystical symbols. The following sections explain what they are and how to use them.

Show/Hide

Use the Show/Hide icon (as shown at the left) to hide all objects on a layer (also called *hiding a layer*), reducing clutter while you work. To hide a layer, click below the Show/Hide icon on that layer's row. Flash places a red X under the eye icon. All the objects on that layer disappear. Click the X to get them back again. To hide (or show) all the objects on the Stage, click the Show/Hide icon itself.

Keep in mind, however, that you can't work on a hidden layer. And, don't forget hidden layers because by default they do appear in your published movies. (For information about specifying whether hidden layers appear in published movies, see Chapter 13.)

To show or hide all layers *except* one, Alt+click (Windows) or Option+click (Mac) below the Show/Hide icon on that layer's row. You can also right-click (Windows) or Control+click (Mac) a layer and choose Hide Others from the contextual menu that appears.

Lock/Unlock

 Use Lock/Unlock to prevent objects from being edited by locking their layers. Lock a layer when you want to avoid changing objects by mistake. To lock a layer, click below the lock icon on that layer's row. Flash places a lock in the layer's row. Click the lock to unlock the layer again. The lock disappears, and you can now edit objects on that layer. You can lock *all* layers by clicking the lock icon directly. Click the lock icon again to unlock all the layers.

To lock or unlock all layers *except* one layer, Alt+click (Windows) or Option+click (Mac) below the lock icon on that layer's row. You can also right-click (Windows) or Control+click (Mac) a layer and choose Lock Others in the shortcut menu.

Outlines

Use Outlines to display objects as outlines of different colors. Outlines help you see which layer objects are on because each layer uses a different color, as shown in Figure 6-3. To display outlines, follow these steps:

1. **Click below the Outlines (box) icon on that layer's row.**

   Flash puts a colored box in the layer's row, and all objects on that layer are now shown as outlines in that color. (Text is still filled in, however.)

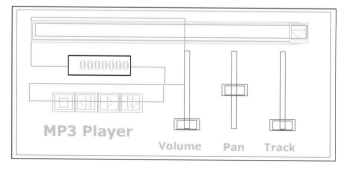

Figure 6-3: All the objects on the Stage are shown as outlines except for text.

2. **Click the box to display objects on that layer normally.**

To display *all* layers as outlines, click the Outlines icon directly. Click it again to see your objects as normal. You can work on outlined layers, but all new objects appear as outlines — so telling how they appear when displayed normally is difficult.

To display all layers as outlines except for one layer, Alt+click (Windows) or Option+click (Mac) below the Outline icon on that layer's row.

Getting Those Layers Right

Good layer housekeeping can help keep you sane. Delete layers that you no longer need. Rename layers when their content changes. Copy layers with their entire contents rather than re-create them from scratch. Here, we explain how to keep control over layers.

You can select more than one layer at a time. To select a contiguous group, click the first layer, hold down the Shift key, and then click the last layer in the group. To select more than one layer when they're not all together in a group, click the first layer, press and hold Ctrl (Windows) or ⌘ (Mac), and then click any additional layers that you want to select.

Deleting layers

When you work, you might find that a layer no longer has any objects. It's a layer without a purpose in life, so delete it. Select the layer and click the Trash can icon at the bottom of the layer list. You can also drag the layer to the Trash can.

When you delete a layer, you delete everything on the layer. However, some objects on a layer might not be visible because you see only what exists on the Stage in the current frame. For example, if you introduce a circle in Frame 15 of a layer named Circle but you're in Frame 1, you don't see that circle. Deleting the Circle layer, however, deletes the circle, although you can't see it. (We discuss frames in more detail in Chapter 9.)

To check for objects on a layer, right-click the layer and choose Hide Others from the contextual menu. Click the first frame on the Timeline and then press Enter (Windows) or Return (Mac) to run any existing animation. Objects on that layer appear during the animation, if they exist.

Copying layers

You can copy a layer, along with its entire contents, throughout all frames. If you create a great bouncing ball but now want two balls, copy the layer. You can then modify the position of the second ball throughout the Timeline without having to re-create the ball itself. Now you have two bouncing balls.

To copy and paste a layer, follow these steps:

1. **Click the layer name to select the layer.**

2. **Choose Edit⇨Timeline⇨Copy Frames.**

3. **Click the Insert Layer button to create a new layer.**

4. **Click the new layer to make its frames active.**

5. **Choose Edit⇨Timeline⇨Paste Frames.**

Renaming layers

Rename a layer whenever you want. By default, Flash names layers Layer 1, Layer 2, and so on. When you use a layer, rename it to reflect its contents. To rename a layer, double-click the layer name and type a new name. Then press Enter (Windows) or Return (Mac).

Reordering layers

In Chapter 4, we explain how to change the order of objects on the Stage when they're on the same layer. When objects are on different layers, though, a new rule applies: The order of the layers indicates the display order of objects on the Stage. Therefore, objects on the uppermost layer in the list are always on top, objects on the second layer appear one level down, and so on. Objects on the last layer in the list appear on the bottom level of the Stage, behind everything else.

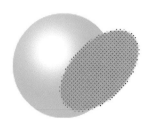

In fact, a simple and effective way to control object stacking is to put objects on different layers and then move the layers higher or lower in the layer list. To move a layer, just click and drag it within the layer list to the desired position. Figure 6-4 shows an example before and after moving a layer. The ball and the oval are on different layers. The top image looks a little odd, but when you reorder the layers, their objects are reordered as well — you can then see a ball and its shadow.

Figure 6-4: Change layer order to change the object order on those layers.

Changing the layer order can help you more easily select and edit objects that are covered by other objects. Simply drag the layer to the top of the list, and the objects in that list then appear on top. When you finish editing the objects, drag the layer back to its original location.

Organizing layers

Sometimes layers can get out of hand. You might have several layers with sounds on them or several layers for each animation. Tame those layers by putting them into folders. Instant organization! For example, you could create a Sounds folder and folders for each animation group.

To create a folder, click the Insert Layer Folder icon below the layer list. You see a new folder just above the active layer. Name the folder the same way you name a layer: Double-click it, type the name, and then press Enter (Windows) or Return (Mac). You can distinguish a folder from a layer by its folder icon.

After you have a folder, you fill it up with layers by dragging layers into it. Click and drag a layer just under the folder's name and then release the mouse button. At the same time, the layer's name becomes indented so that you can easily tell that it's in a folder, as shown in Figure 6-5.

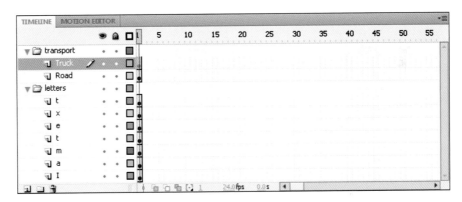

Figure 6-5: Put your layers into folders to keep yourself organized.

You can even put folders in folders. Just drag one folder into another. A folder within a folder is a *nested* folder, and the folder that it's in is the *parent* folder.

Here are some other things that you can do with folders:

- **Remove a folder from a folder.** Drag the nested folder above its parent folder.

- **Remove a layer from a folder.** Drag the layer above the folder name or to another location where it doesn't darken a folder.

- **Collapse or expand individual folders.** Click the folder's arrow, at the left of its icon.

- **Expand or collapse all folders.** Right-click (Windows) or Control+click (Mac) and then choose Expand All Folders or Collapse All Folders from the contextual menu.

- **Hide or lock an entire folder and its layers.** You can hide or lock a folder just like you hide or lock a layer. (See the "Changing layer states" section, earlier in this chapter.) Click below the eye (Show/Hide) or lock (Lock/Unlock) icon on the folder's row.

✔ **Reorder folders.** You can change the order of folders, which automatically changes the order of the layers that they contain. Just drag any folder up or down. For more information, see the preceding section.

✔ **Copy the contents of a folder to another folder.** To make a quick shortcut for copying layers and their contents, you can copy folders. Collapse the folder and click the folder name. Choose Edit➪Timeline➪Copy Frames, and then create a new folder. With the new folder active, choose Edit➪Timeline➪Paste Frames.

✔ **Delete folders.** Delete folders the same way you delete layers. Select the folder and then click the Trash can icon.

Deleting a folder deletes all layers in the folder and everything on those layers. Luckily, Flash warns you before you take the plunge.

Modifying layer properties

You can use the Layer Properties dialog box, as shown in Figure 6-6, to change certain layer properties, such as the color used for the layer's outlines and the layer height. Most settings, however, are easily accessible from the layer list. Select a layer (or a folder) and choose Modify➪Timeline➪Layer Properties to open the Layer Properties dialog box.

Here's how to use this dialog box to get the most from your layers:

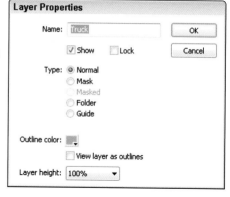

Figure 6-6: Fine-tune layer settings here.

✔ **The Name text box displays the current name of the layer.** You can rename the layer here if you want.

✔ **Change the layer states by selecting (or deselecting) the appropriate check boxes.** Usually, you change these states directly in the layer list, as we explain earlier in this chapter, in the "Changing layer states" section.

✔ **You can change the type of layer (guide or mask) by choosing from the list of layer types.** We cover guide and mask layers later in this chapter.

✔ **You can change the color that Flash uses when the layer is displayed as outlines.** Click the Outline Color swatch and choose another color in the color palette.

- ✓ **Select the View Layer as Outlines check box to turn on outlines.** As we explain earlier in this section, you can accomplish this task easily from the layer listing.

- ✓ **You can change the layer height to two or three times the normal height.** One reason to change the height of a layer is to more easily view sound waves on a layer that contains a sound. Open the Layer Height drop-down list and choose a value.

After you finish using the Layer Properties dialog box, click OK.

Another reason to display a larger layer height is to see larger previews of your keyframes in the Timeline. (Click the Options menu in the upper-right corner of the Timeline and choose Preview or Preview in Context from the pop-up menu.)

A *guide layer* is a layer that's invisible in the final, published animation. You can use guide layers for the following purposes:

- ✓ **Layout:** Although you can display onscreen guides to help you draw precisely (as we describe in Chapter 3), you can also place gridlines on guide layers to help you lay out the Stage, as shown in Figure 6-7. Graphic designers use these types of gridlines to figure out how to create a balanced, pleasing effect in their art.

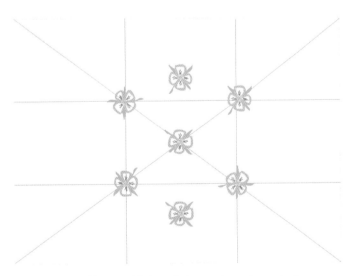

Figure 6-7: A grid on a guide layer helps you lay out your design.

✏ **Drawing:** You can import a bitmap graphic onto a guide layer and draw over the graphic on a regular layer by using the Flash drawing tools. This technique of drawing over a graphic can be a big help when creating your artwork.

In previous versions of Flash, guide layers also allowed you to guide an animated object along a path. You don't need guide layers for this purpose any more. However, you can still create the type of tween used in previous versions; it's now called a Classic Tween. For more information on animation, see Chapter 9.

Of course, you could use a regular layer and then erase whatever you don't want to appear in the final movie. But if you need to go back and make changes, you would have to create the guide layer again. Using a guide layer gives you the flexibility of keeping the layer in the movie file, knowing that it will never appear in the published animation.

Hidden layers appear in the published SWF file, but guide layers don't appear.

To create a guide layer, create a new layer. Then right-click (Windows) or Control+click (Mac) and choose Guide from the contextual menu. The layer is now a guide layer. Use the same procedure to convert a guide layer back to a regular layer.

Opening Windows with Mask Layers

A *mask layer* hides every object on its related layers except those inside a filled shape or text object. You can use mask layers to create peepholes or spotlight effects. Figure 6-8 shows a keyhole shape on a mask layer that hides the entire scene except for the part within the keyhole. The Indian bazaar scene is a rectangle much larger than the section displayed through the keyhole.

Figure 6-8: You can use a mask layer to create a hole through which you can see the layer or layers below.

Creating a mask layer

Follow these steps to create a mask layer, the object on the mask layer, and the objects behind the mask layer:

1. **Create the objects that you want to show through the hole in the mask layer.**

   These objects can be on one or more layers. Place all the layers that you want to be masked next to each other and at the top of the layer list.

2. **Select the topmost layer in the layer list and then click the Insert Layer button to create a new layer at the top of the list.**

   This layer will become the mask layer.

3. **Create, insert, or import one filled shape, text, or an instance of a symbol on the new layer.**

   See Chapter 7 for more about symbols.

   The filled part of the shape, text, or instance will become the hole. In other words, it will be transparent. For an example, see the keyhole shape in Figure 6-8. Unfilled portions of the object will become opaque, so everything will become the opposite of its current state.

4. **Right-click (Windows) or Control+click (Mac) the layer's name and then choose Mask from the contextual menu.**

   Flash turns the layer into a mask layer and locks the mask layer as well as the layer just below it in the layer list. The masked layer is indented in the layer list. You see the mask effect displayed. (To link more than one layer to the mask layer, see the next section, "Editing mask layers.")

Editing mask layers

Because Flash locks both the mask layer and the layer or layers that are masked, you cannot edit them until you unlock them. Click the lock icon above the layer list to unlock all the layers, or unlock the mask and masked layers only. Flash removes the mask effect. After you finish editing the layers, lock them again to redisplay the mask effect.

When you create a mask layer, Flash links only the layer directly below it to the mask layer. A layer linked to a mask layer is masked. If you place objects that you want to be masked on several layers, you need to change the property of all those layers from normal to masked.

All the layers that you want to be masked must be directly under the mask layer.

Here's how to link a layer to a mask layer:

- Drag a normal layer directly below a mask layer, and Flash links it to the mask layer in addition to existing masked layers.

- Right-click (Windows) or Control+click (Mac) the layer and choose Properties. Then select the Masked option in the Layer Properties dialog box.

Similarly, you can unlink a layer from its mask layer by using one of these methods:

- Drag the linked layer above the mask layer.

- Right-click (Windows) or Control+click (Mac) the layer and choose Properties. Then select the Normal option in the Layer Properties dialog box.

Animating mask layers

Mask layers are more fun when you animate them. You can move them, change their sizes, and change their shapes. If you create a keyhole like the one shown in Figure 6-8, you can move the keyhole past the masked layers, revealing what lies beneath while the keyhole moves. You can use the same technique to create an effect of a spotlight moving around a stage, revealing whatever it lights up. (Chapter 9 explains how to animate masks and other objects.) You can create more complex mask animations by using ActionScript. For the steps to do this, see the section on creating animated masks with movie clips in Chapter 10.

Look for `ffd_reveal.fla` on this book's Web site at `www.dummies.com/go/flashcs4fd`. To see the mask, open the file and unlock all the layers. Thanks to Shane Mielke for this file. Check out Shane's fantastic portfolio at `www.shanemielke.com`.

Part III
Getting Symbolic

The 5th Wave   By Rich Tennant

"Well, shoot. I know the animiation's moving a might fast, but dang if I can find a 'mosey' function anywhere in the toolbox!"

In this part . . .

Symbols can represent the deeper levels of life, and Flash symbols let you get down deep into the mechanics of animation. In this part, you discover the three kinds of symbols — graphic symbols, button symbols, and movie clip symbols — and how to use them.

Manipulating symbols is a critical feature of Flash. Symbols enable you to easily place duplicate graphics in your movie without significantly increasing the movie's size, and symbols are necessary when you start to animate. This part of the book also gives you the lowdown on buttons, which are central to the Web lifestyle in the 21st century. Flash lets you create buttons that change when you pass the mouse cursor over them and again when you click them. You can even make animated buttons. Part III provides you with the basis for creating great animations.

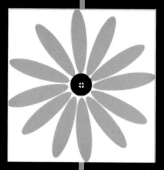

Heavy Symbolism

*F*lash offers a way to simplify your work, using symbols. A *symbol* can be any object or combination of objects, animation, or a Web button. When you create a symbol, the objects (or animation or Web button) become one object. Sounds like grouping, yes? (If you've already read Chapter 4, you know what we mean.) The difference is that Flash stores the definition of the symbol in the Library. From the Library, you can now effortlessly insert multiple copies of the symbol into your movie. Each copy is called an *instance.*

Besides making your life easier when you want to use a set of objects more than once, the use of symbols significantly reduces the size of your files. Instead of storing each instance that you use, Flash stores one definition for the symbol and refers to that definition each time you display an instance of the symbol. You can place symbols inside other symbols, which is called *nesting.* Used this way, symbols are the building blocks for complex graphics and animation. Motion-tweened animation requires symbols, groups, or text, so you often create symbols when preparing to animate. (Chapter 9 explains tweened animation.)

So, symbols are all-around good guys, and you should use them as much as possible.

Understanding Symbol Types

Flash offers three types of symbols: graphic, movie clip, and button. Each type is made up of one or more objects or animation, but each type has a different purpose. Understanding these types is important to understanding symbols and Flash animation in general.

Using graphic symbols

Graphic symbols are the simplest and most obvious type of symbol. When you create a Flash movie, you create objects on the Stage. Some objects may remain still, such as backgrounds. Other objects are animated — after all, what would Flash be without animation? Use graphic symbols for collections of static objects or for simple animation. Figure 7-1 shows a graphic symbol created from several curves and circles.

You create graphic symbols to reduce the size of your file and to make it easier to add multiple copies of a graphic to your movie. Symbols are

Figure 7-1: A graphic symbol.

stored in the Library and are available to not only the movie in which you create them but also to any other movie. You don't have to re-create the wheel. Flash ignores sounds and ActionScript inside graphic symbols. ActionScript code (which we explain in detail in Chapter 10) is the key to creating interactive movies. For that reason, don't use graphic symbols if you want to use ActionScript to directly control them — use movie clips instead.

Using movie clip symbols

A *movie clip* is like a movie within your movie that you can manipulate by using interactive controls (which you can read about in Chapter 10). Movie clips are crucial for complex animation and especially for interactive animation. A movie clip has its own Timeline independent of the movie's main Timeline. For example, you can go to a movie clip at any point in the movie, play it, and then return to where you left off on the Timeline. You can also attach movie clips to buttons. We explain how to create movie clips in this chapter; Chapter 8 discusses using movie clips with buttons. Chapter 9 covers using movie clips in animation, and Chapter 10 explains how to use and control movie clips by using interactive controls.

Flash comes with a library of *components,* which are special movie clips that allow you to add user-interface elements — such as radio buttons, check boxes, and scroll bars — to your movies. Choose Window⇨Components and drag one of your choices to the Stage. Then choose Window⇨Component Inspector to set the parameters of the component. For example, you can insert a list box and then add all the items (called *labels* on the Component Parameters panel) that you want on the list. For more information on components, see Chapter 12.

Using button symbols

Button symbols create *buttons* — those little graphics that you click on Web pages to take you to other pages on the site or the Internet. In Flash, you can use buttons for this type of navigation, but you can also use buttons to interact with your site. For example, you can let viewers decide whether they want to see a movie — when they click the button, the movie starts. You can also use advanced scripting to create buttons that control interactive games and other viewer activities. However you want to use buttons, button symbols are the way to start. You can add movie clips and interactive controls to buttons. Find out about buttons in Chapter 8.

Creating Symbols

For graphic symbols and button symbols, usually you create the objects that you need and then turn them into a symbol. The same is true of movie clips if they are static and you use ActionScript to control them. However, when you use a movie clip as a type of animation, you can use one of two approaches:

- ✔ Create an animation on the Stage and then convert it to a movie clip symbol.
- ✔ Create the movie clip symbol, create the initial objects, and then create the animation.

In the next few sections, we explain the various ways of creating symbols, for whichever purpose you want to use them.

Each type of symbol has its own icon that's used in the Library. The following table shows what type of symbol each icon represents:

Symbol	What It Represents
	Movie clip
	Button
	Graphic

Creating symbols from existing objects

To create a symbol from unanimated objects you've already created, follow these steps:

1. **On the Stage, select the objects that you want to convert to a symbol.**

2. **Right-click and choose Convert to Symbol, or press F8.**

   The Convert to Symbol dialog box opens, as shown in Figure 7-2.

3. **In the Name text box, type a name for the symbol.**

A common convention is to name the symbol in a way that's unique and also indicates the symbol type. For example, help_btn could be the name for a button symbol that will become a Help button on a Web site.

Figure 7-2: The Convert to Symbol dialog box.

4. **In the Type list, select the type of symbol you want to create: graphic, button, or movie clip.**

5. **Click OK to create the symbol and close the dialog box.**

The objects that you selected become one object, indicated by a single selection border around all the objects. Flash also stores the symbol in the Library. (Chapter 2 explains how to use the Library.)

Creating empty symbols

Rather than create a symbol from existing objects, you can create an empty symbol and then create the objects for the symbol. If you know in advance that you want to create a symbol, you can use this method.

To create an empty symbol, follow these steps:

1. **With no objects selected, choose Insert⇨New Symbol, or press Ctrl+F8.**

The Create New Symbol dialog box opens.

2. **In the Name text box, type a name for the symbol.**

3. **In the Type list, select the type of symbol you want to create — graphic, button, or movie clip — and then click OK.**

Flash switches to symbol-editing mode, which we describe in the section "Editing symbols," later in this chapter.

4. **Create the objects or animation for the symbol in the same way you do in regular movie-editing mode.**

5. **Choose Edit⇨Edit Document to leave symbol-editing mode and return to your movie.**

Your new symbol disappears! Don't worry — Flash saved the symbol in the Library. To find out how to insert an instance of the symbol on the Stage, see the "Inserting instances" section.

Converting an animation to a movie clip symbol

You can create a movie clip symbol by converting regular animation to a movie clip. Use this method when you already have the animation created on the Timeline. To convert an animation on the Stage to a movie clip symbol, follow these steps:

1. **On the layer listing, select all frames in all layers containing the animation by clicking the first layer and pressing Shift while you click the last layer in the group.**

   Alternatively, you can press Ctrl (Windows) or ⌘ (Mac) and click additional layers.

2. **On the Timeline, right-click (Windows) or Control+click (Mac) and choose Copy Frames to copy all the frames of the animation to the Clipboard.**

   Alternatively, you can choose Edit⇨Timeline⇨Copy Frames.

3. **With no objects selected (click somewhere off of the Stage to be sure that no objects are selected), choose Insert⇨New Symbol.**

   The Create New Symbol dialog box opens.

4. **In the Name text box, type a name for the movie clip.**

5. **In the Type list, select Movie Clip as the type of symbol. Then click OK.**

   Flash switches to symbol-editing mode so that you can edit the symbol.

6. **Click the first frame of the Timeline to set the start of the movie clip symbol.**

7. **Choose Edit⇨Timeline⇨Paste Frames to paste the animation into the Timeline and create the symbol.**

   You now see the animation on your screen in symbol-editing mode, as shown in Figure 7-3. We discuss editing symbols later in this chapter.

8. **To return to the main movie and Timeline, choose Edit⇨Edit Document.**

9. **To delete the animation from the main movie (now that you've saved it in a movie clip), select all layers as you did in Step 1 and choose Edit⇨Timeline⇨Remove Frames.**

   You can delete the animation from the main movie because your Library now has a movie clip that contains that animation. When you choose the movie clip in the Library panel, you can click the small Play button in the Library panel's window to play the animation.

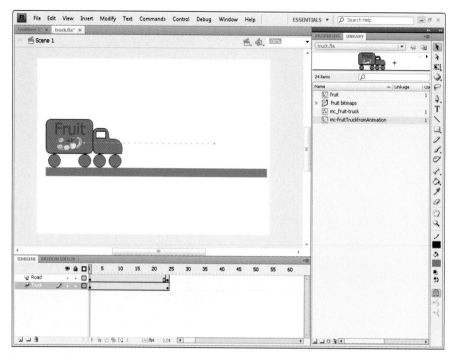

Figure 7-3: If you want lots of fruit trucks, turn the animation into a movie clip symbol.

Creating a symbol by duplicating a symbol

One more way to create a graphic, button, or movie symbol is to duplicate an existing symbol. To duplicate a symbol, follow these steps:

1. **Open the Library. (Choose Window⇨Library).**

2. **Select the symbol that you want to duplicate.**

3. **Click the Options menu in the upper-right corner of the Library window and choose Duplicate.**

   Flash opens the Duplicate Symbol dialog box.

4. **In the Name text box, type a name for the duplicate. Select the type of symbol that you want to create if you want a different kind from the original.**

5. **Click OK to close the dialog box and create the duplicate symbol.**

Modifying Symbols

Flash is a master of flexibility, and sometimes you need to make changes. Of course, you can change symbols after you create them. Here we explain the procedures you need to know.

Changing the properties of a symbol

You might need to change a symbol's properties. For example, you might create a graphic symbol and then realize that you need it to be a movie clip. No problem!

To change the properties of a symbol, follow these steps:

1. **Choose Window⇨Library to open the Library.**

2. **Right-click (Windows) or Control+click (Mac) the symbol's icon (not its name) and choose Properties.**

   The Symbol Properties dialog box opens.

3. **If the symbol is a graphic, button, or movie clip, select the type of symbol that you want in the Type list and then click OK.**

   Note that this change doesn't affect symbols that you've already inserted on the Stage.

Look on our companion Web site at `www.dummies.com/go/flashcs4fd` for `ffd_reveal.fla` — a good example of a short movie with lots of symbols. (The Flash movie is courtesy of Shane Mielke. You can see his other work at `www.shanemielke.com`.)

Editing symbols

An *instance* is a copy of a symbol that you insert into your movie. Part of the power of symbols lies in their control over instances. If you edit a symbol, Flash updates all instances of that symbol in the movie. You can change a symbol once and save yourself the time of creating the same change for every instance of that symbol. For that reason, it's worthwhile to make a symbol whenever you want to use a certain shape or group of shapes more than once.

You can edit a symbol in three modes:

- **Edit in symbol-editing mode.** Switches you to symbol-editing mode. You see only the symbol. Right-click (Windows) or Control+click (Mac) a selected symbol and choose Edit.

- **Edit in place.** Lets you edit a symbol while still viewing other objects on the Stage. Other objects are dimmed while you edit the symbol. Right-click (Windows) or Control+click (Mac) a selected symbol and choose Edit in Place.

- **Edit in a new window.** Opens a new window where you can edit your symbol. You see only the symbol. Right-click (Windows) or Control+click (Mac) a selected symbol and choose Edit in New Window.

The value of editing in place is that you can see how your change works with the rest of the objects that you have on the Stage. For example, if you want to make your symbol bigger, you may need to make sure that it doesn't obscure some nearby text. However, if you have lots of stuff on the Stage, editing in symbol-editing mode or in a new window can help you focus more easily on the symbol itself.

To edit a symbol, follow these steps:

1. **Select any instance of the symbol on the Stage.**

2. **Right-click (Windows) or Control+click (Mac) the instance and choose Edit, Edit in Place, or Edit in New Window.**

   Figure 7-4: One symbol, which includes a wedge and some circles, is being edited.

   (Choosing Edit puts you into symbol-editing mode.) Flash displays the symbol name at the top of the screen. If you choose Edit in Place, other objects are dimmed, as shown in Figure 7-4.

   This kaleidoscope animation is in the Ch07 folder on the companion Web site at www.dummies.com/go/flashcs4fd.

3. **Edit the symbol in any way you want.**

4. **After you finish editing, do the following:**

   • *If you chose Edit or Edit in Place, click the scene name to the left of the symbol name or choose Edit⇨Edit Document.*

   • *If you chose Edit in New Window, click the Close button.*

   You are now back in your main movie.

Using Symbols from Other Movies

After you create a symbol and store it in the Library, you can use that Library in any other movie. You can also open the Library from any other movie and use its symbols in your current movie. If the other movie is open and its Library is open, you can access that movie's Library from within your current movie. Libraries of any open movie are available from any other open movie.

Just choose that other movie in the drop-down list at the top of the Library panel. (Choose Window⇨Library.)

To use a symbol from the Library of another movie that is closed

1. **Choose File⇨Import⇨Open External Library.**

2. **From the Open as Library dialog box, select the movie file.**

3. **Click Open.**

    Flash displays the Library of the other movie in a new Library window.

The new Library might hide your current movie's Library. Just drag the new Library by its title bar so that it rests under the current Library until it docks there. In the new Library, many Options menu items and icons are disabled to prevent you from making changes in the other movie's file.

To use a symbol from the other Library, drag the symbol onto the Stage. Flash places a copy of the symbol in the current movie's Library. (See Chapter 2 for more about the Library.) You can also update or replace any graphic, button, or movie clip symbol in your movie's Library with the content of a symbol from any other Library on your hard drive or network. Accessing a symbol in this way is _author-time sharing_ of symbols or assets.

When you share a symbol while you're creating a movie (during _authoring_), the symbol in your current movie keeps its original name, but the contents take on the properties of the symbol you're sharing. If you have already replaced a symbol and the outside symbol changes (because it has been edited), use author-time sharing to update the symbol in your current drawing.

To update or replace a graphic, button, or movie clip symbol in your movie with the properties of another symbol, follow these steps:

1. **Open the Library (choose Window⇨Library) and select the symbol you want to update or replace.**

2. **From the Library Options menu, choose Properties.**

    The Symbol Properties dialog box opens.

3. **Click Advanced, if necessary, to see the expanded dialog box. In the Source section, click Browse.**

    The Locate Adobe Flash Document File dialog box opens.

4. **Navigate to the movie (`.fla`) file that contains the symbol you want to use. Select it and click Open.**

    The Select Source Symbol dialog box opens. You see a list of the symbols in the movie that you selected.

5. **Choose a symbol and click OK.**

   When you choose a symbol, you see a preview in the preview box, so you can easily find the symbol you want, as shown in Figure 7-5. When you click OK, you're back in the Symbol Properties dialog box.

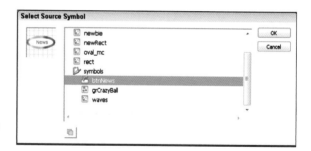

Figure 7-5: Choose another symbol to take on its properties.

6. **In the Source section of the Symbol Properties dialog box, select the Always Update Before Publishing check box if you want to automatically update the symbol if the original has changed.**

   Enable this check box to create a link between the source symbol and the symbol in your current movie.

7. **Click OK.**

You now have a symbol in your Library that has its original name but looks like the symbol you chose from the other movie.

Using the Flash Library

Flash comes with three common libraries you can use. To access these libraries, choose Window➪Common Libraries and then select the one you want. Flash includes buttons, sounds, and classes (building blocks for developing ActionScript applications). These libraries are also a good place to pick up ideas and see what you can create in Flash.

Using the Flash For Dummies Library

The Flash Libraries contain some good examples, but they miss many basic shapes and simple objects, some of which are hard to draw in Flash. We decided to fill in the gaps! We created a Library of art, geometric shapes, and fun shapes that you can use in your movies. You'll find 79 items in all! The *Flash For Dummies* Library is named `Flash CS4 For Dummies Library.fla`. You can find it at `www.dummies.com/go/flashcs4fd`.

To use this Library, go to `www.dummies.com/go/flashcs4fd` and download `Flash For Dummies Library.fla`. In Windows, download it to the `Program Files\Adobe\Adobe Flash CS4\en\Configuration\Libraries` folder on your hard drive. (The en folder indicates an English version of Flash.) On the Mac, download it to the `Applications/Adobe Flash CS4/Configuration/Libraries` folder on your hard drive.

After that, you can open this Library the same way you open other common Libraries: Choose Window⇨Common Libraries⇨Flash CS4 For Dummies Library.fla. We hope you enjoy it!

Working with Instances, for Instance

After you create a symbol, you can use it in many ways. You can insert it in your movie, inside other symbols, or even in other movies. Each copy of the symbol is called an *instance.* You can change the properties of an instance so that it differs from its parent symbol. For example, you can change the color of an instance — the original symbol remains unchanged.

Inserting instances

To insert an instance of a symbol, follow these steps:

1. **Choose Window⇨Library (Ctrl+L or F11 for Windows or ⌘+L or F11 for the Mac) to open the Library, as shown in Figure 7-6.**

2. **In the layer list, choose the layer where you want the instance to be placed.**

   See Chapter 6 for the full story on layers.

3. **Click a keyframe on the Timeline where you want the instance to be placed.**

   Flash places instances only in *keyframes* (frames that define a change in your animation). If you don't select a keyframe, Flash puts the instance in the first keyframe to the left of the current frame. (See Chapter 9 for more about keyframes.)

4. **Drag the symbol from the Library to the Stage.**

   You can drag from the list of items or directly from the preview at the top of the Library.

Figure 7-6: Insert an instance of a symbol by dragging it from the Library.

When you insert a graphic instance, you need to consider how it fits in your entire animation. For example, the instance might be the starting point for some animation, or it might be part of the background that remains static throughout the animation. Perhaps you want the instance to suddenly appear at some point in the animation. If the instance contains animation, you need to insert it at its proper starting point. (Chapter 9 explains how to copy graphics across any number of frames to create a static background and covers the entire topic of animation in detail.)

A movie clip instance, however, takes up only one frame on the Timeline. It plays and loops automatically unless you create ActionScript code to control it. (Chapter 10 talks about ActionScript.)

Editing instances

A symbol's children don't have to be carbon copies of their parents, thank goodness. Instances of a symbol can differ from their parent symbol by color, type, and play mode. You can also rotate, scale, or skew an instance, leaving the parent symbol unchanged.

When you edit an instance, Flash remembers the changes. If you later edit the symbol, Flash doesn't forget the changes you made to the instance. Suppose that you create a red circle graphic symbol, and then you create several instances of it and change one instance to pink. Then you edit the (still red!) circle symbol to change it to an oval. All the instances are now ovals, but the one you turned pink is still pink. The instance's shape has been updated, but the pink color remains.

In the Property inspector (choose Window➪Properties➪Properties), you can change an instance's color (or tint), brightness, or transparency, giving you some useful control over the appearance of your instances. To change an instance's color, brightness, or transparency, follow these steps:

1. **Select the instance.**

2. **Choose Window➪Properties to open the Property inspector.**

3. **Expand the Color Effect section and select one of these options in the Style drop-down list:**

   - *None:* Adds no color effect.

   - *Brightness:* Changes the lightness or darkness of the instance.

   - *Tint:* Changes the color of the instance.

   - *Alpha:* Changes the opacity/transparency of the instance.

   - *Advanced:* Changes both the color and the alpha.

4. **Make the desired changes, as we explain in the next few sections.**

   You see the changes that you make in the Property inspector immediately in your selected instance.

Changing brightness

When you choose Brightness in the Style drop-down list, a text box and a slider appear. Type a brightness percentage or drag the slider and see the result in the symbol instance. High brightness makes the image light, and 100-percent brightness makes the instance white. (It disappears if you have a white background!) Low brightness makes the image dark; 0-percent brightness turns the instance black.

Changing tint

When you choose Tint in the Style drop-down list, you can choose the color and then the amount of the color (the tint), by percentage, that you want to apply. Figure 7-7 shows the controls for this option. You can select a color by clicking the Tint Color swatch and choosing from the color swatches, by dragging the sliders, or by typing red, green, and blue values, if you know them.

Specify the percentage of the color you want to apply by typing a value in the Tint text box or by dragging the slider to choose a percentage. When the percentage is set to 100%, the instance changes to the color you specified. If the percentage is set to 0%, Flash leaves the instance unchanged.

The Flash method of specifying a color gives you great flexibility and precision. You can choose a color and use the tint control to create a meld of the current color and your chosen color.

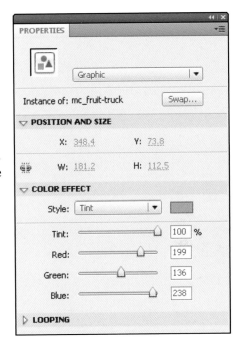

Figure 7-7: Changing the tint used on a symbol instance

Changing transparency

Choose Alpha in the Style drop-down menu to change the transparency of an instance. (*Alpha* enables levels of transparency, and you can think of the term as somewhat synonymous to *opacity.*) Use the slider or type a value in the text box. A value of 0 means that your instance becomes completely transparent — in that case, when you return to the Stage, all you see is the selection border and the small plus sign that marks the symbol's registration point. When you deselect the instance, you see absolutely nothing! (Chapter 4 explains more about a symbol's registration point, including how to move it. See the section on groups.)

Partial transparency lets your background show through. A partially transparent instance blends in with your background, creating a softer effect. However, transparency is a complex feature and can slow down the loading and playing of a movie.

Changing color and transparency at the same time

Select Advanced in the Style drop-down menu to change the red, green, and blue color values and the transparency at the same time. Figure 7-8 shows the controls, which are complex.

Use the controls on the left to specify the color or transparency as a specific percentage of the current value. Use the controls on the right to change the color or transparency to a specific, absolute amount. Flash calculates the new color value by multiplying the current value by the percentage you specified and then adding the value from the right side. As you can see, this method provides lots of control — but it might make you crazy first.

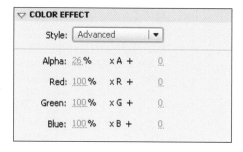

Figure 7-8: The Advanced controls for instances.

To simply change both the color and the transparency of an instance, choose Tint from the Style drop-down list to change the color and then choose Advanced, changing only the left Alpha setting.

Adding filters and blends

You can apply special graphic effects called *filters* to text, buttons, and movie clips — but not to graphic symbols. Select the item and expand the Filters section of the Property inspector, if necessary. Click the Add Filter button and choose one (or more) of the following filters: Drop Shadow, Blur, Glow, Bevel, Gradient Glow, Gradient Bevel, or Adjust Color. The Filters tab then displays further controls so that you can specify how you want the filter to look. You can get some cool effects this way. You can even add multiple filters.

To apply filter settings from one object to another, you can copy and paste one or more filters.

1. **Select the object that has the filter (or filters) that you want.**

2. **In the Filters section of the Property inspector, select the filter that you want to copy.**

3. **Click the Clipboard button. In the pop-up menu, choose Copy Selected or Copy All.**

4. **Select the object that you want to have the filters.**

5. **Click the Clipboard button. In the pop-up menu, choose Paste.**

You can also apply *blend modes* to movie clips. Blend modes determine how movie clips that overlap blend with each other at the point of overlap. To apply a blend, select a movie clip instance and adjust the color and transparency as we explain in the previous sections. Then choose a blend mode in the Blend drop-down list in the Property inspector. The names of the blend modes are not self-explanatory, so try them to see their effects. (The blend mode names may be familiar to you from other Adobe applications.)

Changing an instance's type

The instance type — graphic, movie clip, or button — comes from the symbol type, but you might want to change it. For example, if you created some animation and saved it as a graphic symbol, you might want to use it as a movie clip. Rather than change the symbol type, you can change only the type of the instance that you have inserted. To change the instance type

1. **Select the instance.**

2. **Choose Window⇨Properties to open the Property inspector.**

3. **In the Instance Behavior drop-down list, select one of the following:**

   - *Graphic:* If the graphic contains animation, select Graphic in the Instance Behavior drop-down list. Then determine how the animation will run by expanding the Looping section of the Property inspector. In the Options drop-down list, choose one of these:

     Loop plays the animation contained in the instance over and over during the frames occupied by the instance.

     Play Once plays the animation once from the frame you specify.

     Single Frame displays any one frame of the animation. In other words, the animation doesn't play; you specify which frame the movie displays.

   - *Button:* To create a button, select Button in the Instance Behavior drop-down list. Then specify how the button will function in the Tracking section of the Property inspector. In the Options drop-down list, select Track as Button if you're creating single buttons. Select Track as Menu if you're creating pop-up menus.

   - *Movie Clip:* To create a movie clip, select Movie Clip in the Instance Behavior drop-down list. Then specify an Instance name in the Instance Name text box at the top of the Property inspector. You use this name with certain ActionScript controls so that you can refer to and control the instance. (For more information about ActionScript, see Chapter 10.)

If you select a movie clip or button instance, you can select the Cache as Bitmap check box in the Property inspector. *Runtime bitmap caching* optimizes playback of a Flash movie in a browser. Use bitmap caching only when you have a complex background that remains the same throughout the movie. By storing the background as a bitmap, the Flash player can play the animation faster and more smoothly because it doesn't have to redraw the image throughout the movie.

Replacing an instance

Suppose you create a complex animation with bouncing bunnies all over the Stage. Suddenly your boss decides that some of the bouncing bunnies should be bouncing squirrels. Meanwhile, you had already edited all the bunnies to make them different sizes and colors. You need to replace some of the bunnies with squirrels without losing their sizes and colors. To replace an instance, follow these steps:

1. **Create the squirrel symbol (or whichever new symbol you need).**

   Flash stores the new symbol in the Library.

2. **Select an instance of the bunny — that is, your original instance — on the Stage.**

3. **Choose Window⇨Properties to open the Property inspector.**

4. **Click the Swap button to open the Swap Symbol dialog box, shown in Figure 7-9.**

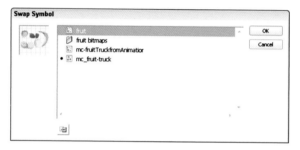

Figure 7-9: The Swap Symbol dialog box makes life easy when you change your mind.

5. **In the dialog box, select the squirrel or any other symbol.**

6. **Click OK to swap the symbols and close the Swap Symbol dialog box.**

   Flash retains your color effects and size changes but changes the symbol.

Unfortunately, you must repeat this process for all the bunnies you want to change on the Stage, but it's better than reinserting all your instances and re-creating the instance changes.

If your boss actually wants you to change all the bunnies to squirrels, your job is much simpler. Just edit the bunny symbol (as we describe in the "Editing symbols" section, earlier in this chapter) to replace the bunny image with a squirrel. Then all the instances of that symbol instantly change to squirrels yet retain the color effects and size changes that you gave them while they were still bunnies.

Duplicate a symbol when you want to use one symbol as a springboard for creating a new symbol. Follow the instructions in the "Creating Symbols" section, earlier in this chapter. Make any changes that you want to the new symbol and place instances on the Stage.

Breaking apart an instance

You can break apart an instance into its component objects. The original symbol remains in the movie's Library. You might want to use the instance as a starting point for creating a completely new symbol, or you might want to animate the components of the symbol so that they move separately. Other instances remain unchanged.

To break apart an instance, select it and choose Modify⇨Break Apart. If an instance contains symbols or grouped objects within it, you can use the Break Apart command again to break apart those internal objects as well.

Changing 3D position and rotation

You can move and rotate movie clip instances in 3D space. (Other symbols aren't invited to this 3D party!) When you change a movie clip instance in this way, it's considered a 3D object. This feature let's you create the appearance of depth and adds to the realism of your movies.

When you use Flash's 3D features, you must publish your movie using the default Flash Player 10 and ActionScript 3.0 settings. Earlier versions of the Flash Player and ActionScript don't support these 3D features. For more information on publish settings, see Chapter 10.

Moving movie clip instances

You can move movie clip instances in all three directions (called *translation),* using the 3D Translation tool. Of course, moving an object in the X (horizontal) and Y (vertical) directions doesn't require a special tool; however, you often want to move a movie clip instance in all three directions at once, so the 3D Translation tool is very handy. Figure 7-10 shows an instance of a movie clip before using the 3D Translation tool (on the left) and after moving it toward the viewer (on the right).

The 3D Translation tool has two modes:

- **Global mode:** Moves the movie clip relative to the Stage. The 3D Translation tool defaults to Global mode.
- **Local mode:** Moves a nested movie clip relative to its parent movie clip.

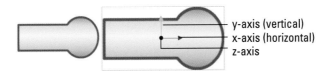

Figure 7-10: The 3D Translation tool moves movie clips in all three directions.

Here's how to move a movie clip instance:

1. **Choose the 3D Translation tool from the Tools panel.**

   The 3D Translation tool is part of a flyout that also contains the 3D Rotation tool. If necessary, click and hold the 3D Rotation tool (discussed next) and then choose the 3D Translation tool from the flyout.

2. **Click an instance of a movie clip symbol on the Stage.**

   The 3D axis appears on the movie clip.

3. **Set the mode, global or local, using the Global Transform button in the Options section of the Tools panel.**

   Select the Global Transform button to use global mode. Deselect the button to use local mode.

4. **To move the movie clip, do one of the following:**

   - To move the clip horizontally, drag the x-axis arrow to the left or right.

   - To move the clip vertically, drag the y-axis arrow up or down.

   - To move the clip in the z direction (toward or away from the viewer), drag the blue dot at the center of the axes up (away from the viewer) or down (toward the viewer). If you move the movie clip toward you, it appears larger; if you move it away from you, it appears smaller.

Note that if you rotate the movie clip instance so that you're not looking directly down at it, as we explain in the next section, you see a z-axis, rather than just a dot.

For greater control over 3D position, you can use the Property inspector. Display the Property inspector (Window⇨Properties) and select a movie clip instance. Expand the 3D Position and View section to display the controls. To change one of these controls, click the current value and type a new value or drag up or down on the value. You can set the following controls:

- ✔ **X:** The horizontal position on the Stage of the movie clip instance.

- ✔ **Y:** The vertical position on the Stage of the movie clip instance.

- ✔ **Z:** The z-axis position of the movie clip instance. Values below zero are closer to the viewer; the instance looks larger. Values above zero are farther away and look smaller.

  The W value is the perspective width. It shows how wide the object looks. The H value is the perspective height and shows how high the object looks. These values are for information only; you can't change them.

- ✔ **Perspective Angle:** The apparent angle of view. This value works like a camera lens' angle of view. The default value is 55°, which is a normal camera lens. Values can range from 1° to 180°. A higher value makes the object appear closer; a lower value makes the object appear farther away. Try adjusting the value. With certain types of rotation, the results can be positively weird!

✐ **Vanishing Point X Position:** The horizontal position of the z-axis.

✐ **Vanishing Point Y Position:** The vertical position of the z-axis.

The location of the vanishing point controls how an object moves along the z-axis. The vanishing point affects all movie clips on the Stage that have a 3D transformation or rotation. By default, the vanishing point is at the center of the Stage.

Rotating movie clip instances

You can rotate the position of a movie clip instance in all three directions using the 3D Rotation tool. As with translation, described just previously, you can rotate globally or locally. Figure 7-11 shows a movie clip instance in its initial state (on top) and rotated in all three directions (on the bottom).

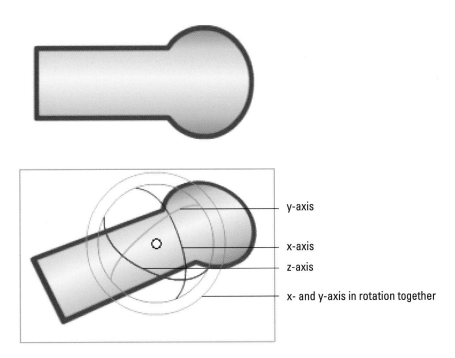

y-axis

x-axis

z-axis

x- and y-axis in rotation together

Figure 7-11: The 3D Rotation tool lets you drag your movie clips any which way.

Follow these steps to rotate your movie clip instance:

1. **Choose the 3D Rotation tool from the Tools panel.**

   The 3D Rotation tool is part of a flyout that also contains the 3D Translation tool. If necessary, click and hold the 3D Translation tool and then choose the 3D Rotation tool from the flyout.

2. **Click an instance of a movie clip on the Stage.**

   The 3D Rotation control appears on the movie clip instance. If the control appears in a different location, double-click the control's center point to move it back to the selected instance.

3. **Set the mode, global or local, using the Global Transform button in the Options section of the Tools panel.**

   Select the Global Transform button to use global mode. Deselect the button to use local mode.

4. **To rotate the movie clip instance, do one of the following:**

   - To rotate the movie clip around the x (horizontal) axis, drag the x-axis control.

   - To rotate the movie clip around the y (vertical) axis, drag the y-axis control.

   - To rotate the movie clip around the z axis, drag the z-axis control. This movement is like a 2D rotation.

   - To rotate the movie clip around the x and y axes simultaneously, drag the orange circle on the outer edge of the control. This control allows you to freely rotate the movie clip in 3D space.

The small circle in the 3D Rotation control is the center point of the rotation; you can drag it to control the rotation's center. Double-click it to return it to the center of the object.

8

Pushing Buttons

When you view a Web page, you click buttons to move to other pages or sites. As you probably know, these buttons are graphical images, but they're hyperlinks as well. If you start to pay attention to these buttons, you see that some of them change when you pass your mouse cursor over them. They change again when you click them. Occasionally, they make a sound when you click them.

Flash can create these types of buttons and more. You can animate Flash buttons so that they move or rotate when viewers pass their cursors over them or click them. You can add interactive controls (actions) to buttons so that passing over or clicking them starts other movies or creates other effects.

In this chapter, you find out how to create buttons that look the way you want. You also discover how to make more complex buttons that include sounds, movie clips, and simple ActionScript. To discover more about ActionScript and interactivity, see Chapter 10.

Creating Simple Buttons

Before you create a button, stop and think about what you want the button to accomplish on a Web page and how you want it to look. When designing a Web site's navigation, designers often create a series of similar buttons that lead to pages within a site. This similarity provides a coherent style for the site. Buttons usually include some text to identify the button's purpose.

A *button* is a symbol that responds to a mouse. (See Chapter 7 for the low-down on how to create and edit symbols.) In this chapter, we cover the entire process of creating buttons.

Understanding button states

A button has four states that define characteristics of the button. Figure 8-1 shows a button in its four states.

- ✔ **Up:** What the button looks like when the mouse pointer is not over the button. The viewer initially sees the Up state of a button.

- ✔ **Over:** What the button looks like when the pointer is over the button but it hasn't been clicked.

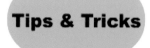

- ✔ **Down:** What the button looks like when it is clicked.

- ✔ **Hit:** The area of the button that responds to the mouse. The user doesn't see this area — it's invisible. When you pass the pointer over the hit area, the pointer is considered to be over the button. When you click anywhere in the hit area, the button works.

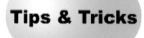

A typical, simple button might show a lit-up effect for the Over state and an indented look (as though the button is pressed in) for the Down state. In this example, the Down state moves the highlight to the right, giving the impression of movement when the user clicks the button.

Radial gradients are useful for creating a lit-up or pushed-in look. Use a light color or white to create the appearance of a highlight. Use a dark color or black to create an indented look. Just changing the color of the fill (often to a lighter color) is enough to make it seem lit up.

Figure 8-1: The four button states.

The button shown in Figure 8-1 is on the companion Web site at `www.dummies.com/go/flashcs4fd`. Look for `capsule.fla`. To try out the buttons in this movie, choose Control⇨Test Movie.

Making a basic button

To create a simple button, follow these steps:

1. **Choose Insert⇨New Symbol to open the Create New Symbol dialog box.**

2. **In the Name text box, type a name for the button.**

   When you have many symbols in a movie, it helps to name them according to their type and purpose. For example, if a button will be labeled Submit a Resource, you might name it btnSubmitResource.

3. **From the Type drop-down list, select the Button option.**

4. **Click OK.**

   You're now in symbol-editing mode. Flash displays the special Timeline for buttons, with four frames: Up, Over, Down, and Hit, as shown in Figure 8-2. Note the dot in the Up frame, indicating that the frame is a keyframe. (For more information about keyframes, see Chapter 9.) The word *Up* is highlighted, indicating that the Up frame is active.

Figure 8-2: The Flash symbol-editing mode for buttons displays a Timeline with four frames.

5. **Create the graphic for the Up state.**

   You can use the Flash drawing tools, an imported graphic, or an instance of a graphic or movie clip symbol. You can create as many layers as you want for the button. For an animated button, use a movie clip symbol. We explain how to create an animated button in the "Adding a movie clip to a button" section, later in this chapter.

   If you want the button image for the four states to be in the same place, place the graphic in the center of the display and build the other states in the center as well. To do this, cut and paste the graphic. (See Chapter 4 for more about centering objects on the display.) If the button images aren't in the same place, the button shifts when the viewer passes the cursor over or clicks the button.

6. **Right-click (Windows) or Control+click (Mac) the Over frame and choose Insert Keyframe from the contextual menu.**

   Flash inserts a keyframe in the Over frame of the button. You can also choose Insert⇨Timeline⇨Keyframe or press F6. The graphic for the Up state remains on the Stage.

7. **Create the graphic for the Over state.**

   You can use the graphic for the Up state as a starting point and change it. (Or leave it the same if you don't want the button to change when the mouse pointer passes over the button.) You can also delete the graphic and put a new one in its place. If you have more than one layer, place a keyframe on each layer before creating the artwork for that layer.

8. Right-click (Windows) or Control+click (Mac) the Down frame and choose Insert Keyframe.

9. Create the graphic for the Down frame.

   Repeat as in Step 7. Note that if the button functions as navigation to another page, your viewer will see this state for only a split second.

10. Right-click (Windows) or Control-click (Mac) the Hit frame and choose Insert Keyframe.

11. If necessary, create the shape that defines the active area of the button.

   This shape should completely cover all the graphics of the other state. Usually, a rectangle or circle is effective. If you ignore the Hit frame, Flash uses the boundary of the objects in the Up frame, which might be what you want. Figure 8-3 shows the Timeline when a button is completed.

Figure 8-3: When you complete a button, all four frames are keyframes.

   If you use text for the button, viewers have to click the letters precisely unless you create a rectangular hit area around the text. To cover an area of text, create a filled-in shape on a new layer. (We explain how to create shapes in Chapter 3.)

12. Click the scene name at the upper left of the screen (or the Back arrow to the left of the scene name) to return to the regular Timeline and leave symbol-editing mode.

13. If the Library isn't open, choose Window⇨Library and drag the button symbol that you just created to wherever you want it on the Stage.

   You created a button!

A button is a symbol, but when you want to place a button on the Stage, you must drag the button from the Library to create an instance of the symbol. See Chapter 7 for a full explanation of symbols and instances.

Putting Buttons to the Test

After you create a button, you need to test it. You can choose from several methods. The fastest way to test a button is to enable it on the Stage. An enabled button responds to your mouse as you would expect — it changes as you specified when you pass the mouse over it or click it. To enable the buttons on the Stage, choose Control⇨Enable Simple Buttons. All the buttons on the Stage are now enabled. Have fun with your button! Pass the mouse over it, click it, and watch it change.

After you test your button, suppose that you want to select the button to move it. You try to click it to select it, and it only glows at you, according to the Down frame's definition. Choose Control⇨Enable Simple Buttons again to disable the buttons. Now you can select a button as you do any other object. In general, you enable buttons only to test them.

However, if you really want to select an enabled button, you can do so with the Selection tool by dragging a selection box around it. You can use the arrow keys to move the button. If you want to edit the button further, choose Window⇨Properties⇨Properties to open the Property inspector and edit the button's properties, as we explain in Chapter 7.

If you have other animations on the Stage, you can play an animation with the buttons enabled. Choose Control⇨Play or press Enter (Windows) or Return (Mac). By playing the animation, you can see how the buttons fit in with the rest of your movie.

Another way to test a button is to test the entire movie. Choose Control⇨Test Movie. Flash creates an SWF file based on default publishing settings, just as it would if you were publishing the movie. Any animation plays, and you can test your buttons as well. When you're finished, click the Close box of the window. If your button contains movie clips, you must use this method of testing the button because the animation doesn't play on the Stage.

Creating Complex Buttons

Buttons can do more than just change color or shape. You can enhance a button in three ways:

- **Add a sound.** For example, you can add a clicking sound to the Down frame of a button so that users hear that sound when they click the button.

- **Add a movie clip.** To animate a button, you add a movie clip to it. You can animate the Up, Over, and Down frames, if you want.

- **Add an action (interactive control).** To make a button do something, you need to add an action to it by using ActionScript. Actions are covered in Chapter 10, but we discuss some of the basic concepts here.

Adding a sound to a button

For fun, you can add a sound to a button. Usually, sounds are added to the Over or Down frame — or both, if you want. Chapter 11 explains lots more about sound, but in this section, we explain how to add a simple sound to a button.

On the companion Web site at `www.dummies.com/go/flashcs4fd`, look for `click.wav`. You can add this sound to the Down frame of a button.

To add a sound to a button, follow these steps:

1. **Create the button symbol.**

2. **Choose File⇨Import⇨Import to Library to open the Import dialog box.**

3. **Select the sound file (in `.wav`, `.aiff`, or `.mp3` format) and click Open.**

   Flash stores the file in the Library.

4. **Choose Window⇨Library to open the Library.**

5. **If you aren't in symbol-editing mode, double-click the button's icon in the Library to enter symbol-editing mode.**

6. **Click the Insert Layer button at the bottom of the layer list to add a new layer.**

   See Chapter 6 for a full explanation of layers.

7. **Name the new layer *Sound* or something similar.**

8. **In the new layer, right-click (Windows) or Control-click (Mac) the frame where you want to place the sound — for example, the Down frame — and choose Insert Keyframe.**

9. **Display the Property inspector.**

   Choose Window⇨Properties⇨Properties to open the Property inspector if it's not already open.

10. **In the Sound section, in the Name drop-down list, select the sound file that you want.**

    Flash lists all the sounds you've imported into the Library. When you select the sound file, you see the sound wave indicator on the sound's layer in the frame where you inserted the sound, as shown in Figure 8-4.

Figure 8-4: When you add a sound to a button, the sound wave appears in the Timeline.

11. **With the new keyframe still selected, click the Sync drop-down list in the Property inspector and choose Event.**

    The Event setting synchronizes the sound to the occurrence of an event: in this case, the clicking of the button. Event is the default setting.

12. **Click the scene name in the upper-left area of the layer list or the back arrow to the left of the scene name.**

    Flash returns you to the regular Timeline and leaves symbol-editing mode.

13. **Drag the button symbol that you just created from the Library to wherever you want the button on the Stage.**

    You're finished! Now test the button as we explain in the earlier section, "Putting Buttons to the Test."

Be sure to look in Chapter 11 for more information on adding sounds to buttons and movies.

If you already added the sound to another movie, choose File➪Import➪Open External Library and choose the other movie. Click the desired keyframe and drag the sound from the Library to anywhere on the Stage. Flash places the sound in the selected keyframe.

Adding a movie clip to a button

If you think that simple buttons are b-o-r-i-n-g, you can animate them. To animate a button, you must create a movie clip symbol and then insert the movie clip into one of the frames. Generally, button animation is localized in the area of the button. If you want to make an elaborate button, you can animate all three frames — Up, Over, and Down.

To add a movie clip to a button, first create the movie clip. Chapter 7 explains how to create a movie clip symbol, and Chapter 9 explains how to create the animation to put in the movie clip.

For the following steps, you can use the movie clip that we provide on the companion Web site at `www.dummies.com/go/flashcs4fd`. Open `flower power.fla`. It's a blank movie with a Library that contains the symbols necessary to create a button with a movie clip.

If you've never created a button, review the steps in the "Making a basic button" section, earlier in this chapter. Then to create a button with a movie clip, follow these steps:

1. If you're using the movie file included on the Web site, open `flower power.fla`; otherwise, open any new movie file.

2. Choose Insert⇨New Symbol to open the Create New Symbol dialog box.

3. In the Name text box, type a name for the button.

4. In the Type list, select the Button option. Then click OK.

5. Create the graphic for the Up state.

   If you're using the movie from the Web site, choose Window⇨Library and drag the graphic symbol named Flower to the Stage. Press the arrow buttons on the keyboard (left, right, up, and down, as necessary) to center the flower symbol's registration point (shown by a little plus sign) exactly over the registration point (also a plus sign) on the Stage. (See upcoming Figure 8-5.) You can also cut and paste the symbol to center it. The flower graphic symbol is static, not animated.

6. Right-click (Windows) or Control+click (Mac) the Over frame and choose Insert Keyframe from the contextual menu.

   Flash inserts a keyframe.

7. Create the graphic for the Over state.

   For this example, delete the graphic on the Stage (it's still there from the Up frame) and drag the movie clip called Flower Rotating to the center of the Stage. Click the Stage and use the arrow keys to perfectly center the flower. The Flower Rotating movie clip animates the flower by rotating it.

8. Right-click (Windows) or Control+click (Mac) the Down frame and choose Insert Keyframe.

9. Create the graphic for the Down state.

   In this example, delete the graphic on the Stage and drag the Flower Light graphic symbol to the exact center of the Stage.

10. Right-click (Windows) or Control+click (Mac) the Hit frame and choose Insert Keyframe.

11. Use the Rectangle tool and drag a square to cover the entire area of the symbol, leaving the symbol on top. Use the Selection tool to select and delete the symbol, leaving only the square.

    If you don't perform this step, viewers must place the mouse cursor exactly over one of the petals to see the animation. By defining the Hit frame as a square, placing the cursor anywhere within that square activates the button. Your screen should look like Figure 8-5, shown with the Up frame active.

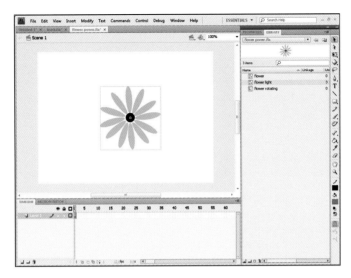

Figure 8-5: You can use the Flower Power library to create an animated button.

12. Click the scene name (Scene 1) above the layer list to return to the regular Timeline.

13. Drag the button symbol that you just created from the Library to wherever you want the button placed on the Stage.

Congratulations! You have just created a button with a movie clip.

To test the button that you just created, choose Control➪Test Movie. Place the cursor over the button, click the button, and watch the animation. If you used the Flower Power movie from the Web site, first save the file on your computer by choosing File➪Save As and choosing a location on your hard drive. When you test this movie, the flower rotates and lightens when you pass the cursor over it. When you click the flower, it seems to freeze. When you're finished, click the Close box of the window.

If you want to see the final result of the preceding steps, check out `flower power final.fla` on the companion Web site at `www.dummies.com/go/flashcs4fd`.

Adding an action for a button

A button doesn't do anything except look pretty until you give it the proper instructions. For example, a button can link you to another Web page or start a movie. See Figure 8-6 for an example of a navigation button. You find out about ActionScript in Chapter 10, but in this section, we explain the basic principle of adding an action to a button — in this case, an action that links the user to another Web page.

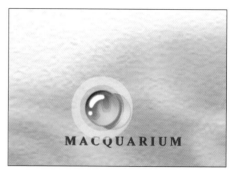

Courtesy Macquarium, Inc.

Figure 8-6: This movie sports beautiful bubble buttons.

As we explain in Chapter 10, by default, Flash CS4 uses ActionScript 3.0 as its programming language. After you have the ActionScript code for a button, you can use it as a template to create your own buttons.

You add an action for a button by placing the action on the Timeline, usually in the first frame. To create ActionScript for a button, follow these steps:

1. If you haven't already done so, drag an instance of the button onto the Stage. If the button isn't selected, select it.

2. Open the Property inspector (choose Window⇨Properties⇨ Properties). In the Instance Name text box at the top, enter a name for this instance of the button symbol, as shown in Figure 8-7.

   The name can't include spaces. You can use an underscore or hyphen for readability.

   Each instance of a button symbol should have a different instance name.

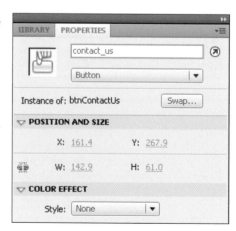

Figure 8-7: Enter an instance name for your button.

3. **Click anywhere off the Stage to deselect the button.**

4. **Create a new layer and name it Actions.**

   Chapter 6 explains how to create layers.

5. **Click the first frame of the Actions layer.**

   This instruction assumes that you want the button to appear at the beginning of the movie. If you want the button to appear later, right-click (Windows) or Control+click (Mac) the frame where you want the button to appear and choose Insert Keyframe. When you click a keyframe of a layer, all actions that you add go in that keyframe and on that layer.

6. **Open the Actions panel. (Choose Window⇨Actions.) Type the following ActionScript, substituting the following:**

   • Your function name for `goHome` (in two places)

   • Your instance name for `btnHome`

   • The URL you want for the URL in the code you see here

   ```
   function goHome(event:MouseEvent):void
   {
       var targetURL:URLRequest = new
               URLRequest("http://www.ellenfinkelstein.com/");
       navigateToURL(targetURL);
   }
   btnHome.addEventListener(MouseEvent.CLICK, goHome);
   ```

   This code creates a function, called `goHome`, that references an instance of a button, called `btnHome`. It "listens" for a click and then executes the function. Be sure to keep the same capitalization and line endings as shown here.

7. **Close the Action panel and save your movie.**

   If the Compiler Errors panel opens when you close the Actions panel or test your button (Control⇨Test Movie), it means that you made a mistake in your typing. Check your code, correct any errors, and try again.

You can add your button to an existing Web page. In such a case, the button might be the only Flash element on the page. You can also include buttons as part of an environment created completely in Flash. Either way, buttons are a valuable piece of the Flash arsenal.

Testing your button's URL navigation

To properly test a button, you need to publish your movie, upload it to your Web page, go online, and try it out. However, you can test the button on your hard drive first so that you can be fairly sure that it will work when you put it on your Web page.

To test your button without publishing it, choose Control⇨Test Movie and click the button. If you used an absolute (complete) URL, you should have no problem. Your browser should open and display the appropriate Web page. However, a relative (local) URL might not be available. For example, if your URL is `tips.html`, the button won't work unless you have a file named `tips.html` in the same folder as the Flash movie.

You can still test a relative URL on your hard drive. Continuing with the example of a link to `tips.html`, assume that on your Web server, `tips.html` is in the same folder as the Web page containing your Flash button so that you can use this simple local URL.

To test your button's ActionScript, follow these steps:

1. **After creating the button and its Action Script containing a URL of `tips.html` (or whatever's appropriate in your situation), choose File⇨Save to save the movie file.**

2. **Choose File⇨Publish.**

   Flash publishes the file, creating an HTML file and an SWF file in the same folder as your FLA file. (These are default settings. See Chapter 13 for more information on publishing movies.)

3. **You need a file on your hard drive with the same URL that you used for your button. Create a file named `tips.html` (or whatever URL you used) on your hard drive in the same folder as your movie.**

   You can use either of two methods:

   - **Make a copy** of the existing `tips.html` (if you have it on your hard drive) and move it to the folder containing your movie.

   - **Create a new HTML document** and save it as `tips.html` in the same folder as your movie. This document can be a dummy document — you can put any text you want in it. For example, you can type **This is a test HTML document**. If you create this document in a word processor, be sure to save it as an HTML document. Otherwise, use the software that you normally use to create HTML documents.

4. **Working offline, open your browser, choose File⇨Open, and open the HTML file for your Flash movie. (It has the same name as your movie.)**

5. **Click your button.**

   You should see `tips.html` displayed. If you don't, go back and check your ActionScript.

Part IV
Total Flash-o-Rama

The 5th Wave By Rich Tennant

"You might want to adjust the value of your 'Nudge' function."

In this part . . .

Moving imagery is the heart and soul of Flash, and in this part you make your Flash creations come to life through the power of animation and video. You find out about moving objects and changing their shapes, letting Flash create animation for you, and easily integrating video into your Flash extravaganzas.

After you create your movie, you can make it interactive so that the viewer's Web experience is more meaningful and engaging. Flash ActionScript offers infinite potential, so let your imagination soar. We show you how to combine your animation with your symbols and then add ActionScript to script your entire movie.

The world is not silent, and your Flash movies don't have to be either. Find out how to add sounds and music to your movies — from the simplest sound of a button click to the majestic tones of a full-fledged symphony.

9

Getting Animated

*I*n this chapter, we explain animation and making your graphics move. Are you ready to plunge into a world where you can make almost anything seem to happen? Hold on to your hat!

We start by explaining the basics of animation, including how to prepare for animation and how to work with the Timeline. Then we go into the specific techniques — frame-by-frame animation, tweening, and bones — that you can use to create great, animated effects in Flash. We cover motion tweening, shape tweening, and inverse kinematics, and we give you the details of editing your animations.

Who Framed the Animation?

The secret of animation in Flash, like in the movies, is that nothing ever really moves. A Flash movie creates the illusion of movement by quickly displaying a sequence of still images. Each still image is slightly different. Your brain fills in the gaps to give you the impression of movement.

One of the great things about Flash is that you can easily create complicated, spectacular extravaganzas of animation. And Flash stores lots of information in the super-compact vector format. Because the files can be small, they can be transmitted over the Web quickly. That's good for your Web site viewers.

Just like in a movie on film, each still image is contained in a frame. Each *frame* represents a unit of time. You create the animation by placing images in the frames, as shown in Figure 9-1. A frame can contain one object or none or many, depending on how crowded of a scene you want to create.

Figure 9-1: Movies are simply still images in sequence.

Time is your ally in Flash because you have complete control over it. You can look at each individual image in time and tweak it to your heart's content. Then you can step on the gas, play everything back at full speed, and watch everything appear to move.

In Flash, you create animation in three ways:

✔ **Frame by frame:** You move or modify objects one frame at a time. Frame-by-frame animation is time consuming but is sometimes the only way to create complex animated effects. This method can certainly satisfy your appetite for total control.

✔ **Tweening:** You specify starting frames and ending frames and let Flash figure out where everything goes in the in-between frames — which is why it's called *tweening*. Tweening is much more fun and much easier than frame-by-frame animation. If you can create the animation you want by tweening, it's definitely the way to go. Flash offers three types of tweening: motion tweening, shape tweening, and classic tweening, all of which we describe later in this chapter, in the section "The Animation Tween."

✔ **Inverse Kinematics (IK):** You use the new Bone tool to draw a chain of bones (an *armature*) that connects your objects. Then, when you move one of the bones, the whole chain of objects is pulled along with it. Just like when you shake someone's hand, her wrist, forearm, elbow, and upper arm move, too. This cool feature of Flash takes the automatic creation of animation to a whole new level.

Preparing to Animate

Before you can start animating, you need to set the stage first so that your animation works properly. Here are the steps you need to take before you can begin creating your animation:

1. **Choose Insert⇨Timeline⇨Layer to create a new layer for your animation, and then put your starting graphic or graphics on that layer.**

   When tweening, always animate each object on a separate layer that has no other objects on it. Otherwise, your animated objects might erase, connect to, or segment other objects — with messy results. And your animation probably won't work. Read Chapter 6 for more on layers.

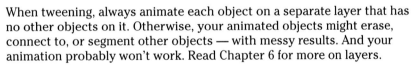

   If you're animating using bones, however, you want to put all the objects for one set of bones on a single layer. Otherwise, Flash doesn't let you connect your objects with the bones.

2. **Choose the object type:**

   - *If you plan to use motion tweening or bones,* turn your objects into instances of symbols.

   - *If you plan to use shape tweening,* make sure that your object is a shape and not a symbol.

   If your graphic is a symbol or a group or both, you can't shape tween it; so, for shape tweening, just create a shape by using the drawing tools. Or keep breaking apart your symbol or group until it becomes a shape. (Check out Chapter 4 for breaking objects apart.)

   Lines and shapes can have disastrous results when used together in shape tweens. Try to stick to one or the other. Shapes seem to work the best.

   - *If you plan to do frame-by-frame animation,* your graphic can be anything you want.

   See the section "The Animation Tween," a little later in this chapter, to find out more about motion tweening and shape tweening.

3. **Set a frame rate.**

   See the later section "Turtle or hare?" for more information.

When you animate, you often need to play back your animation during the process. The simplest way is to press Enter (Windows) or Return (Mac), which plays the movie. Sometimes, however, you might want more control — perhaps to play part of your movie. In this case, using the Controller can be handy. The Controller, as shown in Figure 9-2, is a simple toolbar that looks like the controls on a tape recorder. Use it to play, rewind, fast-forward, and stop your animation.

Figure 9-2: The Controller.

Pressing Enter/Return or using the Controller is a quick way to see your animation. However, if your Timeline includes a movie clip or a button or ActionScript, you typically won't see those elements function until you choose Control⇨Test Movie.

Master of the Timeline

The *Timeline* is the map of your animation sequence. If the Timeline isn't visible, choose Window⇨Timeline. Each layer has its own Timeline row. The Timeline has its own coding to help you understand the structure of your animation, as shown in Figure 9-3.

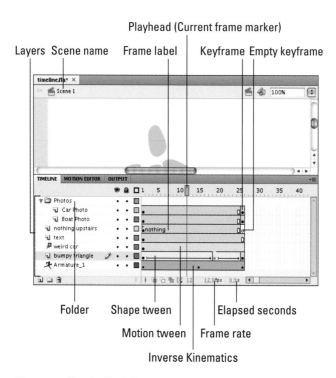

Playhead (Current frame marker)

Layers Scene name Frame label Keyframe Empty keyframe

Folder Shape tween Elapsed seconds

Motion tween Frame rate

Inverse Kinematics

Figure 9-3: Use the Flash Timeline to control your animations.

To customize your workspace, you can undock the Timeline from the main Flash window and also resize it. Just click the tab labeled Timeline (at the top of the Timeline) and drag the Timeline where you want it. Then you can resize it as an independent window. (Drag its left, right, or bottom edge.) If you get lost with the new arrangement, you can always go back to Window⇨ Workspace⇨Default.

Half the power of the Timeline is that it divides motion into *frames* — bits of time that you can isolate and work with — one at a time. The other half of the Timeline's power is that you can organize different components of your animation into different layers.

Click any frame to make it active. Remember to click in the row of the layer containing the graphics you want to animate. By clicking a frame, you can view your animation frozen at that moment of time. As you read through the examples and steps in this chapter, you'll quickly get the hang of working with the Timeline.

Hide the layers that you're not interested in (click below the eye icon) to help you visualize the animation. Don't forget, though, to check the animation with all the layers displayed to see how everything looks together. You should also lock layers when you're finished with them to avoid unwanted changes. See Chapter 6 for further instructions on hiding and locking layers.

Turtle or hare?

All you need to do to make animation work is to view your sequence of still images over time at high speed. Unless you have a remarkable attention span, one image per second is way too slow. Silent movies typically ran at 16 or 18 frames per second (fps). With the arrival of talkies, the speed got bumped up to 24 fps for better quality sound. On your television, the speed is roughly 30 images per second.

The smoothness of the playback of your animation depends not only on the frame rate that you specify but also on the complexity of the animation and the speed of the computer that's playing it. Generally, 24 fps is a good choice for Web animation, and that's the default rate in Flash.

To change the frame rate for your animation, click the Frame Rate value (which displays a number and the letters fps) at the bottom of the Timeline, type a new number (in frames per second), and then press Enter (Windows) or Return (Mac). You can set only one frame rate for all the animation in your current Flash file. You should set the frame rate before you start animating.

A Flash movie's frame rate represents the maximum speed at which the movie runs. Flash animation has no guaranteed minimum speed. If your animation is lagging or bogging down, increasing the frame rate doesn't help at all; in fact, it might make things worse.

Animating with Keyframes

Keyframes are the frames that are, well, key to your animation. They are the key moments in time that the software uses to calculate the in-between frames. You specify the state of each object only at a few keyframes, and the computer does all the work of calculating and rendering the changing state of each object in all the in-between frames — which is called *tweening.*

Tweening not only means less work for you but also creates smaller files (which download faster) because you're describing your animations more concisely. In frame-by-frame animation, every frame is a keyframe because every frame defines a change in the action.

You can change the display of the appearance of frames on the Timeline by choosing from the Frame View pop-up menu in the upper right of the Timeline, shown in Figure 9-4. With this menu, you can

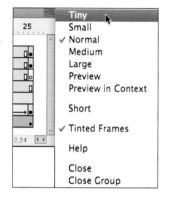

- ✓ Set the width of frame cells to Tiny, Small, Normal, Medium, or Large.

- ✓ Decrease the height of frame cells by choosing Short.

- ✓ Turn on or off the tinting of frame sequences.

- ✓ Choose to include a preview image of the contents of each frame in the Timeline display.

Figure 9-4: Customize your Timeline display here.

This is an awesome feature, like unspooling a reel of film. If you choose Preview, the preview image is scaled to fit the Timeline frame; if you choose Preview in Context, the preview image also includes any empty space in the frame.

Frame After Frame After Frame

If your animation isn't a simple motion in an easily definable direction or a change of shape or color — and isn't a sequence you'd create by inserting and animating bones in your objects — you probably need to use frame-by-frame animation.

If you must, you must. Some complex animations just have to be created frame by frame. The basic procedure is simple:

1. **Select a frame in the row of the layer that you want to use.**

   The animation starts in that frame.

2. **Right-click (Windows) or Control+click (Mac) the frame and then choose Insert Keyframe.**

   The first frame on a movie's Timeline is automatically a keyframe, so you don't have to create it.

3. **Create the graphic for the first frame.**

   You can import a graphic, paste a graphic from the Clipboard, or use the Flash drawing tools. (See Chapter 3 for help with creating or importing a graphic.)

4. **Right-click (Windows) or Control+click (Mac) the next frame and then choose Insert Keyframe again.**

   The next frame on the Timeline now has the same graphic as the preceding one.

5. **Modify the graphic to create the second frame of the animation.**

6. **Repeat Steps 4 and 5 until you create all the frames that you need for your animation.**

   While you work, you can continually check your cool animation by pressing Enter (Windows) or Return (Mac) to play it back.

Figure 9-5 shows frames of an animation as the word *New!* is created from a few specks on the page.

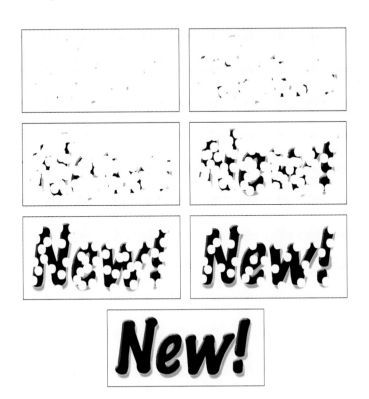

Figure 9-5: Sometimes a complex animation must be created frame by frame.

The Animation Tween

You can save yourself lots of work (and reduce your file size, too) by using Flash to automatically calculate the frames in-between the keyframes you set up. You create a few keyframes, and Flash figures out what should go in between. In animation technobabble, that's *tweening* — a quick, fun way to create great animations.

You can do a lot with Flash's tweening capabilities, including

- **Motion tweening:** This is the type of tweening you're likely to use most of the time. With motion tweening, you can move your objects in a straight line from here to there. You can use motion tweening also to animate an object along any path that you create, even one with lots of curves.

  In Flash CS4 motion tweens, you can also animate your movie clip's 3D position on the *z axis* (that is, its position in front of or behind other objects) and its rotation in 3D space. This requires that you specify ActionScript 3.0 and Flash Player 10 in your Publish Settings, which we describe in Chapter 13.

- **Shape tweening:** This type of tweening gradually changes any shape to another shape, as shown in Figure 9-6. You create the first and last shapes. These days, kids call it *morphing.* The results may be quite unpredictable and require a lot of computer processing but are usually interesting. You can add shape hints to try to tell Flash exactly how you want your shape to morph.

Figure 9-6: Shape tweening automatically morphs your shapes.

- **Classic tweening:** This is how motion tweening was accomplished in earlier versions of Flash. Classic tweening functions similarly to motion tweening, but it's more work to use, more error prone, and usually has fewer benefits. In almost every case, using Flash CS4 motion tweening is simpler, easier, and more powerful, so we explore Flash CS4 motion tweening rather than classic tweening.

With motion tweening and shape tweening, you can also

- **Animate an object's size.** For example, to make their movements more expressive, you can make objects appear to squash and stretch, as shown in Figure 9-7.

✔ **Rotate an object.** You specify the amount of the rotation. Flash combines the motion or shape tweening with the rotation so that you get both effects at one time.

✔ **Animate color or transparency.** Flash creates a gradual change in color based on your starting and ending colors.

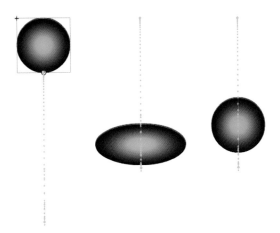

Figure 9-7: Squash and stretch makes objects more expressive.

Animating your graphic's transparency is a particularly cool effect because it lets you fade objects in and out, making them magically appear and disappear at just the right moment. And with motion tweens you can animate all filter properties, which can also produce really cool effects. For example, you can specify how much a glow or drop shadow changes during the tween. (See Chapter 7 to read about filters.)

Of course, you can create several animations, one after another, to mix and match effects. You can also combine frame-by-frame animation with tweened animation. Let your imagination soar!

From here to there — motion tweening

In motion tweening, you move an object from one place to another. The movement can be a straight line or any path that you can draw with the Pencil tool. Figure 9-8 shows a few frames from a motion tween that uses a looped path. While the animation progresses, the skateboarder image also scales down to 50 percent of its original size so that it appears to be moving away from you. In this example, the path is visible so that you can see how the animation works. When you play the finished animation the path is invisible.

Figure 9-8: You can draw any path and animate an object along the path.

Making a motion tween

When you motion tween your objects, you can not only move them but also tween their size, rotation, skew, transparency, and even their position in three-dimensional space.

For info on skewing an object, check out Chapter 4.

To create a simple motion tween animation, follow these steps:

1. **Create a new layer by choosing Insert⇨Timeline⇨Layer.**

   For each motion tween, you must put each object on a separate layer.

2. **Right-click (Windows) or Control+click (Mac) an empty frame in the new layer where you want the animation to start. From the contextual menu that appears, choose Insert⇨Keyframe.**

3. **Put a symbol instance, text field, or shape on the Stage.**

You can create one there, or paste it there, or drag it onto the Stage from the Library. (See Chapter 2 for info on the Library.)

4. **Right-click (Windows) or Control+click (Mac) the keyframe you created and then choose Create Motion Tween from the menu that appears.**

5. **If your object is a shape, a dialog box appears asking whether you want to convert it to a symbol so that Flash can create a tween. In this case, click OK.**

   Flash adds a motion tween starting in the frame you choose. In Step 2, if you choose the very first frame in the layer, Flash automatically creates a motion tween with a duration of one second. Otherwise, Flash creates a motion tween with a duration of only one frame.

6. **To increase the number of frames in which the image appears in your animation, click the last frame (or the only frame, if that's the case) of the tween and then drag the mouse on the Timeline to the right for the desired number of frames.**

   Flash duplicates your image throughout all intermediate frames.

7. **To decrease the number of frames in which the image appears in your animation, click the last frame of the tween and drag the mouse on the Timeline to the left for the desired number of frames.**

8. **Click a frame in the tween other than the first frame of the tween.**

9. **Move the object to a new position.**

   A property keyframe appears in the current frame; and a _motion path_ appears on the Stage (as shown in Figure 9-9, showing the path of the object from the previous frame to the current frame.

10. **If you want to change the object's size, rotation, color, or position in 3D space (as we explain in the sections that follow), make the adjustments at this point.**

Figure 9-9: The motion path shows the path your animation takes.

   See the next three sections of this chapter for details.

   You're done! Press Enter (Windows) or Return (Mac) to play the animation.

In motion tweened animation in Flash CS4, keyframes and property keyframes are defined differently. _Motion tween keyframes_ are the frames where a new symbol instance appears in the Timeline. A _property keyframe_ is a frame where you specify a change in one or more properties of the object that you're animating in a motion tween.

You can also use the preceding steps to create an image that remains still over a number of frames. Follow the steps, but stop before Step 8. This simply copies an object over a number of frames. You might want to do this for several reasons. Sometimes, you want a still image to sit unmoving for a while on a layer of your animation — as a background image, for example — while your animation moves in front. A background gives context to your animated objects. Even animated objects often need to remain on the Stage after they've finished moving about. A key element of animation is timing, and an animated character is often still for a few moments (even in elaborately animated Disney cartoons) before taking its next action.

Scaling and rotating an animated object

Okay, so you're creative and ambitious and want to do more. Changing other properties of your graphic while you're moving it is easy. In Step 10 of the procedure in the preceding section, you can scale and rotate (including skewing) your object, as shown in Figure 9-10.

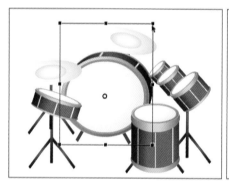

Figure 9-10: Use the Free Transform tool to create animated changes in scale.

Use the Free Transform tool, located on the Tools panel, or any other method of changing size or rotation. (See Chapter 4 for instructions on scaling and rotating objects.)

Symbols have transformation points that are usually at the center of the graphic. When you tween along a path, you might want another point to follow the path. In the section on groups in Chapter 4, you find out how to change the transformation point to get the results you want.

Tweening color or transparency

To change a motion tweened object's color, transparency, or brightness, follow these steps:

1. **Click the frame in the motion tween span on the Timeline where you want to change its color.**

A *tween span* is the group of frames in the Timeline in which a motion tween occurs. The tween span appears as a group of frames in the Timeline with a blue background, as shown in Figure 9-11.

Figure 9-11: The tween span is the group of frames in your motion tween.

2. **Click the object.**

3. **Choose Window⇨Properties to open the Property inspector (if it's not already open). In the Property inspector (if necessary), click the disclosure triangle to the left of the Color Effect section to reveal the contents of that section.**

4. **Select one of the options (such as Tint or Alpha) in the Color Effect drop-down list and make the desired adjustments.**

   Chapter 7 provides more detail about using the options in the Color Effect drop-down list.

You can mix and match motion animation with scaling, rotation, and color or transparency changes to create exciting effects. Animating semitransparent objects in front of each other creates interesting mixtures of color and gives a semblance of texture and depth in the 2D world of the Web. Decreasing Alpha (opacity) during a tween makes the object appear to fade as it becomes more transparent. Try out some possibilities and come up with ideas of your own.

Color fades are less work for the computer than alpha fades. If you need an object to fade in or out, your movie loads faster on older computers if you tween to or from the background color rather than tween to or from transparency.

Animating your movie clip's position in 3D space

Objects that you create in Flash are two-dimensional vector graphics. But with Flash CS4, you can now easily animate the position of your 2D movie clips in 3D space, to make your animations even more dazzling. (For more information on 3D changes to movie clips, see Chapter 7.) To animate your 2D movie clips in 3D space, follow these steps:

1. **Create a movie clip and motion tween it as described in the steps in the earlier section, "Making a motion tween."**

   Flash can only change 3D properties for movie clips. If you want to animate an object other than a movie clip, convert it to a movie clip first. (Check out Chapter 7 for info on converting objects to movie clips.)

2. **(Optional) Create additional movie clips on separate layers to provide spatial points of comparison in the scene.**

3. **Click the frame in the motion tween span on the Timeline where you want to change the first movie clip's position in 3D space.**

4. **Click the first movie clip.**

5. Choose Window⇨Properties to open the Property inspector (if it's not already open). In the Property inspector (if necessary), click the disclosure triangle to the left of the 3D Position and View section to reveal the contents of that section.

6. In the 3D Position and View section, click the Z value, type a new number, and then press Enter (Windows) or Return (Mac).

The Z value specifies your movie clip's position forwards or backwards along the z axis. Negative numbers move the movie clip closer to the viewer. Positive numbers move the movie clip farther away from the viewer.

7. Press Enter (Windows) or Return (Mac).

The movie clip relocates to its new position in 3D space. This new feature in Flash CS4 isn't necessarily implemented as you might expect: Movie clips move forward and backward in space in their own layer, but movie clips in layers above (or below) them always stay in front (or behind).

8. (Optional) Repeat Steps 6 and 7, but type new numbers in the X and/or Y field, instead, as desired.

The X value specifies your movie clip's position left to right. Y specifies its position up or down. Changing these values modifies your tween's motion path.

If in Step 3, you pick a frame other than the first frame of the motion tween, when you play the movie (choose Control⇨Test Movie), your movie clip appears to start in one position in 3D space and move to the second position you specify, as shown in Figure 9-12.

Figure 9-12: You can animate 2D Flash graphics in 3D space.

Editing or replacing the motion path

When you motion tween an object and make it move, Flash draws a motion path on the Stage that shows the path the object takes during the animation.

You can change the motion path simply by moving the playhead on the Timeline to the time where you want the motion path to change, and then clicking the object and dragging it.

You can create animation that doesn't move in a straight line by editing the motion path that Flash creates, changing it from a straight line to any curves that you desire. You can even replace the motion path that Flash creates with a path that you draw and paste in its place. Suppose that you want to get the skateboarder shown in Figure 9-13 to do some tricks. The following steps show you how to do that. To edit a motion path, follow these steps.

1. **Create an object and motion tween it from one location to another as described in the steps in the earlier section, "Making a motion tween."**

   The object's motion path appears on the Stage.

2. **Choose the Selection tool in the Tools panel. (If the Tools panel isn't visible, choose Windows➪Tools.)**

3. **To move the entire motion path, double-click it and drag.**

   The entire motion path moves, and the object moves along with it.

4. **To change the shape of the motion path, click the motion path where you want it to change and then drag.**

   The shape of the motion path changes where you click and drag.

5. **To edit the curvature of the motion path, choose the Subselection tool from the Tools panel. Click an anchor point on the motion path; then click and drag one of the direction points that appears.**

   The curvature of the motion path changes as you drag the direction point, as shown in Figure 9-13.

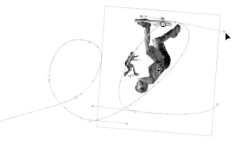

6. **To see the object animate with the revised motion path, choose Control➪Test Movie.**

   The object moves along the new motion path that you created.

   Figure 9-13: You can freely edit your motion path.

In Figure 9-13, we made the skateboarder in *Poser,* which is a cool program for generating 3D people. You can find out more about Poser at http://my.smithmicro.com.

You can also transform the motion path with the Free Transform Tool. Just follow these steps.

1. **Create an object and motion tween it, as described in the steps in the earlier section, "Making a motion tween."**

   The object's motion path appears on the Stage.

2. **Choose the Selection tool from the Tools panel and then click the motion path.**

   The motion path is highlighted, showing that it's the current selection.

3. **Choose the Free Transform tool from the Tools panel.**

   The motion path displays a bounding box with handles and a transformation point.

4. **Click and drag the handles to rotate, scale, or skew the motion path.**

   For all the info on using the Free Transform tool, see Chapter 6.

You can easily add a rotation to a tweened object as it moves on a path. To add a rotation to a tweened object, do the following steps:

1. **Choose the Selection tool from the Tools panel. On the Stage, click the motion path of the tweened object.**

   The motion path is highlighted, showing that it's the current selection.

2. **You can add a rotation to the object in one of two ways:**

   • *In the Rotation section of the Properties inspector,* click the Rotate value, type a number between 0 and 359, and then press Enter (Windows) or Return (Mac). From the Direction drop-down list, choose CW (for clockwise) or CCW (for counterclockwise).

   With this setting, the object rotates clockwise or counterclockwise as it moves along the path, as shown in Figure 9-14.

   • *Select the Orient to Path check box.*

   If you select Orient to Path — say, you're animating a skateboarder — the object rotates so that the nose of the skateboard follows the curvature of the path, as shown in Figure 9-15.

Figure 9-14: You can add a rotation to an object on your motion path.

3. To view your changes, drag the playhead on the Timeline, or choose Control➪Test Movie.

The object rotates along the motion path in the way you specify.

With Flash, you can even draw your own motion path. To replace a motion path with a path that you draw, follow these steps.

Figure 9-15: You can orient your object to rotate according to the curvature of your motion path.

1. **Create an object and motion tween it, as described in the steps in the earlier section, "Making a motion tween."**

The object's motion path appears on the Stage.

2. **Create a new layer, and then select the first frame in that layer.**

3. **Use the Pencil tool or the Pen tool, on the Stage, to draw a stroke that you would like to be the new motion path.**

To read all about the Pencil tool and the Pen tool, see Chapter 3.

4. **Choose the Selection tool from the Tools panel, and then double-click the stroke to select it.**

5. **Right-click (Windows) or Control+click (Mac) the stroke; from the contextual menu that appears, choose Copy.**

6. **If the object with the motion path isn't visible in frame one of the Timeline, click a frame in the Timeline where the object is visible. Right-click (Windows) or Control+click (Mac) the motion path; from the contextual menu that appears, choose Paste.**

Flash replaces the motion path with the stroke that you draw in Step 3.

7. **To view the change, choose Control➪Test Movie.**

The object animates along the new motion path, as shown in Figure 9-16.

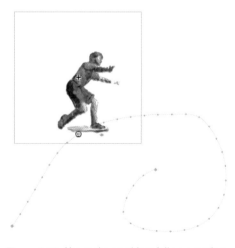

Figure 9-16: You make an object follow a motion path that you draw.

And now you can still edit your new motion path in all the ways that we describe earlier in this chapter.

Using Motion Presets

A fast, cool way to learn about Flash's motion tween capabilities is to use *Motion Presets,* which are prebuilt motion tweens that you can apply to any symbol instance to instantly create a complete motion tween. Flash CS4 comes with dozens of Motion Presets. You can apply a Motion Preset to an object to instantly make it bounce, squash, and stretch; fly on the Stage in a blur; throb and pulse; and more. To apply a Motion Preset, do the following steps:

1. **Put a symbol instance, text field, or shape on the Stage.**

   You can create one there, or drag it onto the Stage from the Library.

2. **Choose the Selection tool from the Tools panel, and then click the object that you put on the Stage.**

3. **If the Motion Presets panel isn't open, choose Window➪Motion Presets. If necessary, click the disclosure triangle to the left of each folder in the Motion Presets to make the contents of each folder visible.**

4. **In the Motion Presets panel, click the Motion Preset that you want, and then click the Apply button at the bottom of the Motion Presets panel.**

5. **If the object on the Stage is a shape, a dialog box appears asking whether you want to convert it to a symbol so that Flash can create a tween. In this case, click OK.**

   Flash creates a motion tween with all the animation from the Motion Preset you choose, as shown in Figure 9-17.

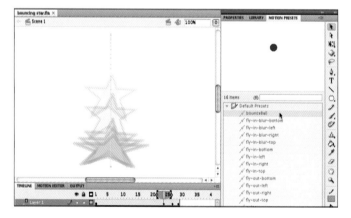

Figure 9-17: You can use Motion Presets to instantly animate an object.

6. To view your new animation, click and drag the playhead in the Timeline, or choose Control⇨Test Movie.

One fantastic feature of Motion Presets is that you can create your own. In this way, you can build up a library of cool animations that you can instantly apply to any symbol instance, any text field, or any shape that you want. To create a custom Motion Preset, follow these steps:

1. Choose the Selection tool from the Tools panel, and then right-click (Windows) or Control+click (Mac) one of the following:
   - A tween span in the Timeline
   - A motion-tweened object on the Stage
   - A motion path on the Stage

2. From the contextual menu that appears, choose Save As Motion Preset.

3. In the Save As Preset dialog box that appears, type a name in the Preset Name text field and then click OK.

   The name of your new Motion Preset appears in the list of presets in the Custom Presets folder in the Motion Presets panel.

Using the Motion Editor

For even more control of your motion tweens, you can use the Motion Editor, which makes it easy for you to view every property keyframe in your animation and tweak each transformation with precision and in great detail. To use the Motion Editor, select a tween span in the Timeline, or select a tweened object or a motion tween path on the Stage. Then click the Motion Editor tab (if it's docked somewhere; probably next to the Timeline) or choose Window⇨ Motion Editor (if the Motion Editor isn't visible).

As shown in Figure 9-18, the Motion Editor shows the values of each property of the selected tween in a graph. The value of the property is represented vertically, and the time on the Timeline is represented horizontally. Thus, when the value of a property (transparency, for example) increases or decreases, the graph line goes up or down; and as time moves forward, the graph line moves forward. Then if, for example, you want to change how the transparency of an object is animated, you can add or delete keyframes; and you can move keyframes up, down, or sideways on the graph. This really makes you the master of Flash space and time!

You can even adjust the curvature of the graphs by clicking a keyframe. (For the X, Y, and Z position properties, you can't adjust the curvature of the graph, but you can add and remove control points in the graph.)

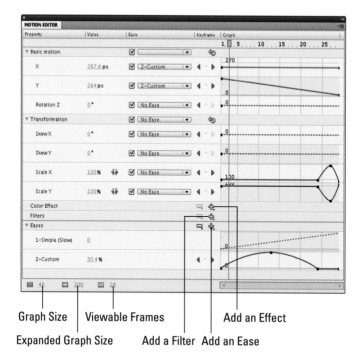

Figure 9-18: The Motion Editor gives you tremendous control over every property keyframe.

You can control the number of frames you see in the Motion Editor by clicking the Viewable Frames value near the bottom left of the Motion Editor, typing a new number, and then pressing Enter (Windows) or Return (Mac). If the number of Viewable Frames is set to 1, you might want to increase that number.

You can add a new color effect or filter to a tween by choosing the new item that you want from the Add drop-down menu (the plus sign) in the color effect or filter column in the Motion Editor. A graph for the new item then appears in the Motion Editor.

Tweening shapes

In shape tweening, you change an object's shape at one or more points in the animation, and the computer creates the in-between shapes for you. You can get some great animation effects by using shape tweening. This process is often called *morphing*. You can see an example in Figure 9-19.

When shape tweening, you can combine changes in shape with changes in position as well as changes in size, color, and transparency. You should work with one shape per layer to avoid problems.

You can shape tween objects that you have created by using the Flash drawing tools.

You can't shape tween a symbol instance, text (type), or a group unless you break them apart into shapes by selecting them and choosing Modify⇨Break Apart. And you have to break apart text blocks twice — once to break the text block into individual letters and again to break the letters into shapes. You can also try to shape tween a bitmap image after breaking it apart, but the results are sure to be unpredictable.

If you break apart a symbol instance, text block, bitmap image, or group by using Modify⇨Break Apart, you might have a number of shapes to animate. Be sure to put each animated object on a separate layer. You can do this easily by selecting the objects and choosing Modify⇨Timeline⇨Distribute to Layers, which we explain in Chapter 6.

To create a simple shape tween, follow these steps:

1. **Right-click (Windows) or Control+click (Mac) an empty frame where you want the animation to start and then choose Insert⇨Timeline⇨Keyframe.**

2. **Use the drawing tools to create the beginning shape.**

   You can create complex objects by merging objects of the same color or creating cutouts with objects of differing colors. (See Chapter 3 for details.)

3. **Create a new keyframe after the first keyframe wherever you want it on the Timeline by using the same technique you used in Step 1.**

4. **Create the ending shape.**

   You can erase the old shape and draw a new one, or you can use the first shape, still on the Stage, and modify it. You can also move the shape and change its color or transparency or both. You can quickly change the color by using the Color modifiers in the Tools panel. Use the Color panel to change opacity (Alpha). See Chapter 3 for more information on colors and transparency.

5. **Click anywhere in the tween before the last keyframe.**

6. **Choose Insert⇨Shape Tween.**

   An arrow signifying a shape tween appears in the Timeline (as shown in Figure 9-20), connecting the first and second keyframes.

Figure 9-19:
A circle becomes a star!

7. **Choose Window⇨Properties to open the Property inspector (if it's not already open).**

8. **In the Tweening section of the Properties inspector, from the Blend drop-down menu, select an Angular Blend or a Distributive Blend.**

Figure 9-20: The arrow in the Timeline signifies a shape tween.

• *Angular Blend:* Select the Angular Blend type for blending shapes with sharp corners and straight lines. It preserves corners and straight lines in the in-between shapes of your animation.

Using the Angular Blend on irregular shapes might cause the animation to vanish!

• *Distributive Blend:* If your shapes don't have sharp corners, use the Distributive Blend type (the default) for smoother in-between shapes.

9. **You're finished! Click the first frame and press Enter (Windows) or Return (Mac) to play the animation.**

Getting Flash to take a hint — using shape hints

Does the transformation of your shape animation look strange? Flash tries to figure out the simplest and most probable way to change one of your shapes into another, but this solution might not turn out the way you expect or want.

You can use the Flash shape hints feature to attempt to correct this problem. A *shape hint* is a marker you attach to a point on a shape at the beginning and end of a shape change. The shape hints signal to Flash exactly how you want this point and the area around it to move from the start to the end of the shape tweening process.

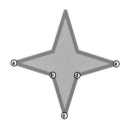

You can use up to 26 shape hints per layer. Shape hints are displayed on the Stage as small, colored circles with a letter *(a–z)* inside. On the starting keyframe, the shape hint is yellow; and on the ending keyframe, it's green. When you first insert a shape hint — before you move it onto your shape — it's red. Figure 9-21 shows an example of beginning and ending shapes with shape hints.

Figure 9-21: Shape hints guide Flash as it tweens your shape.

From this book's companion Web site, at www.dummies.com/go/flashcs4fd, you can download the Flash movie file shown in Figure 9-21. It's the 4 to 5 point star with shape hints.fla file.

To use shape hints, follow these steps.

1. **If you haven't already done so, create a shape animation by using shape tweening.**

   Refer to the set of steps in the preceding section for help with this task.

2. **Click the keyframe where you want to add your first shape hint.**

3. **With the object selected, choose Modify➪Shape➪Add Shape Hint or press Ctrl+Shift+H (Windows) or ⌘+Shift+H (Mac).**

   Your beginning shape hint appears as the letter *a* in a small, red circle somewhere on the Stage, as shown in Figure 9-22.

4. **Click the small, red circle and drag it to the part of your graphic that you want to mark.**

5. **Click the keyframe at the end of the shape animation.**

   The ending shape hint appears somewhere on the Stage, again as the letter *a* in a small, red circle.

6. **Click the small, red circle and drag it to the point on your shape where you want your beginning point to move.**

   The ending shape hint turns green. If you go back to the first frame of the animation, the beginning shape hint turns yellow, as shown in Figure 9-23.

7. **Press Enter (Windows) or Return (Mac) to play your movie.**

Figure 9-22: Shape hints are red until you position them.

You can drag shape hints off the Stage to remove them. You can also choose Modify➪Shape➪Remove All Hints to nuke them all, but the layer with shape hints must be selected. (Your animation then reverts to its original tween.) Choose View➪Show Shape Hints to see all the shape hints in your current layer and keyframe. Choose it again to hide them. (Again, the layer and keyframe with shape hints must be selected.)

Figure 9-23: The beginning shape hint is yellow, and the ending shape hint is green.

Adjusting shape hints

To tweak your animation, click the keyframe at the start or end of your shape animation and move your shape hint. Then play your animation again to see the new result. The more complicated your shape animation, the more shape hints you need to use. For more complicated shape animations, you can also add more keyframes between your original starting and ending keyframe. This creates intermediate shapes at the new keyframes that you can then tween (using plenty of shape hints, of course). In other words, you can create two or more shape tweens, one immediately following the other.

If you aren't getting the results you want, make sure that you have placed your shape hints logically. If you have a curve with shape hints *a, b,* and *c* (in that order), don't have them tween to a curve with the shape hints in *c, b, a* order unless you want some unusual effects. Flash does a better job with shape hints when you arrange them in counterclockwise order, starting from the upper-left corner of your object.

Editing Animation

You might find that you usually don't get your animation to move perfectly the first time, but fortunately, Flash is quite forgiving. You can edit keyframes in assorted ways. For example, you can edit motion-tweened frames directly by Ctrl+clicking (Windows) or ⌘+clicking (Mac) a frame and then changing the position or other properties of the object on Stage.

You can't edit shape-tweened frames directly: You can view them, but you can edit your objects only in the keyframes, not in the in-between frames. You can overcome this restriction and edit your shape-tweened frames by inserting a new keyframe between your beginning and ending keyframe and then editing the new keyframe. You do this by clicking a frame in the Timeline and then choosing Insert⇨Timeline⇨Keyframe (or pressing F6). **Note:** Don't choose Insert⇨Timeline⇨Blank Keyframe unless you want to nuke your existing shape-tween animation. Of course, you can always edit shape-tweened frames by simply changing the starting or ending keyframe that defines them.

When you edit a keyframe of a tweened animation, Flash automatically recalculates the entire tween.

The following sections explain some useful techniques for editing and managing your animations.

Adding labels and comments

Animation can get complicated after a while. You might find it helpful to add comments to the Timeline to explain what each part of the Timeline is doing. Also, when you start adding interactivity to your movies, you can add labels to shape tween frames and then refer to them in your ActionScript. (You can find out more about ActionScript in Chapter 10.)

To add a label or a comment to a frame (as shown in Figure 9-24), follow these steps:

1. **Select a frame.**

   See the next section for information on selecting a frame.

2. **Choose Window➪Properties to open the Property inspector (if it's not already open).**

3. **In the Frame Label text box, type the text for the label or comment and then press Enter (Windows) or Return (Mac).**

   To make the text function as a comment, choose Comment from the Type drop-down list, below the Label Name text box.

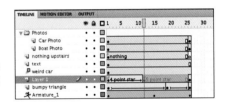

Figure 9-24: Adding comments as Frame Labels can help you keep track of what is going on in your Timeline.

Adding frame labels can be a nice way to lay out the timing of a movie — by typing what you want to happen where on your Timeline — for a kind of brief verbal storyboard. This can be particularly helpful when you're working with others on a project.

Selecting frames

Flash offers two styles of making selections on the Timeline:

- **Frame-based selection:** This is the default method for shape animations. In this method, if you click a frame or a keyframe, it's selected. To select a range of frames, you can click and drag over the frames that you want to select. Or, you can click the first frame, press Shift, and then click the last frame in the range.

- **Span-based selection:** In this method, if you click a frame, it selects the entire sequence containing that frame, from one keyframe to the next. Clicking and dragging moves the entire sequence (between the keyframes) along the Timeline in either direction. To select an individual frame, press Ctrl (Windows) or ⌘ (Mac).

   Motion tweens and armature animations (inverse kinematics) use this method. Shape tweens can also use this method, but it's not the default for shape tweens. You can change the style of selection for shape tweens by first choosing Edit➪Preferences (Windows) or Flash➪Preferences (Mac). Then in the General category in the Preferences dialog box, select or deselect the Span Based Selection option in the Timeline section.

Copying and pasting frames

You can copy frames of motion tweens and shape tweens that contain content you want. Then you can paste the frames in another location.

To copy and paste frames, follow these steps:

1. **Select one or more frames, as shown in Figure 9-25.**

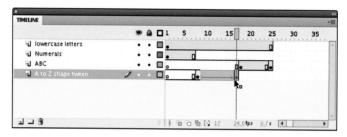

Figure 9-25: You can select the frames of one tween and paste them to another.

2. **To copy the frames to the Clipboard, choose Edit⇨Timeline⇨Copy Frames.**

3. **Select the first frame of your destination or select a sequence of frames that you want to replace.**

4. **To paste the frames into their new location, choose Edit⇨Timeline⇨ Paste Frames.**

You can also copy frames by pressing and holding Alt (Windows) or Option (Mac) while you drag the keyframe or range of frames to a new location. You see a small plus sign while you drag.

Copying and pasting motion

You can copy motion tween information in Flash from one object to another. If you've created some nice animation for one character, for example, you can easily copy that same animation to other characters in your scene — or in another scene or movie.

To copy and paste motion from one symbol instance to another, follow these steps:

1. **In the Timeline, select the frames that contain the motion tween that you want to copy.**

   To get this to work properly, be sure to copy all the frames.

2. **To copy the motion information to the Clipboard, choose Edit⇨ Timeline⇨Copy Motion.**

3. **Select the symbol instance that you want to copy the motion information to.**

   The symbol instance should only be one frame long at this point; Flash will add the needed frames.

4. **To copy the motion information to the symbol instance you selected, choose Edit⇨Timeline⇨Paste Motion.**

   The pasted motion tween appears, starting in the frame of the Timeline that contains the destination symbol instance.

This copies all the motion tween information from one symbol instance to another, including the information about the symbol's changes in position, changes in scale, changes in rotation and skew, changes in color (including tint, brightness, or alpha), changes in filter values, and changes in blend modes. (See Chapter 7 for information on filters and blend modes.)

Moving frames

You can easily move frames and their contents. Just select the layer, place the cursor over a frame or range of frames, and then drag them to their new home, as shown in Figure 9-26.

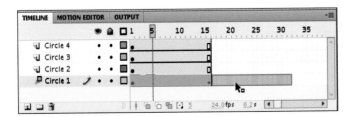

Figure 9-26: Move frames by selecting and dragging them.

Reversing your animation

You can make your animation play backward by selecting the relevant frames in one or more layers and choosing Modify⇨Timeline⇨Reverse Frames. (This is an amazing and useful feature.) ***Hint:*** For shape tweens, your selection must start and end with keyframes.

Changing speed

After you set up your animation, play your movie to check the speed. If one part of your tweened animation is too fast or too slow, you can slide keyframes around on the Timeline to shorten or lengthen the time between keyframes. You can do this by simply clicking a shape tween keyframe or Ctrl+clicking (Windows) or ⌘+clicking (Mac) a motion tween keyframe to select the keyframe and then dragging it to another point on the Timeline. This technique gives you lots of control over the timing of your animation.

If you have difficulty dragging an ending keyframe, create a new keyframe somewhere to the keyframe's right and then drag the obstinate keyframe.

Figure 9-27 shows two possible versions of the Timeline for the shape tween shown in Figure 9-16. The black dots on the Timeline are the keyframes. To create the version on the bottom, we dragged the last keyframe to the right, thereby lengthening the tween. Because the same change in shape now occurs over a longer period, the tween appears slower.

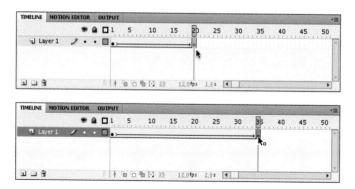

Figure 9-27: You can change the length of a tween.

The effect is even more noticeable when an object is moving across the stage during a tween. For example, if a symbol (or shape) moves from the left of the Stage to the right and you shorten the tween, the symbol (or shape) appears to move across the Stage more quickly because it must get from the left to the right in fewer frames.

Using onion skins

To help you visualize the flow of your animation, you can turn on the onion skinning feature. *Onion skinning* lets you see a "ghost image" of some or all of the frames in your animation. (Normally, you see only the current frame on the Stage.) Figure 9-28 shows an example of both regular and outlined onion skinning. Onion skinning displays frames as transparent layers, like the transparent layers of an onion skin.

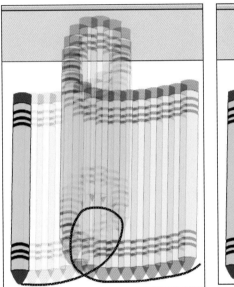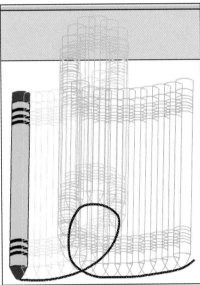

Figure 9-28: Onion skinning helps you see where your animation is going.

To display onion skinning, click the Onion Skin button at the bottom of the Timeline.

To display onion skinning with outlines, click the Onion Skin Outlines button. Sometimes this makes it easier to see how your objects are animating.

When you display onion skinning, Flash places markers at the top of the Timeline around the frames that are displayed as onion skins. (See Figure 9-29.) Usually, these markers advance automatically when the current frame pointer advances. You can manually adjust the beginning and ending of the onion-skinning effect by clicking and dragging either the left or right marker to a new location on the Timeline.

To edit any of the frames on the Timeline no matter where your current frame pointer is, click the Edit Multiple Frames button. If you also have onion skinning turned on, you can then edit any frame while viewing all the other onion-skinned frames.

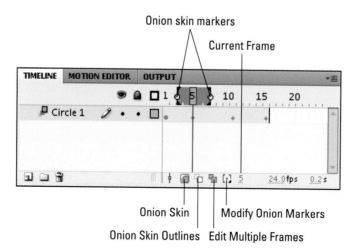

Figure 9-29: When you display onion skinning, markers are placed on the Timeline.

 Click Modify Onion Markers to display a menu to help you adjust the way your onion markers work:

- ✏ **Always Show Markers:** Shows onion markers even when you turn off onion skinning.

- ✏ **Anchor Onions:** Locks the onion markers in their current position and prevents them from moving along with the current frame pointer, as they normally do.

- ✏ **Onion 2:** Applies onion skinning to the two frames before and the two frames after the *playhead* (the current frame pointer).

- ✏ **Onion 5:** Applies onion skinning to the five frames before and the five frames after the playhead.

- ✏ **Onion All:** Applies onion skinning to all the frames on your Timeline.

 Hidden or locked layers never show as onion skinned. Hide or lock layers to isolate them from the layers you really want to change and to keep your onion skinning from getting out of control. Chapter 6 explains how to hide and lock layers.

Moving everything around the Stage at once

If you move a complete animation on the Stage without moving the graphics in all frames and all layers at one time, you might quickly go nuts when you discover that every little thing must be realigned. Instead, retain your sanity and move everything at one time.

To move a complete animation, follow these steps:

1. **Unlock all layers that contain the animation you want to move and then lock or hide any layers that you don't want to move.**

   To lock (or unlock) a layer, click below the lock icon on that layer's row. To hide (or unhide) a layer, click below the eye icon on that layer's row. See Chapter 6 for more information on working with layers.

2. **Click the Edit Multiple Frames button at the bottom of the Timeline.**

   If you ever need to resize a project, this button is your new best friend.

3. **Drag the onion skin markers to the beginning and ending frames of your animation.**

   Alternatively, if you want to select all frames, click the Modify Onion Markers button at the bottom of the Timeline and then choose Onion All.

4. **Choose Edit⇨Select All.**

5. **Drag your animation to its new place on the Stage.**

   Here is a workaround if you run into difficulties making this work.

   - *In Step 3,* click the Modify Onion Markers button at the bottom of the Timeline and choose Onion All.

   - *In Step 5,* use the keyboard arrows to move your animation to its new place on the Stage.

Connecting the Hip Bone to the Thigh Bone

With the new Flash CS4 Inverse Kinematics (IK) tools, you can draw a chain of bones (an *armature*) to connect a set of objects and then animate all the objects automatically, simply by animating the position of one of the bones in the chain. Flash simulates the physics of your objects moving as if they were all connected by the chain. You can also draw a chain of bones inside a single shape so that when you move a bone, the part of the shape near the bone flexes. The bones are visible when you're creating your movie yet are invisible when you play the movie. Thus, your audience sees only the effect of the bones — not the bones themselves.

These tools can make it much easier, for example, to create animated characters and to animate their arms and legs (as shown in Figure 9-30, for example) as well as facial expressions.

In the study of mechanics, when objects are connected in a dangling chain and caused to move by changing the position of the objects at the top, that's a *kinematic chain.* If the motion is created by moving the position of the objects at the bottom (for example, when you shake someone's hand, and that motion moves their forearm, elbow, and upper arm), that's *inverse kinematics.*

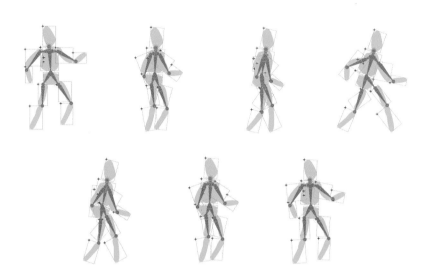

Figure 9-30: Use inverse kinematics to quickly create a "walk cycle."

Putting bones into your symbols

You can quickly and easily set up an armature of bones in your animation. The armature can contain a linear chain of bones. Or, the bones can be in a branched structure, like the branches of a tree; or the torso, legs, and arms of a human. The armature can connect movie clips, graphic symbols, or buttons. Or, as you can see in the next section of this chapter, the armature can be inside a shape, which bends and flexes when the armature is animated.

As usual, any movie clips and buttons you use can contain other movie clips for nested animations, if you like. (See Chapter 7 for more info on movie clips and graphic symbols, and see Chapter 8 for the lowdown on buttons.)

To create an armature that connects a set of symbol instances, follow these steps:

1. **Create movie clips, graphic symbols, or buttons; and then place instances of them on the Stage approximately how you want them to appear, all in one frame on one layer in the Timeline.**

   Your graphics absolutely must be instances of movie clips, graphic symbols, or buttons for animation with bones to work. (See Chapter 7 for more about symbols and instances.)

2. Select the Bone tool from the Tools panel.

The Bone tool is part of a flyout that also contains the Bind tool. If necessary, click and hold the Bind tool (discussed next), and then choose the Bone tool from the flyout.

3. Click and drag from one symbol instance to another.

This creates a bone that connects the two symbol instances, as shown in Figure 9-31. The bone and the symbol instances appear in a new layer labeled Armature. The new layer is a *pose layer.* The bone has a head (which is rounded) and a tail (which is pointed).

For this step to work, you must click in an area of the symbol instance that isn't empty and drag to a non-empty area in the other symbol instance.

4. Repeat Step 3 for each of the symbol instances that you want to connect.

- *To make a chain of bones:* Click and drag from the tail of the bone in the last symbol instance to a new symbol instance.

  Another bone appears, connecting the previous symbol instance and a new one, as shown in Figure 9-32. The original bone is the *parent,* and the new bone is the *child.*

  Repeat this step for as many symbol instances as desired.

Figure 9-31: Connect your symbol instances with a bone.

Figure 9-32: You can build armatures as chains.

- *To make a branch:* Click a symbol instance that has a bone connected to the tail of its bone, and then drag to a new symbol instance that doesn't yet contain a bone.

  Another bone appears, connecting the previous symbol instance and a new one, as shown in Figure 9-33.

  Repeat this step for as many symbol instances as desired.

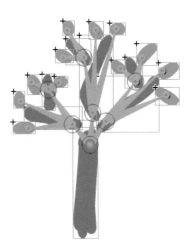

Figure 9-33: You can also build armatures as branches.

On our companion Web site (`www.dummies.com/go/flashcs4fd`), download the `person-with-bones.fla` file for a simple example of a person with animated bones that you can work with.

To join two armatures, select the Bone tool from the Tools panel, click a bone in one armature, and then drag to a bone in the second armature. This connects the second armature to the first one, in a single new armature in a single pose layer, as shown in Figure 9-34.

Unlike layers that contain a shape tween or a motion tween, which contain only one animated object per layer, an Armature layer contains multiple objects — a set of connected bones — animating on a single layer.

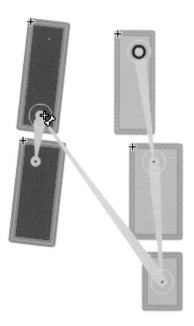

Figure 9-34: Join two armatures by clicking a bone in one and dragging it to the other.

Binding bones to shapes

You can also use the Bone tool to build an armature (a set of bones) inside a single filled shape. For example, if you put the bones inside the shape of an arm, as shown in Figure 9-35, Flash bends the forearm and elbow part of the arm shape automatically when you move the bone in the forearm.

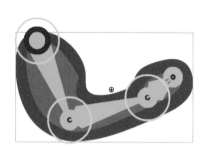
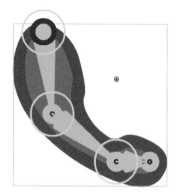

Figure 9-35: You can put a set of bones inside a shape.

To build an armature inside a filled shape, follow these steps:

1. **Create a new layer by choosing Insert⇨Timeline⇨Layer.**

2. **Right-click (Windows) or Control+click (Mac) an empty frame in the new layer where you want your animation to start. From the contextual menu that appears, choose Insert⇨Keyframe.**

3. **Draw a shape, or paste one onto the Stage.**

   The shape can be as simple or complex as you like, but it must be a single filled shape. (Check out Chapter 3 for all the info on creating fills.)

4. **Select the Bone tool from the Tools panel.**

5. **Click and drag inside the shape.**

   A bone appears inside the shape.

6. **Click the tail of a bone and then drag to create a new bone inside the shape.**

   A new bone appears, connected to the previous bone.

7. **Repeat Step 6 as desired.**

To see how the shape flexes, choose the Selection tool from the Tools panel, click the tail of a bone, and then drag. The shape should bend and bulge as the tail moves.

To change how the shape flexes when you move a bone, you can use the Bind tool. With the Bind tool, you can control which points on the shape's stroke are bound to which bones, which allows you to make the shape flex the way you want. These points are called *control points*. To adjust which points on the shape's stroke connect to which bones, follow these steps:

1. **Select the Bind tool from the Tools panel.**

   If the Bind tool isn't visible, press and hold the Bones tool in the Tools panel. From the pop-up menu that appears, choose the Bind tool.

2. **Click the shape in the Armature layer that you want to work on.**

   The control points on the selected shape appear.

3. **Click any bone to see which control points in the Stroke of the shape are connected to the bone.**

   The control points that are connected to the bone appear highlighted in yellow, as shown in Figure 9-36. You can press Shift and then click to select multiple bones.

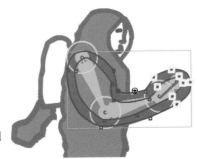

Figure 9-36: Click a bone to see the control points connected to it.

4. **To connect a control point to a bone, click the bone (if it's not already selected), and then Shift+click a control point not highlighted in yellow.**

   The control point becomes highlighted in yellow, showing that it's now connected to the selected bone.

   You can Shift-drag to connect multiple control points.

5. **To disconnect a control point from a bone, click the bone (if it's not already selected), and then Ctrl+click (Windows) or Option+click (Mac) a control point highlighted in yellow.**

   The control point is no longer highlighted in yellow, showing that it's no longer connected to the selected bone.

   You can Shift-Ctrl-drag (Windows) or Shift-Option-drag (Mac) to disconnect multiple controls.

6. **If a control point is connected to more than one bone, Flash highlights the control point with a yellow triangle. If you select that triangle, Flash highlights the bones it connects to.**

7. **Click any control point to see which bone or bones are connected to it.**

   The bone or bones that are connected to the control point appear highlighted in yellow. You can press Shift and click to select multiple bones.

8. **To connect a bone to a control point, click the control point (if it's not already selected), and then Shift+click a bone.**

   The bone becomes highlighted in yellow, showing that it's now connected to the selected control point.

9. **To disconnect a bone from a control point, click the control point (if it isn't already selected), and then Ctrl+click (Windows) or Option+click (Mac) a bone highlighted in yellow.**

   The bone is no longer highlighted in yellow, showing that it's no longer connected to the selected control point.

To see the results of your adjustments, choose the Selection tool from the Tools panel, click the tail of a bone and drag, and watch how your shape flexes differently.

Working with constraints

If you click the tail of any bone and drag, by default, you can move the bone up and down and rotate it 360 degrees around the bone connected to its head.

To make it easier to create realistic animations, you can constrain each bone's freedom of motion. That way, for example, if you put bones in a character's thigh and shin, the knee doesn't bend in the wrong direction.

To change a bone's freedom of motion, follow these steps:

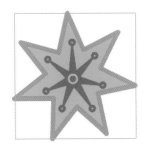

1. **Choose the Selection tool from the Tools panel, and then click an armature on the Stage.**

    The bones in the armature appear, highlighted in purple, as shown in Figure 9-37.

2. **Click a bone to select it.**

    The selected bone is highlighted in a different color.

    Figure 9-37: These bones are all selected.

    To set the constraint properties for several bones at once, Shift+click additional bones to select several bones.

3. **Choose Window⇨Properties to open the Property inspector (if it's not already open). In the Property inspector (if necessary), click the disclosure triangle to the left of each section to reveal the contents of that section.**

4. **To enable or disable the bone's freedom of rotation around the joint at its head, select or deselect (respectively) the Enable check box in the Joint:Rotation section of the Property inspector.**

    If you deselect the Enable check box, the bone is connected rigidly to its parent, and only its children can move.

5. **To constrain the bone's freedom of rotation around the joint at its head, select the Enable check box and the Constrain check box in the Joint:Rotation section of the Property inspector. To limit the amount of counterclockwise rotation, click the Min value, type a number between 0 and –359, and then press Enter (Windows) or Return (Mac). To limit the amount of clockwise rotation, click the Max text field, type a number between 0 and 359, and then press Enter (Windows) or Return (Mac).**

6. **To enable or disable the bone's freedom of motion left and right, select or deselect the Enable check box in the Joint:X Translation section of the Property inspector.**

    If you select the Enable check box, the bone can move freely left and right, stretching the length of its parent to accommodate the motion. If you deselect the Enable check box (the default setting), you can move the bone left to right, but the length of the parent bone won't stretch.

7. **To constrain the bone's freedom of motion right and left, select the Enable check box and also the Constrain check box in the Joint:X Translation section of the Property inspector. To limit the amount of motion to the left, click the Min value, type zero or a negative number, and then press Enter (Windows) or Return (Mac). To limit the amount of motion to the right, click the Max value, type 0 (zero) or a positive number, and then press Enter (Windows) or Return (Mac).**

The number you type specifies the maximum number of pixels the bone can move right or left.

8. **To enable or disable the bone's freedom of motion up and down, select or deselect (respectively) the Enable check box in the Joint:Y Translation section of the Property inspector. To limit the amount of motion upward, click the Min value, type 0 (zero) or a negative number, and then press Enter (Windows) or Return (Mac). To limit the amount of motion downward, click the Max value, type 0 (zero) or a positive number, and then press Enter (Windows) or Return (Mac).**

The number you type specifies the maximum number of pixels the bone can move up or down.

To test the changes you make in your bones' constraints, choose the Selection tool from the Tools panel, click the tail of a bone, and drag to see how the armature moves with the new constraints.

Animating your bones

After you build your armatures, animating them is easy. To animate the bones in an armature, follow these steps:

1. **To make room on the Timeline for your animation, right-click (Windows) or Control+click (Mac) a frame in a pose layer to the right of any existing frame. From the contextual menu, choose Insert Frame. Or, click the last frame of the pose layer and drag to the right.**

A layer that contains an armature (a set of bones) is called a pose layer.

On the Timeline, the frames of the pose layer are highlighted from the frame containing the first pose to the last frame you added.

2. **To add a new pose to the pose layer, move the playhead to the desired location in the highlighted area on the Timeline. Choose the Selection tool from the Tools panel. On the Stage, reposition the bones in your armature as desired, by clicking the head or tail of a bone (or clicking a symbol connected to the bone) and dragging, as shown in Figure 9-38.**

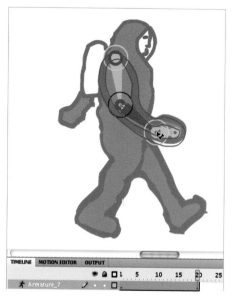

Figure 9-38: Adding new poses to your armature animation is easy.

A keyframe marker appears in the current frame on the Timeline.

3. **You can also add a new pose to the pose layer by right-clicking (Windows) or Control+clicking (Mac) a frame in the pose layer. From the contextual menu that appears, choose Insert Pose. Or, move the playhead to the desired frame on the Timeline and then press F6.**

   Each time you add a new pose, a keyframe marker appears in the current frame on the Timeline.

4. **To adjust a pose, move the playhead to the frame with the desired pose, and reposition the bones in the armature as you wish.**

5. **To see the armature animate, click and drag the playhead in the Timeline, or choose Control⇨Test Movie.**

You can give a bone a feeling of weight by giving it a joint speed of less than 100%. To limit a bone's joint speed, do the following steps:

1. **Choose the Selection tool from the Tools panel and then click a bone to select it.**

2. **Choose Window⇨Properties to open the Property inspector (if it's not already open). In the Property inspector (if necessary), click the disclosure triangle to the left of each section to reveal the contents of that section.**

3. **In the Location section of the Property inspector, click the Joint Weight value, type a number between 0 (zero) and 100, and then press Enter (Windows) or Return (Mac).**

If you want to move an armature to another location on the stage, choose the Selection tool from the Tools panel and double-click the armature to select it. In the Position and Size section of the Properties inspector, click the X or Y value, type a new number, and then press Enter (Windows) or Return (Mac).

If you decide that a bone isn't the right length in a particular pose, you can change its length by Alt+clicking (Windows) or ⌘+clicking (Mac) the bone and then dragging it to the new length that you desire. To delete a bone, select the bone and press Delete.

You can make your armature animations more compelling and realistic by controlling the acceleration and deceleration of motion near pose frames in your animations — *easing*. To add easing to an animation of an armature, do the following steps:

1. **In your pose layer on the Timeline, click a frame between two pose frames.**

2. **In the Ease section of the Properties inspector, from the Type drop-down menu (shown in Figure 9-39), choose the type of easing that you want.**

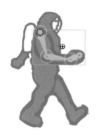
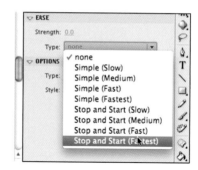

Figure 9-39: Add an ease with ease.

- *Simple:* Simple eases slow down the motion in the frames prior to the second pose frame.

- *Stop/Start:* Stop and Start eases slow down the motion in the frames after the first pose frame, then accelerate the motion, and then slow down the motion in the frames before the second pose frame.

3. **In the Ease section of the Properties inspector, click the Strength value, type a number from −100 to 100, and then press Enter (Windows) or Return (Mac).**

   This specifies the strength of the easing. Zero (0) is equivalent to no easing at all.

4. **To view your changes, move the playhead in the Timeline or choose Control⇨Test Movie.**

If you want to add motion tween effects to your armature animation, convert it to a movie clip or graphic symbol. To convert your armature animation to a movie clip or graphic symbol in a motion tween, follow these steps:

1. **Choose the Selection tool from the Tools panel.**

2. **Double-click the armature.**

   The armature and all its associated objects are selected.

3. **Right-click (Windows) or Control+click (Mac) the selection. From the contextual menu that appears, choose Convert to Symbol.**

4. **In the Convert to Symbol dialog box that appears, type a name, choose Movie Clip or Graphic from the Type drop-down menu, and then click OK.**

5. **Right-click (Windows) or Control+click (Mac) the new symbol instance. From the contextual menu that appears, choose Create Motion Tween.**

   Now you can add motion tween effects to the symbol, including scaling, rotation, color effects, and 3D positioning, as described previously in this chapter.

 To use inverse kinematics in your Flash movies, you must specify ActionScript 3.0 in the Flash tab of the Publish Settings dialog box. (See Chapter 13 for all the info about the Publish Settings dialog box.)

Making the Scene

Animations can get complicated fast, and one way to manage that complexity is by organizing them in layers and layer folders. (Hop to Chapter 6 for the lowdown on layers and layer folders.) Another way to manage the complexity of your animations is to break them into chunks of time — into scenes. You can then use scenes as the modular building blocks of your movies, which you can then rearrange any way you want.

Breaking your movie into scenes

When you create a new Flash movie file (for example, by choosing File⇨New and selecting a Flash File ActionScript 3.0 under the General tab), by default, the file contains one empty scene, cleverly titled Scene 1. Any animations that you create then become part of Scene 1. If you want to add a scene, choose Insert⇨Scene. The Stage clears, and the Timeline is labeled Scene 2.

Manipulating that scene

To keep track of your scenes, open the Scene panel by choosing Window⇨Other Panels⇨Scene, as shown in Figure 9-40. The Scene panel lists all the scenes in your movie. When you choose Control⇨Test Movie, the scenes play in order from the top of the list down.

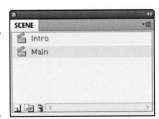

Figure 9-40: The Scene panel lets you make a big scene.

Here's how to use the Scene panel to control your scenes:

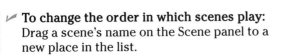 ✓ **To change the order in which scenes play:** Drag a scene's name on the Scene panel to a new place in the list.

✓ **To rename a scene:** Double-click the scene's name in the Scene panel, type the new name, and then press Enter (Windows) or Return (Mac).

To delete a scene, select that scene and then click the Delete Scene button at the bottom of the Scene panel.

To duplicate a scene, click the Duplicate Scene button at the bottom of the Scene panel.

To view a particular scene, click its name on the Scene panel. Or choose View⇨Go To and choose the name of the scene that you want from the submenu.

(10)

Getting Interactive

The real fun with Flash begins when you start to make your art and animations interactive. *Interactivity* means that a computer user's input triggers immediate changes on the computer screen, which the user can then respond to further, as if a conversation is taking place between the user and the computer. Examples can be as simple as clicking a button to go to another Web page, or as complex as a video jukebox.

Flash uses a computer language called ActionScript to specify how the interactivity works. ActionScript statements are short instructions that tell Flash what to do next. By combining them, you can produce complex sets of instructions to create amazing animated graphics and give your Flash movies sophisticated interactive capabilities. ActionScript provides you with tremendous flexibility in designing animations and interactivity, and only your imagination limits what you can do.

Our Proc

PRODUCTS

ERVICES

Understanding ActionScript

The most recent version of ActionScript is 3.0, which was thoroughly redesigned to better support big, complex applications that have lots of data. For those just starting out with Flash, one advantage of ActionScript 3.0 is that Flash movies powered by ActionScript 3.0 can perform up to ten times faster than those using earlier versions of ActionScript.

Flash CS4 supports earlier versions of ActionScript, too. To use some of the latest features in Flash CS4, though, you need to use ActionScript 3.0. In this book, all our code is written in ActionScript 3.0 because that's the wave of the future.

To run Flash movies written with ActionScript 3.0, your users need Flash Player 9 or later. At this writing, more than 96 percent of the computer users in the world have Flash Player 9 or later, and that percentage is rising.

 ActionScript is based on the same language specification as JavaScript, the popular computer language used extensively in Web page design. ActionScript is basically a powerful version of JavaScript with extensions for controlling Flash animations. If you know JavaScript, you can use much of that knowledge when working with ActionScript, and vice versa.

Making objects work for you

ActionScript has numerous software building blocks that are ready for you to use. These building blocks are organized into *classes* that share similar properties and capabilities. (The capabilities are called *methods.*) You create instances of a class in ActionScript to use them in your Flash movies. These instances are called *objects.* Buttons, for example, are one kind of object in ActionScript, and sounds are another.

Objects such as buttons, text, movie clips, and sounds have properties and methods built into them in ActionScript, and this makes it easy to use ActionScript to control them.

Method acting

You can make an object work for you by calling on one of its built-in methods. Doing this is pretty easy: You specify the object by name, followed by the dot (.) operator, followed by the method and the parameters that you want to pass to it.

For example, if you have a movie clip with an instance named `owl`, you can create a variable (using the definition keyword `var`) named `my_color` that can use the ActionScript built-in `ColorTransform` class and its `transform` and `colorTransform` properties to transform the color of the instance:

```
var my_color:ColorTransform = owl.transform.colorTransform;
```

You can set `my_color` by specifying it by name, followed by the dot (.) operator, followed by the `color` property (which describes its red, green, and blue intensity), and then setting all that equal to a number for the color you want, like this:

```
my_color.color = 0x990099;
```

In ActionScript, you specify a color by using hexadecimal format preceded by `0x`. Then you can apply the change to `owl` by specifying the name of the instance you want to change (`owl`), followed by the dot (.) operator, the `transform` property, another dot operator, and the `colorTransform` property, and then setting all that equal to `my_color` variable:

```
owl.transform.colorTransform = my_color;
```

You can see the result of setting the `colorTransform` property in Figure 10-1. By setting the `colorTransform` property equal to the color 990099, the owl turns purple (99 red mixed with 0 green and 99 blue).

As usual, Flash makes it easy for you to control objects and their built-in methods. As we show you in the next section of this chapter, you can just choose methods, events, and properties from a list in the Actions panel, and Flash shows you the parameters you need to fill in.

Figure 10-1: Specify a color in hexadecimal format.

Flash lets you put ActionScript 3.0 in only two places:

- A keyframe on the Timeline
- A separate ActionScript text file

Adding ActionScript to Frames

You can add ActionScript to any frame, but to manage your Flash project more efficiently, it's a good idea to put all your ActionScript code in one place — such as in Frame 1 in the first layer of your FLA file — to make it easy to find and modify.

Before we take a look at a specific example of adding ActionScript to a keyframe, get an overview of the process. First, you select the keyframe where you want to store the ActionScript; then you open the Actions panel (shown in Figure 10-2, where the window is shown with Script Assist enabled); and finally, you add the ActionScript.

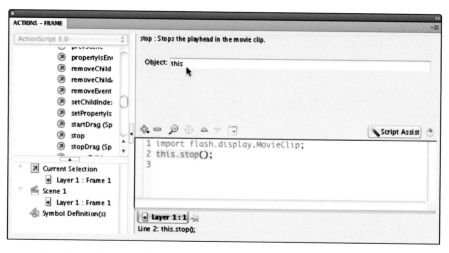

Figure 10-2: The Actions panel is your key to adding ActionScript to your frames.

Now take a look at how to proceed through those steps in a simple example of using ActionScript in a frame: placing a Stop method at the beginning of the movie. You might want this, for example, if you provide a button that starts the movie, so that viewers can choose whether they want to see it. The movie loads, but the first thing that it encounters is a command to stop. Nothing happens until someone clicks a button to start the movie. (Of course, the Web page should also contain other buttons and information that viewers can use to navigate through your Web site.)

To add the Stop method to your movie, follow these steps:

1. **Create your animation.**

2. **Choose Control⇨Test Movie and watch your animation run.**

3. **Create a new layer for your ActionScript and name it Actions.**

Chapter 6 explains how to create and name layers.

4. **Click the keyframe where you want to add the ActionScript.**

5. **Choose Window⇨Actions to open the Actions panel if it isn't open already.**

If necessary, to expand the Actions panel, click the Actions panel's icon or double-click the Actions panel's tab. The Actions panel is divided into a right and left pane, and the left pane is divided into a top and bottom pane. If the left pane isn't showing, find the tiny triangle at the left of the panel and click it. If both the top and bottom panes in the left pane aren't showing, find the tiny triangle at the top or bottom of the pane and click it.

6. **Click the Script Assist button on the right side of the Actions window if it isn't already enabled.**

In Script Assist mode, the right side of the Actions window is split into two horizontal sections so that the upper-right pane of the Actions window can display any parameters you need to type to write your ActionScript.

Using Script Assist makes creating ActionScript much easier. We love it and leave it on almost all the time. We suggest that you do, too.

7. **In the left pane, choose flash.display⇨MovieClip⇨Methods, and then double-click Stop in the list of methods.**

This code appears in the Script pane on the right of the Actions panel:

```
import flash.display.MovieClip;
not_set_yet.stop();
```

The first ActionScript statement imports information about the `MovieClip` class into your Flash project so that your movie will have access to the prebuilt methods and properties of the `MovieClip` class. The second ActionScript statement uses the `stop` method to stop the `not_set_yet` instance. We change `not_set_yet` in the next step.

Each instruction in ActionScript is called a *statement,* and it's written with a semicolon at the end.

To get an idea of the scope of ActionScript, take a peek at the many categories and subcategories that you can choose from the left pane of the Actions window. For starters, you might browse briefly through the flash.display category and its subcategories.

8. **In the Object text box in the Actions panel, type the word this.**

The word *this* refers to the currently running movie clip, which in our case is the movie defined by Flash's main Timeline. In the Script pane on the bottom right of the Actions panel, the second line of code changes to

```
this.stop();
```

9. **Choose Control➪Test Movie again.**

   This time, the movie doesn't run; the `stop` method halts it.

Using ActionScript with Buttons

A common way to add interactivity is to create a button. The viewer clicks the button and something happens (or stops happening). Usually, you add text near or on the button so that your viewers know what the button is for.

If you've already worked on a Web site, you're familiar with the concept of hyperlinks. If you know HyperText Markup Language (HTML) — the language behind Web pages — you know that you can create hyperlinks by using the `<a>` tag and its `href` attribute. This tag links text or an image to another URL (that is, another Web address). When people click the text or the image, they are teleported to that URL. You can create Flash buttons that accomplish the same purpose but with much greater flair. And you can use buttons for so many other useful tasks — to start or stop animation, jump to different parts of a movie, turn music on and off, and much more.

Here's an example of how to create ActionScript that plays a movie clip when you click a button. To do that, follow these steps:

1. **Create the button and place an instance of the button on the Stage.**

   Chapter 8 tells you about creating buttons.

2. **Open the Property inspector if it isn't already open. (Choose Window➪Properties.)**

   If necessary, expand the Property inspector to its full size.

3. **In the Instance Name text box near the top of the Property inspector, type a unique instance name for the button, such as** myButton.

4. **Create a new layer for your ActionScript and name it Actions. Click the first keyframe in the new layer.**

   The ActionScript that you create in the next steps is stored in this frame.

5. **Choose Window➪Actions to open the Actions panel if it's not already open.**

   If necessary, to expand the Actions panel, click the Actions panel's icon or double-click the Actions panel's tab. And if the left pane of the Actions panel isn't visible, click the tiny triangle in the middle of the left side of the Actions panel.

6. **If the Script Assist button on the right side of the Actions panel is enabled, click the button to disable Script Assist.**

7. In the Script pane of the Actions panel, type

```
import flash.display.MovieClip;
this.stop();
```

This stops your movie on the first frame, as described in the previous section.

8. **Click the Script Assist button on the right side of the Actions window to enable Script Assist.**

9. **In the left pane of the Actions panel, choose Language Elements⇨ Statements, Keywords & Directives⇨Definition Keyword⇨Function.**

Language Elements is up near the top of the list. Note the code that appears in the Script pane now, just below `this.stop();`

```
import flash.display.MovieClip;
this.stop();
function not_set_yet() {
}
```

10. **In the Name text box (in the Parameters area in the upper-right pane of the Actions panel), type** startMovie. **In the Parameters text box, type** event:MouseEvent. **In the Type text box, type** void.

Now the code in the Script pane on the right of the Actions panel looks like this:

```
import flash.display.MovieClip;
this.stop();
function startMovie(event:MouseEvent):void {
}
```

11. **In the left pane of the Actions panel, choose flash.display⇨ MovieClip⇨Methods⇨gotoAndPlay.**

Now the code in the Script pane on the right of the Actions panel looks like this:

```
import flash.display.MovieClip;
this.stop();
function startMovie(event:MouseEvent):void {
        not_set_yet.gotoAndPlay();
}
```

12. **In the Object text box (in the Parameters area of the Actions panel), type** this. **In the Frame text box, type a frame number (such as** 20) **or a frame label (in quotes) — for example,** "products".

See Chapter 9 for information on creating a frame label.

Now the code in the Script pane on the right of the Actions panel looks like the following.

```
import flash.display.MovieClip;
this.stop();
function startMovie(event:MouseEvent):void {
    this.gotoAndPlay("products");
}
```

The code creates a function named startMovie. When Flash runs the function startMovie, it goes to the frame labeled "products". The word this is ActionScript shorthand for the currently running (or stopped) movie clip — in this example, it's the Flash movie running from the main Timeline.

Be sure your code is within the final bracket, which is what closes the function.

13. **In the Script pane at the bottom right of the Actions panel, select the final line of code (the curly bracket), and in the left pane of the Actions panel, choose flash.events➪EventDispatcher➪Methods➪ addEventListener.**

Now the code in the Script pane on the right of the Actions panel looks like this:

```
import flash.events.EventDispatcher;
import flash.display.MovieClip;
this.stop();
function startMovie(event:MouseEvent):void {
    this.gotoAndPlay("products");
}
not_set_yet.addEventListener();
```

14. **Add the following:**

> a. *In the Parameters area of the Actions panels, in the Object text box, type* **myButton**.
>
> b. *In the Type text box, type* **MouseEvent.CLICK**.
>
> c. *In the Listener text box, type* **startMovie**.

Now the code in the Script pane on the right of the Actions panel looks like this:

```
import flash.events.EventDispatcher;
import flash.display.MovieClip;
this.stop();
function startMovie(event:MouseEvent):void {
    this.gotoAndPlay("products");
}
myButton.addEventListener(MouseEvent.CLICK, startMovie);
```

The last line of ActionScript code adds an event listener to myButton that "listens" for a mouse click and executes the startMovie function when it detects a mouse click on myButton. So when the user clicks the mouse, Flash goes to the frame labeled "products", as shown in Figure 10-3.

15. If you want to change the `MouseEvent.CLICK` parameter, click it in the lower-right pane of the Actions panel. Then in the Parameters area of the Actions panel, replace `CLICK` with another parameter, such as `MOUSE_OVER`.

    See Table 10-1 for more information on some of the event parameters that you can use to define when a button action goes into effect.

16. Choose Control➪Test Movie.

    When you click your button, your Flash movie jumps to the frame labeled `products` in your Timeline.

Figure 10-3: When the user clicks myButton, Flash goes to the frame labeled products.

Table 10-1	Mouse Events
Event	*When the Action Occurs*
CLICK	When the user clicks the mouse button
MOUSE_DOWN	When the mouse cursor is over the object (or the button's hit area) and the user is pressing the mouse button
MOUSE_UP	When the mouse cursor is over the object (or the button's hit area) and the user releases the mouse button
MOUSE_OVER	When the mouse cursor moves over the object (or the button's hit area) without clicking
MOUSE_OUT	When the mouse cursor moves out of the object (or the button's hit area) without clicking
MOUSE_WHEEL	When a mouse wheel is spun over the object

The hit area of a button is the button's *active area* — the area that responds to mouse clicks and other user interactions. See Chapter 8 to find out all about buttons.

Here's a variation of the preceding ActionScript code. This version makes use of different mouse events — the MOUSE_DOWN and MOUSE_UP events. With this code, pressing the mouse button makes the movie on the current Timeline play, and releasing the mouse button stops it.

```
import flash.events.EventDispatcher;
import flash.display.MovieClip;
this.stop();
function startMovie(event:MouseEvent):void {
        this.play();}
function stopMovie(event:MouseEvent):void {
        this.stop();}
myButton.addEventListener(MouseEvent.MOUSE_DOWN,startMovie);
myButton.addEventListener(MouseEvent.MOUSE_UP,stopMovie);
```

Using ActionScript with Movie Clips

You use ActionScript with a movie clip in much the same way that you use it with a button; both are instances of objects that you can control with ActionScript.

You can use ActionScript with movie clips to do all kinds of things, such as starting or stopping a movie clip from playing and replacing one movie clip with another. You can use ActionScript to make one movie clip control a second movie clip — the ActionScript could set the second movie's properties, for instance, and change its size, visibility, and so on, based on the user's interaction with the first movie clip. For example, you might make a movie clip that contains a cartoon of a dancing TV set, and you add ActionScript so that each time the user clicks the movie clip, the TV shows a different cartoon.

In this section, we look at two examples of how you can use ActionScript with movie clips. In the first, you make one movie clip into an animated mask that reveals another movie clip underneath it. In the second, you find out how to make a movie clip draggable.

Creating animated masks with movie clips

Flash has loads of useful methods and properties built into its objects. One is the DisplayObject class's mask method, which you can use, for example, to create an animated mask. When a mask is animated, the mask reveals the background beneath while it moves, as shown in Figure 10-4. (For more on masks, see Chapter 6.)

To use the `mask` property to make a movie clip into a mask, follow these steps:

1. **Create a movie clip and place an instance of it on the Stage.**

   This instance will be the background movie clip behind the mask. For example, you may want to make a wide movie clip a landscape. (If you need to know how to create movie clips, check out Chapter 9.)

2. **Choose Window⇨Properties to open the Property inspector.**

   If necessary, expand the Property inspector to its full size.

Figure 10-4: In this Flash movie, letters change shape while revealing the background movie.

3. **In the text field near the upper-left corner of the Property inspector, enter an instance name for the movie clip (such as** background**).**

4. **Create another movie clip and place an instance of it on a new layer on the Stage. In the Property inspector, enter an instance name (such as** binoculars**) for the second movie clip.**

   This instance will be the mask movie clip. Check out Chapter 6 for information on creating new layers.

5. **Create some animation for this movie clip so that it moves over the background movie clip.**

   See Chapter 9 for information on creating animation.

6. **Create a new layer in the Timeline, and select Frame 1 of the new layer.**

7. **Choose Window⇨Actions to open the Actions panel.**

   If necessary, to expand the Actions panel, click the Actions panel's icon or double-click the Actions panel's tab.

8. **Click the Script Assist button on the right side of the Actions window if it isn't already enabled. In the left pane of the Actions panel, choose flash.display⇨DisplayObject⇨Properties and double-click** `mask`**.**

   This code appears in the Script pane to the right of the Actions panel:

   ```
   import flash.display.DisplayObject:
   not_set_yet.mask();
   ```

The first line of code imports information about the `DisplayObject` class into your Flash project so that your movie will have access to the prebuilt methods and properties of the `DisplayObject` class.

9. **In the Expression text field at the upper-right pane of the Actions panel, change not_yet_set to the first movie clip's instance name (such as background). Before the ending semicolon, type an equal sign and the mask movie clip's instance name (such as binoculars).**

If your mask movie clip's instance name is `binoculars` and your other movie clip instance is named `background`, the code in the Actions panel should now look like this:

```
import flash.display.DisplayObject:
background.mask = binoculars;
```

10. **Choose Control⇨Test Movie and enjoy the new animation.**

Dragging movie clips

Flash lets you create objects that your audience can drag around the screen. Draggable movie clips can be both fun and useful. You can create draggable movie clips to use for games, drag-and-drop interfaces, or, as shown in Figure 10-5, slider bars.

To create a draggable movie clip, follow these steps:

1. **Choose Insert⇨New Symbol to create a new symbol.**

2. **In the Create New Symbol dialog box that appears, name your new symbol, select the option for the Movie Clip behavior, and click OK.**

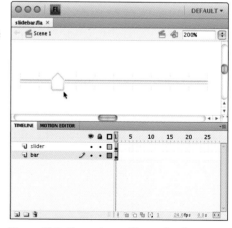

Figure 10-5: Use a draggable movie clip to create a slider on a bar.

3. **On the Stage, create an object that you want the viewer to be able to drag.**

4. **Choose Edit⇨Edit Document to return to the main Timeline.**

5. **Drag the movie clip that you created from the Library to the Stage.**

An instance of the movie clip appears on the stage.

To open the Library if it's not visible, choose Window⇨Library.

6. **Choose Window⇨ Properties to open the Property inspector if it's not already open.**

7. **In the Property inspector, type in a name in the Instance Name text box.**

   Your instance now has a name — snowflake, for example.

8. **Create a new layer in your movie and select the first frame in the new layer.**

9. **Choose Window⇨Actions to open the Actions panel if it's not already open.**

   If necessary, to expand the Actions panel, click the Actions panel's icon or double-click the Actions panel's tab.

10. **Click the Script Assist button to turn it off if it's selected.**

    Now you can type your code directly, without interference from Script Assist.

11. **Type the following code in the right pane of the Actions panel:**

    ```
    import flash.events.EventDispatcher;
    import flash.display.Sprite;
    function dragMovie(event:MouseEvent):void {
        snowflake.startDrag();
    }
    snowflake.addEventListener(MouseEvent.MOUSE_DOWN,
        dragMovie);
    function dropMovie(event:MouseEvent):void {
        snowflake.stopDrag();
    }
    snowflake.addEventListener(MouseEvent.MOUSE_UP, dropMovie);
    ```

    If your instance isn't named snowflake, substitute the name you gave to your instance instead.

    This code tells Flash to start dragging your movie clip instance when you click it, and it tells Flash to stop dragging it when you release the mouse button. You might have noticed that it's similar to the code in the "Using ActionScript with Buttons" section, earlier in this chapter.

12. **Choose Control⇨Test Movie and then click and drag your movie clip.**

    Your mouse drags the movie clip!

You can constrain the movement of the movie clip to certain areas. For example, on a slider bar, you don't want the movie clip going all over the page — only along the bar. You can constrain the movement by specifying a constraint rectangle for the movie clip. See startDrag in the description of the Sprite class in the ActionScript 3.0 Language Reference for more details. (In the Actions window, select startDrag and click the Help button next to the Script Assist button to view the discussion of startDrag in the Help section.)

Exploring ActionScript Further

Flash contains approximately one zillion more ActionScript methods and properties than the ones that we cover in this chapter. For more information, choose Help⇨Flash Help, and in the Help window that appears, browse through the ActionScript 3.0 Language and Components Reference. In the following sections, we briefly explain a few more aspects of ActionScript programming to give you an idea of some of the possibilities.

Programming constructs

If you're familiar with programming, you'll recognize many commands in ActionScript, such as `For` and `While`, which let you process certain ActionScript statements repeatedly while certain conditions that you specify are true. The `If` and `Else` statements create conditional expressions.

Making comments

To help make your ActionScript clear when you look back at it a few months from now, you should add comments that explain the purpose of the ActionScript. As shown in Figure 10-6, you can add comments when Script Assist is on by choosing Language Elements⇨Operators⇨Comment⇨// (or Language Elements⇨Operators⇨Comment⇨/*..*/) and then typing your comments in the Comments text box, located in the Parameters area in the upper-right pane of the Actions panel.

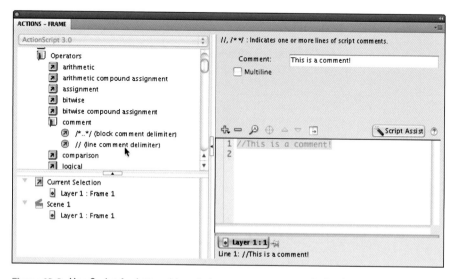

Figure 10-6: Use Script Assist to add reminder comments to your ActionScript.

It is definitely easier, though, to type your comments with Script Assist off. Temporarily turn off Script Assist in the Actions panel by clicking the Script Assist button. Then in the Script pane, type two slashes (//) and then your comments. Anything on the line after the two slashes is ignored when running the animation. If you need more than one line for comments, type the two slashes at the beginning of each comment line.

If you're like us, you love Script Assist and will want to turn it on again (by clicking the Script Assist button) after typing your comments.

External scripting

You can keep your ActionScript in separate text files that your Flash movie can load when needed. This makes it easier to reuse your beautiful ActionScript code in multiple movies. You can create your ActionScript files with any text editor that you like.

Adobe recommends that instead of adding ActionScript to frames all over the place, you put all of your ActionScript code in a single place, making it easier to find and debug all your code. To make your code easy to find and manage, it's probably best to put all your code in the first frame of the first layer of the Timeline or in a separate text file.

To create a separate new ActionScript file within Flash, choose File⇨New and then choose ActionScript File from the General tab of the New Document dialog box. You can type your ActionScript code in this file and save it.

You can also create ActionScript files by using Dreamweaver or a separate text editor, such as Notepad (Windows) or TextEdit (Mac). Be sure to save the file with the .as suffix, which stands for ActionScript, of course.

To create ActionScript files in TextEdit on a Mac, first choose TextEdit⇨ Preferences. In the Preferences window that appears (see Figure 10-7), on the New Document tab, select Plain Text rather than Rich Text in the Format section. On the Open and Save tab of the Preferences window, deselect Add ".txt" Extension to Plain Text Files in the section labeled When Saving a File (as shown in Figure 10-8).

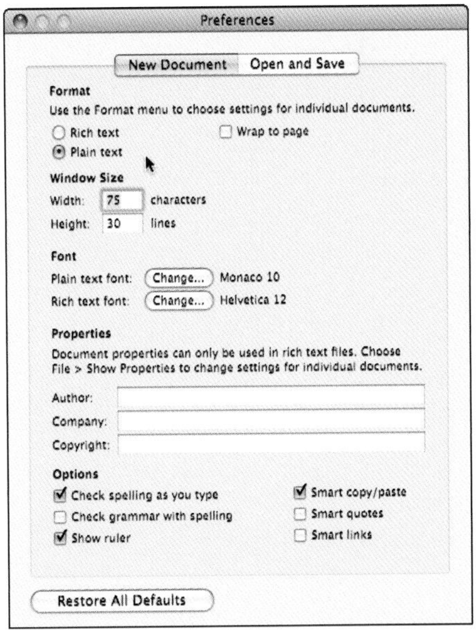

Figure 10-7: Select Plain Text rather than Rich Text.

To include the code from a separate ActionScript file in any part of your movie, simply add this ActionScript into a frame:

```
include "your-filename-goes-here.as"
```

This specifies an ActionScript file in the same directory as your FLA or SWF file.

Discovering more about ActionScript

ActionScript gives you tremendous power over your Flash movies. If you enjoy using ActionScript, you might want to check out some of the great resources we list in Chapter 15.

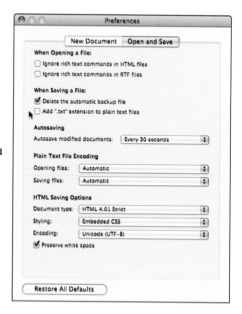

Figure 10-8: Deselect adding a `.txt` extension to plain text files.

11

Extravagant Audio, High-Velocity Video

Silent movies have been gone for a long time now. Why should your Flash movies be silent? You can create music and sound effects that play continuously or are controlled by your animation Timeline. You can also add sounds to buttons to liven things up a little. You can edit sounds and control when they start and stop. But be aware that sound adds overhead to a movie, which slows down loading on a Web site, and some audiences might not be in the mood to hear any sound. If you're careful about how you use sounds, however, you can get great results.

You can also include video clips in your Flash animations. You can import video clips in a variety of file formats and then scale them, rotate them, tween them, stack them in layers, animate their transparency levels, and do all the other creative things that you're used to doing in Flash, just as though the video clips were regular Flash animations. And you can stream your video clips in Flash so that your audience may view the clips while they're downloading.

Acquiring Amazing Audio

To add some great sound to your Flash movie, you must first import the sound. You can import AIFF, WAV, and MP3 sounds. Flash places these sounds in your Library. (See Chapter 2 for more about the Library.)

Sounds vary in sample rate, bit rate, and channels. These statistics are important because they affect the quality and size of the sound file. Of course, the length of the sound also affects its size. Here's what you need to know:

- ✓ **Sample rate:** The number of times the recorder samples an audio signal when it's recorded in digital form; measured in kilohertz (kHz). Try not to use more than 22 kHz unless you want CD-quality music.

- ✓ **Bit rate:** The number of bits used for each audio sample; sometimes called *bit resolution.* A 16-bit sound file is clearer with less background noise, but use 8-bit sound if you need to reduce file size.

- ✓ **Channels:** Typically one channel of sound *(monophonic)* or two channels *(stereophonic).* In most cases, mono is fine for Flash files and uses half the amount of data that stereo uses.

Often, you need to take a sound as you find it unless you have software that can manipulate sounds. Luckily, you can set the specs of sounds when you publish your movie to an SWF file. You generally get the best results by starting with high-quality sounds and compressing during publishing. (Turn to Chapter 13 for details on settings for publishing Flash files.)

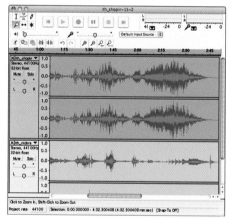

Audacity, shown in Figure 11-1, is an excellent program for recording and manipulating sound for your Flash movies — and it's free. Download it from `http://audacity.sourceforge.net`.

Figure 11-1: Use Audacity to record and edit sound for your Flash movies.

You can check a sound's stats after you import the sound into Flash. The next section explains how to import a sound.

Importing sounds

Importing a sound is easy. To import a sound, follow these steps:

1. Choose File➪Import➪Import to Library to open the Import dialog box.

2. Locate the sound that you want to import.

3. Click Import to Library.

Nothing seems to happen, but Flash places your sound in the Library. Choose Window➪Library to check it out (if the Library window isn't already open). To see the sound's stats, click the name of the sound in the Library window. Then click the Properties button (with the little *i* symbol) at the bottom of the Library window.

Placing sounds into a movie

After you import a sound into your movie's Library, you need to place it and set its parameters. To place sounds in a movie, follow these steps:

1. **Create and name a new layer for the sound.**

   Click the Add Layer icon in the lower-left corner of the layer list to add a new layer. Each sound should have its own layer. Sounds are combined (mixed) when the movie is played.

2. **Choose Window➪Properties to open the Property inspector, if it isn't already open.**

   If necessary, expand the Property inspector to its full size.

3. **Select the keyframe in the new layer where you want the sound to start playing.**

4. **In the Sound section of the Property inspector, in the Name drop-down list, select the sound that you want to place in your movie.**

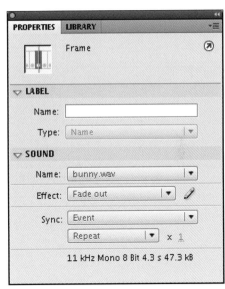

Figure 11-2: Set sound parameters in the Property inspector.

The Name drop-down list shows all sounds that you've imported. Below the name of the sound, at the bottom of the Property inspector, the sound's stats are listed (sample rate, channels, bit rate, duration, and file size), as shown in Figure 11-2.

Flash places the sound on the active layer. The image of the sound waves appears in the Timeline between the keyframe you select in Step 3 and the next keyframe. If there isn't a next keyframe, you can add one to see the sound, or you can add frames until the sound wave line stops. (You can add frames by repeatedly pressing F5, which is equivalent to repeatedly choosing Insert⇨Timeline⇨Frame.)

5. **If desired, select an effect in the Effect drop-down list.**

   These effects are self-explanatory. For example, Left Channel plays the sound from only the left speaker. Fade In starts the sound softly and gradually brings it up to full volume. The default setting is None.

6. **In the Sync drop-down list, select one of the following synchronization options:**

   - *Event:* Plays the sound when its first keyframe plays and continues to play the sound until it's finished, even if the movie stops. If Flash plays the keyframe again before the sound is finished, Flash starts the sound again. Use this setting for button sounds when you want the sound to play each time that the button is passed over or clicked. (Check out Chapter 8 for more information on adding sounds to buttons.) This setting is the default.

   - *Start:* Plays the sound when its first keyframe plays and continues to play the sound until it's finished, even if the movie stops. If the keyframe is played again before the sound is finished, Flash doesn't start the sound again.

   - *Stop:* Stops the sound.

   - *Stream:* Synchronizes the sound to the Timeline. Flash skips animation frames if it can't draw them fast enough to keep up with the sound. The sound stops when Flash plays the last frame containing the sound wave. Use this option when you want to match the sound with a portion of the animation in your movie. You can insert an ending keyframe before placing the sound to control when the sound ends.

   If your sound is set to Event, it will play to its finish even if not all the sound is visible on the Timeline. If your sound is set to Stream, it will only play for the frames on the Timeline where the image of the sound waves is visible.

You may want to edit the sound (as described in the next section, "Editing Sounds") to add a fade out so the sound doesn't end abruptly.

7. **Choose Repeat or Loop from the Repeat/Loop drop-down menu. If you choose Repeat, type the number of times you want to repeat the sound.**

If you set a Stream sound to Repeat, your Flash Player movie's file size is increased by the number of times that the sound is repeated. Adobe recommends that you do not set stream sounds to Repeat.

- *Loop:* If you choose Loop, the sound will repeat continuously.

- *Repeat:* If you choose Repeat, you can calculate the number of times that you need to play a sound throughout an animation by knowing the length (in seconds) of the sound, the number of frames your animation contains, and the frame rate. If your animation is 48 frames and the rate is 24 frames per second (24 fps; the default), your animation is 2 seconds. If your sound is 1 second long, loop it twice to play it throughout your animation. If you don't want to do the math, use a high number of loops, just to make sure.

After you place the sound, press Enter (Windows) or Return (Mac) or use the Controller to play your movie and hear the results.

Editing Sounds

After you place a sound, you can edit the sound to fine-tune its settings. You should delete unused or unwanted portions of a sound to reduce file size. You can also change the volume while the sound plays.

To edit a sound, follow these steps:

1. **Click a frame that contains a sound (or import a sound, as we describe in the preceding section, "Placing sounds into a movie").**

2. **Choose Window⇨Properties to open the Property inspector, if it isn't already open.**

   If necessary, expand the Property inspector to its full size.

3. **Click the Edit button (the Pencil icon to the immediate right of the Effect drop-down list) to open the Edit Envelope dialog box. (See Figure 11-3.)**

Envelope line, left channel

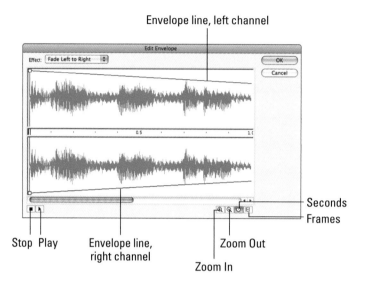

Stop Play　　Envelope line,　　　　　Zoom Out
right channel

Zoom In

Seconds
Frames

Figure 11-3: Use the Edit Envelope dialog box to edit your sounds.

To see a specific section of a sound in more detail, click the Zoom In button. Zoom in when you want to edit small details of a sound.

To see more of a sound's time frame, click the Zoom Out button. Zoom out to edit the sound as a whole.

You can display sounds in terms of seconds or frames. Click the Seconds button (far left) to show sounds in seconds. Click the Frames button to display sounds by frames.

Deleting parts of a sound

Between the left (top) and right (bottom) channel display is a narrow strip that controls the starting and ending points of a sound. By deleting the beginning and end of a sound, you can eliminate unused portions of the sound. Along this strip are two vertical bars: one at the beginning of the sound and another at the end. These bars control when the sound starts and ends. Use them to edit the sound as follows:

✔ **Time In control:** This bar, on the left edge of the sound, specifies the start of the sound. Drag the bar to the right to delete the beginning of the sound.

✔ **Time Out control:** This bar, on the right edge of the sound, specifies the end of the sound. Drag the bar to the left to delete the end of the sound.

Changing the volume

On both the left and right channel displays, Flash shows an envelope line (refer to Figure 11-3) to indicate the approximate direction of the sound's volume. Where the volume changes, Flash places small squares, called *envelope handles*. To change the sound's volume, drag an envelope handle up (to increase the volume) or down (to decrease the volume). This is how you create sound fade ins and fade outs.

You can click an envelope line to add a new envelope handle. This new handle enables you to create a new direction for the sound's volume at the handle's location. To remove an envelope handle, click it and drag it out of the Edit Envelope window.

When you finish editing a sound, click OK to close the Edit Envelope dialog box.

Managing Sound

Sound can increase the size of your movie by such a great extent that you need to pay attention to how you use it. You should make every effort to compress the sound. You can also lower the sampling rate; however, your sound's quality is then reduced. Nevertheless, you should try out all the possibilities until you get the best results.

The *sampling rate* is the rate at which the computer measures sound and converts it into numerical data. The computer makes these sample measurements many thousands of times per second. A higher sampling rate provides more information about the sound and, therefore, better audio quality. But all those extra measurements make for a much bigger data file.

Flash offers two ways to control the properties of a sound:

- ✔ **Use the Publish Settings dialog box to specify properties for all the sounds in a movie.** If you have only one sound or a few similar sounds, specifying settings this way is easy.
- ✔ **Use the Sound Properties dialog box to specify properties of specific sounds.** As long as you don't specifically override these properties when you publish, these settings stick. Use the Sound Properties dialog box when you want to specify different properties for each sound.

Because you specify the publish settings when you publish a movie, we discuss those settings in Chapter 13. In this section, we explain how to fine-tune sound properties in the Sound Properties dialog box.

To open the Sound Properties dialog box, open the Library (choose Window⇨ Library) and double-click the icon of the sound that you want to work with. Figure 11-4 shows the Sound Properties dialog box.

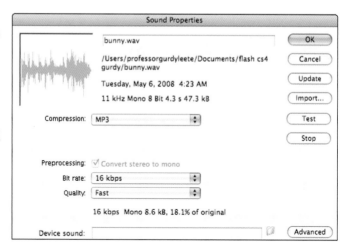

Figure 11-4: Set individual sounds' properties here.

At the top of the dialog box, Flash displays statistics for the sound — its location, date, sample rate, channels, bit rate, duration, and file size. Use the Compression drop-down list to specify how you want to export the file. For each compression type, Flash displays the settings available for that type in the drop-down list. When you choose settings, look at the bottom of the dialog box, where Flash displays the new file size in kilobytes and in percentage of original size. The file size reduction can be pretty amazing. Here are the options in the Compression drop-down list box:

- ✓ **Default:** This option uses the compression settings specified on the Flash tab of the Publish Settings dialog box when you publish your SWF file. (Chapter 13 gives you more information on publishing to SWF files.)

- ✓ **ADPCM:** You can convert stereo to mono to cut down file size. Available sampling rates are 5, 11, 22, and 44 kHz. You can choose from 2, 3, 4, or 5 bits. Choose 5 bits for the best sound; the default is 4 bits. ADPCM is short for Adaptive Differential Pulse Code Modulation. This compression method produces files that take up less storage space than CD-quality audio and is useful for short audio clips, such as button clicks. In case you're wondering what the heck this compression is, it's used to store music on Sony Mini Discs.

- ✓ **MP3:** MP3 is a popular and efficient compression method. (To change the settings of an imported MP3 file, be sure to deselect the Use Imported MP3 Quality check box.) You can convert stereo to mono and choose a bit rate measured in kilobits per second. You can choose from 8 Kbps (poor quality) to 160 Kbps (near-CD quality). Generally, you want something between these two extremes. Try a bit rate between 20 and 84 Kbps for a good balance of file size and quality. You can also choose the quality — Fast, Medium, or Best. The Fast option optimizes the sound for faster download from your Web site but with some quality compromise. For music, MP3 provides the best compression, letting you keep your quality as high as possible.

✔ **Raw:** This option exports the sound with no sound compression. You can convert stereo to mono and select the same sampling rates as for ADPCM.

✔ **Speech:** This option exports the sound with compression techniques specially designed for speech. You can select the same sampling rates as for ADPCM. A good choice for speech is 11 kHz.

After you specify a group of settings, click the Test button. This handy button lets you hear how your sound file sounds with each setting.

The Sound Properties dialog box also lets you update the original sound after you modify it with sound-editing software — just click the Update button. You can also click Import to import a sound file. The Stop button stops playing a sound that you're previewing.

When you're finished, click OK to finalize your settings and close the dialog box.

Video Magic

The Flash Player has achieved more universal adoption than any other Web video technology, so Flash can be a great way to deliver video over the Web. Flash Player version 6 and later can play video, and (as of this writing) Adobe claims that more than 98 percent of U.S. Web surfers have Flash Player 7 or higher, compared with 82.2 percent for Windows Media Player, 66.8 percent for Apple's QuickTime Player, and 47.1 percent for RealPlayer. The Adobe Web site provides more details — you can check it out at

```
www.adobe.com/products/player_census/flashplayer
```

Flash can use a variety of video formats. You can use Flash to create or import Flash Video (FLV) files. (FLV is a file format developed by the Flash team for video on the Web.) If you have QuickTime 7 installed on your Mac or QuickTime 6.5 for Windows on your PC, you can import files in the AVI, MPG/MPEG, MOV, and DV formats. If you have DirectX 9 or higher installed on your Windows PC, you can import files in the AVI, MPG/MPEG, and Windows Media File (WMV and ASF) formats.

Four ways to use video in Flash

You may include video in your Flash movie in various ways. For starters, you may embed video in your SWF file and play it in the Timeline. This lets you play your video from within your SWF file. This can work well for short video clips (perhaps ten seconds or less), but longer video clips might make your Flash file take a loooooooong time to download, and these clips might have problems with audio/video synchronization. For more information, see the next sections in this chapter, "Preparing to embed video in Flash" and "Embedding a video."

And using Flash CS4, you may also

- ✔ **Stream video from your Web server.** You can connect to an FLV video file from within your SWF file and play the video while it downloads from a plain-old Web server. This is a cool feature and definitely a good idea if you have a video longer than around ten seconds. Your audience can start to watch the video while it's still downloading, and the audio and video won't get out of sync. For more information, see the "Streaming a video" section, later in this chapter.

- ✔ **Stream video from a Flash video streaming service.** You can play your video from a Web hosting service provider that specializes in Flash video. This can give you good performance if you want to do fancy things like host video-on-demand applications, webcam chats, live-event broadcasts, and real-time collaboration applications. But it's definitely not cheap, so if you're a new Flash user, you probably don't need to think about this option for now.

- ✔ **Stream video from a Flash Media Server.** You can play your video from a Flash Media Server that you host. This can give you good performance for heavy-duty deployment of multiple Web video streams, as if you were your own Flash video streaming service. However, the Flash Media Server software is complex — and it's not cheap, with prices ranging from free for a developer version to $4,500 for the most powerful version. So unless your boss is investing zillions in a Flash video Web site, you again probably don't need to worry about this option.

Preparing to embed video in Flash

If you have a video file that you want to embed into your Flash file, you first need to find out the frame rate of your video and make sure that your Flash document has the same frame rate, to avoid erratic playback.

On a Mac, you can do this by following these steps:

1. **Click the Finder on the Dock. In a Finder window, open your Applications folder and then double-click the QuickTime Player.**

   The QuickTime Player starts, and the QuickTime Player menus appear.

2. **In the QuickTime Player menus, choose File➪Open File. In the file dialog box that appears, locate and select your video, and then click the Open button.**

   Your video appears.

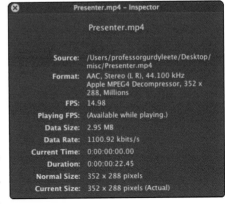

Figure 11-5: The Movie Inspector window in the QuickTime Player.

3. **Choose Window➪Show Movie Inspector.**

   The Movie Inspector window appears, as shown in Figure 11-5.

4. **Make a note of the video's frame rate (shown in the Movie Inspector window as FPS — frames per second).**

   You might also want to note the normal size of the video. (A typical size is 720 x 480 pixels.)

5. **Choose File➪Quit.**

   The QuickTime Player closes.

6. **Return to Flash (perhaps by clicking the Flash icon on the Dock), open or create a Flash movie if one isn't open, and choose Modify➪ Document.**

   The Document Properties dialog box appears, showing the document's dimensions, frame rate, and other properties.

7. **To avoid unstable video playback, change the number in the Frame Rate text box to match your video's frame rate.**

In Windows, you can match your Flash movie's frame rate to your video's frame rate by following these steps:

1. **If your video is not an AVI file or a WMV file, skip to Step 2. If your video is an AVI or a WMV file, right-click the file and choose Properties. On the Summaries or Details tab, note the number of fps (frames per second) for your movie. Close the Properties window and skip to Step 8.**

   You might also want to note the normal size of the video. (A typical size is 720 x 480 pixels.)

2. **From Windows, choose Start⇨Programs⇨QuickTime⇨QuickTime Player.**

   If you don't have the QuickTime Player on your Start menu, point your Web browser to www.apple.com/quicktime/download, follow the instructions there to download and install QuickTime, and then choose Start⇨QuickTime⇨QuickTime Player.

3. **In the QuickTime Player, choose File⇨Open Movie in New Player.**

4. **In the Open dialog box, locate and select your video, and then click the Open button.**

   Your video appears.

5. **Choose Window⇨Show Movie Inspector.**

   The Movie Inspector window appears.

6. **If necessary, click the More Info disclosure triangle to see the detailed information about the movie. Make a note of the video's frame rate (shown in the Movie Inspector window as Movie FPS — frames per second).**

   You might also want to note the normal size of the video. (A typical size is 720 x 480 pixels.)

7. **In the video window, choose File⇨Exit.**

   The QuickTime Player closes.

8. **In Flash, open (or create) a Flash movie if one isn't open and then choose Modify⇨Document.**

   The Document Properties dialog box appears, showing the document's dimensions, frame rate, and other properties.

9. **To avoid unstable video playback, change the number in the Frame Rate text box to match your video's frame rate.**

   If you downloaded QuickTime while Flash was running, you have to quit Flash and restart Flash if you want to import a MOV file.

Embedding a video

You can import video directly into your Flash animations. Flash's Import Video Wizard makes it easy for you to embed your video.

Embedding video in your Flash movie is convenient if your video is short — perhaps ten seconds or less. If the video is longer, downloading your video while the Flash movie plays is probably a better approach.

Before you embed video into Flash, first you should make sure that the frame rate of your video and your Flash movie match, which we show you how to do in the preceding section. After you do that, you can make video clips part of your Flash movie by following these steps:

1. **Click a keyframe where you want to put your video (or create a keyframe by clicking a frame and choosing Insert⇨Timeline⇨ Keyframe).**

2. **Choose File⇨Import⇨Import Video.**

   The Video Import Wizard appears.

3. **Select the On Your Computer option to import a video from your computer.**

4. **Click the Browse button.**

   The Open File dialog box appears.

5. **In the Open File dialog box, find and choose a video file and then click Open.**

   The Import Video dialog box now lists the name of the file you chose.

6. **In the Import Video dialog box, select the Embed FLV in SWF and Play in Timeline option (as shown in Figure 11-6), and then click Next (Windows) or Continue (Mac).**

Figure 11-6: Choose the video that you want to import.

7. **You probably want to select Movie Clip from the Symbol Type dropdown list, and you probably want to mark the check boxes for Place Instance on Stage, Expand Timeline If Needed, and Include Audio.**

   The Video Import Wizard gives you a choice of symbol type for your embedded video. Embedding your video as a movie clip symbol and with the audio track integrated are usually good choices. When you embed your video in a movie clip symbol, the video's Timeline is within the movie clip and plays independently of the main Timeline. This gives you a lot of flexibility and lets you move your video around easily within your Flash movie. However, if your Flash movie is mostly just going to play back the video on the main Timeline without doing much else, Embedded Video in the Symbol Type drop-down menu is an appropriate choice.

8. **Click Next (Windows) or Continue (Mac).**

   The Finish Video Import pane appears in the Video Import Wizard, summarizing your choices.

9. **If you want to change any of your choices, click Go Back. Otherwise, click Finish.**

   The Flash Video Encoding Progress window appears. Encoding your video may take quite a while. When Flash finishes encoding your video, the window disappears, and the movie clip or clips (or embedded video symbol or symbols) containing your video appear on your Stage and in your Library (which you can view by choosing Window⇨Library, if it isn't visible).

Now your video segments are inside movie clips (if you choose that in Step 7), and as with any other movie clips, you can drag them around on the Timeline, rearrange them, rotate them, motion tween them, paint on top of them in other layers, and tween their brightness and transparency — you can mangle them, destroy them, and bring them to life in all the usual Flash ways. This is pretty amazing. (See Chapter 9 for lots more animation ideas.)

Streaming a video

You can set up your Flash movie to stream a video while the video appears inside your Flash movie. That means that viewers can see the video play fairly smoothly even while it's still downloading from the Web — without having to wait until the entire video has downloaded. This is a fantastic feature. You'll certainly want to do this rather than embed your video in Flash if your video is more than a few seconds long.

These streaming video files are in the `.flv` Flash video format. This is the format of all the videos you see at `www.youtube.com` and `http://video.google.com`.

To make an FLV video file to put online and then stream, follow these steps:

1. **Click a keyframe (or create one by clicking a frame and choosing Insert⇨Timeline⇨Keyframe).**

   Your video will start on this keyframe.

2. **Choose File⇨Import⇨Import Video.**

   The Video Import Wizard appears.

   You're about to import a video file into your Flash movie. Ultimately, you will put the file on a Web server, but first you need to create and publish the FLV file.

3. **Select the On Your Computer option if you want to import a video from your computer. If you want to import an FLV video file from the Web, select the Already Deployed to a Web Server, Flash Video Streaming Service, or Flash Media Server option; type the Web address of the video file into the URL text box; and skip to Step 7.**

   Importing a video file from the Web works only for video files that are already in the FLV format.

4. **Click the Browse button.**

5. **In the Open File dialog box, find and choose a movie file and then click Open.**

6. **In the Import Video dialog box, select the radio button for Load External Video with Playback Component.**

7. **Click the Next (Windows) or Continue (Mac) button.**

   The Skinning pane of the Import Video dialog box appears, as shown in Figure 11-7.

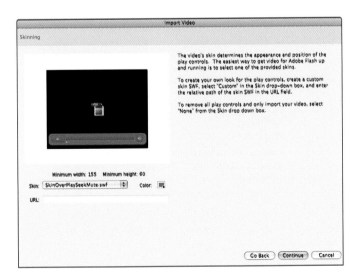

Figure 11-7: Choose the style of play controls you want for your video.

8. **In the Skin drop-down list, select the style of play controls you want for your video.**

   The *skin* is the graphic design of the video play controls. You can infer the characteristics of some skins from their names. For example, the skin named `SkinOverPlaySeekMute.swf` has the play controls placed over the video and include Play, Seek, and Mute buttons. You are probably going to love fooling around choosing your skin — it's so easy. The skin you select in the drop-down list appears as a preview in the pane above the drop-down list.

9. **Click Next (Windows) or Continue (Mac).**

   The Finish Video Import pane appears in the Import Video dialog box, summarizing what happens next, and you may want to make notes on that because unfortunately this information disappears when you click Finish in Step 10. Among other things, this pane tells you where your new FLV file will be located relative to your SWF file.

10. **If you want to change any of your choices, click Go Back. Otherwise, click Finish.**

    When Flash finishes encoding your video, the encoded video and the player controls appear on the Stage. You may find it interesting to compare the file size of your new FLV file to the original video file size. (You can find the new FLV file in the location shown in Step 9.)

11. **Choose Window⇨Component Inspector.**

    The Component inspector appears. If necessary, expand the inspector to its full size.

12. **Click the Parameters tab in the Component inspector and then click the row labeled source.**

    The name of the FLV file is highlighted.

13. **Click the magnifying glass next to the contentPath text box, and the Content Path dialog box appears, as shown in Figure 11-8. Here you can enter the Web address of the final location for your FLV file on your Web server or Flash Media Server.**

    For example, you might type **http://www.helpexamples.com/flash/video/clouds.flv.**

14. **Upload your new FLV file to your Web server, your Flash Media Server, or your Flash Video Streaming Service. Also, upload the video skin you chose in Step 8 — you can find a copy of it on your computer in the same folder as your FLA file.**

    For instance, if you choose SkinOverPlaySeekMute in Step 8, you see a file there called `SkinOverPlaySeekMute.swf`, which you need to upload to your Web server in the same directory as your FLA file. (If you don't upload the skin, the video will still play, but it will have no video playback controls.)

Figure 11-8: Enter the Web address of the FLV file.

15. Choose Control➪Test Movie.

A new window appears showing your Flash movie, and, as shown in Figure 11-9, your video appears with the play controls in the style of the skin you chose in Step 8.

Figure 11-9: An imported video appears with the play controls in the skin style you choose.

16. Use the play controls to play your streaming video.

Your video FLV file plays from within your Flash movie while it downloads from your Web server, your Flash Media Server, or your Flash Video Streaming Service. It probably looks great. This is pretty amazing.

17. Add more elements to your Flash movie if you like.

18. Choose File⇨Publish Settings to choose the settings for your HTML file and SWF file in the Publish Settings dialog box, click Publish, and then click OK.

    Flash creates an HTML file and an SWF file that contains your Flash movie. (See Chapter 13 to find out how to set your publish settings and publish your files.)

19. Upload your HTML file and your SWF file to a Web server.

    For others to see your video, you must upload four elements to the Web: the HTML file and the SWF file that you upload in this step, plus the FLV file and the skin file that you upload in Step 14. The FLV file doesn't need to be hosted at the same site as the other elements, as long as you entered the Web address of the FLV file in Step 13.

Part V
The Movie and the Web

The 5th Wave   By Rich Tennant

"I have to say, I'm really impressed with the interactivity on this car wash Web site."

LOADING...

In this part . . .

*T*he not-so-secret desire of every Flash movie animation is to appear in bright lights on the Web. In this part, we show you how to make that happen. We explain how to put all the pieces together to create a way-cool Flash-only site. You see how to build a Web site that contains a complete navigational system so that viewers can quickly get the information they need. We cover three techniques for creating a complete site.

We also discuss the nitty-gritty details of publishing your Flash movie so a Web browser can display it. Besides the Flash Player file, Flash can create the HTML code you need and the alternative images you might want to use in case a viewer doesn't have the Flash Player. Flash makes it easy: Just specify your settings and click Publish.

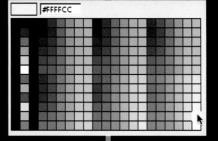

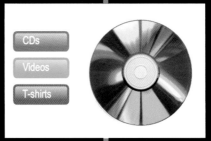

Putting It All Together

*W*hen creating your Flash animation, you need to consider how you will integrate it with your entire Web site. Are you creating a small animation to insert into an existing HyperText Markup Language (HTML) site, or do you want your entire site to be *Flashed?* In this chapter, we cover techniques for creating entire presentations, Web pages, and sites using Flash.

Adding the Power of Components

Components in Flash are built-in, precoded wonders that simplify the creation of interactive Flash movies. Components can be used to add interaction and navigation elements to your Flash movies, allowing you to create surveys, forms, interactive art galleries, or even complete graphical user interfaces for your Flash movies. Among other things, you can also use components (with the help of some fairly sophisticated ActionScript) to access and manipulate data from the Web and other sources.

Flash CS4 ships with more than two dozen ActionScript 2.0 components and more than three dozen ActionScript 3.0 components. You can download more components built by Flash community members by choosing Help⇨Flash Exchange. When you create a Flash document or open an existing one, Flash will display either ActionScript 2.0 components or version 3.0 components in the Components window depending on the document's

ActionScript version. In this book, we focus on ActionScript 3.0 because of its performance improvements and features.

Some of the components that ship with Flash CS4 are

- **RadioButtons:** These let you make one choice from several buttons.

- **CheckBoxes:** You can mark or clear each CheckBox.

- **Buttons:** Clicking one of these makes something happen in your movie. (Button components have more features than button symbols.)

- **ComboBoxes:** These are drop-down lists.

- **Lists:** These are scrolling lists of choices.

- **Video playback controllers:** With these, your audience can start, stop, and adjust the volume of video and audio in your Flash documents.

To add a component to your Flash movie, drag it from the Components panel (see Figure 12-1) onto the Stage.

Components can add significantly to the size of your Flash Player movie, so consider the benefits of including them versus their cost in download time.

In the following sections, we look at how to use several types of components. We skip Button components because button symbols that you make yourself (as described in Chapter 8) are easier to use and usually do everything you need.

Figure 12-1: The Components panel.

Getting ready to work with components

Before you work with any of Flash's components as described in the following sections of this chapter, you need to bring up the Property inspector, the Components panel, and the Parameters tab of the Component inspector. So, to get ready to work with components, you want to do this:

- You'll be typing some ActionScript, so create a layer, perhaps called Actions, where you can place the ActionScript.

- To view the Components panel, if the Components panel is not already visible (either as a separate window or as a tab in a tabbed window), choose Window⇨Components. If the Components panel is docked in a tabbed window with other panels, click the Components tab.

✓ If all the components in a category (for example, the User Interface category) are not displayed in the Components panel, click the plus sign (Windows) or the disclosure triangle (Mac) to the left of the category in the Components panel.

✓ To view the Component inspector, if the Component inspector is not already visible (either as a separate window or as a tab in a tabbed window), choose Window⇨Component Inspector.

✓ To view the Property inspector, if the Property inspector is not already visible (either as a separate window or as a tab in a tabbed window), choose Window⇨Properties.

✓ If the Property inspector is docked in a tabbed window with other panels, click the Properties tab in the tabbed window to make the Property inspector visible.

✓ To view the information on a particular category of properties in the Property inspector, if necessary click the disclosure triangle to the left of the category.

Using RadioButtons in a Flash movie

RadioButtons, shown in Figure 12-2, are groups of buttons that permit you to choose one (and only one) item from the group, like the buttons on a car radio. The following example describes how to create two RadioButtons that display specified text in a dynamic text box.

Figure 12-2: Use RadioButtons to allow the user to choose only one item.

To use a set of RadioButtons in your Flash movie, follow these steps:

1. Decide which elements of your Flash movie will change when a RadioButton is selected; then add those elements to the Flash movie if you haven't already done so.

For example, if you decide that the contents of a dynamic text box will change when a RadioButton is selected, create a dynamic text box on the Stage and give it an instance name, such as *myInfo*. (See Chapter 5 to discover how to create dynamic text.) In the dynamic text box on the Stage, type the initial message you want to display. If you plan to label your RadioButtons *FedEx Air* and *FedEx Ground* with the *FedEx Ground* RadioButton initially selected, you might type the cost of FedEx Ground shipping in the dynamic text box.

2. **Drag two or more RadioButtons from the Components panel onto the Stage.**

You need at least two RadioButtons in every set of RadioButtons for them to work as they're intended. In a Flash movie, when you enable a RadioButton in a set, that button is turned on and all others in the set are turned off.

3. **Select one of the RadioButtons and type a name in the Instance Name field at the top of the Property inspector.**

4. **Repeat Step 3 for each RadioButton, giving each a unique instance name.**

For example, you might give the instance name *option1* to one RadioButton, and the instance name *option2* to another RadioButton.

5. **Select one of the RadioButtons.**

You're going to set its parameters in the next steps.

6. **To change the RadioButton's label, click in the Value field in the Label row of the Parameters tab of the Component inspector, type a new name for the RadioButton (shown in Figure 12-3), and press Enter (Windows) or Return (Mac).**

Figure 12-3: Change a RadioButton's label.

The RadioButton's label changes on the Stage. For example, you could type **FedEx Air** as the label.

In Steps 3 and 4, you give each instance of the RadioButton a name. Here in Step 6, you can change the label near the RadioButton on the Stage. It's helpful to understand that the RadioButton's instance name and the RadioButton's label on the Stage are separate items of information and don't need to be the same.

7. **To change the RadioButton's initial state, click the Selected drop-down list in the Component inspector and select True or False.**

The Selected drop-down list is in the Value field in the Selected row in the Component inspector — it will probably say False by default, but when you click it, a drop-down list of two choices appears.

If you select True, the RadioButton is initially selected. (The RadioButton's circle is filled in.) If you select False, the RadioButton is initially clear.

8. **To change the group to which the RadioButton belongs, type a new name in the Value field in the GroupName row in the Component inspector.**

   For example, you might type **myRadioGroup**. All the RadioButtons with the same group name act as one group. Selecting one RadioButton in the group deselects all the other RadioButtons with the same group name.

9. **To change the position of the RadioButton's label, click in the Value field in the LabelPlacement row in the Component inspector so that the Label Placement drop-down list appears, and make a selection.**

   If you choose top or bottom, you undoubtedly want to type a larger value in the Height box to increase the height of the RadioButton box. The Height (H) box is at the bottom right of the Position and Size section of the Property inspector.

10. **To associate additional information with the RadioButton, enter the information in the Value field in the Value row in the Component inspector.**

    For example, in Step 6 you might label your RadioButtons *FedEx Air* and *FedEx Ground.* Then here in Step 10, in the Value box in the Property inspector for each RadioButton, you could enter the shipping cost for each RadioButton.

11. **Repeat Steps 5 through 10 for each RadioButton.**

12. **Choose Window⇨Actions to open the Actions panel if it isn't open already and in the Actions panel, click the Script Assist button to deselect it (if it's selected).**

    This allows you to type code directly.

13. **Select Frame 1 of your Actions layer in the Timeline and enter the following code in the Script pane of the Actions panel:**

```
import fl.controls.RadioButton;
import flash.text.TextField;
import flash.events.EventDispatcher;
option1.addEventListener(MouseEvent.CLICK,
    myClickHandler);
option2.addEventListener(MouseEvent.CLICK,
    myClickHandler);
function myClickHandler(event:MouseEvent):void {
    myInfo.text = event.target.value;
}
```

You can replace `myClickHandler` with any name that you like. `option1` and `option2` are the instance names of the RadioButtons we use as an example in Step 4, and `myInfo` is the name of the dynamic text field we mention in Step 1.

When the user clicks the FedEx Air RadioButton, the dynamic text box displays the cost for FedEx Air. Likewise, clicking the FedEx Ground radio button displays the cost for FedEx Ground.

Each instruction in ActionScript is called a *statement* and is written with a semicolon at the end. *Function definitions*, by contrast, start with the keyword `function`, followed by the name you give to the function, followed by parentheses that contain the names of any parameters you want to pass to the function, followed by curly brackets that contain one or more statements.

In the first three statements in the preceding code, we import three files to make the application programming interfaces for RadioButtons, text fields, and event listeners available to our Flash movie. Basically, that means we tell our Flash file where to find lots of useful software code that we can call on to easily make our RadioButtons, text fields, and events perform commonly needed tasks.

Statements 4 and 5 in the code connect *event listeners* to the RadioButtons. These event listeners are software instructions that wait for a mouse to click one of the buttons, and they notify Flash when that happens. The code after Statement 5 defines a function that is a click handler so that when you click one of the RadioButtons in `myRadioGroup`, Flash sets the text of the dynamic text field to whatever is in the `value` parameter of the RadioButton that you click.

The following code is an example of how to change the contents of the dynamic text box that we describe in Step 1:

```
myInfo.text = event.target.value;
```

As you learn more ActionScript, you can use RadioButtons to perform entirely different actions, and you can replace this code with other ActionScript code to do something else. For example, the value of the RadioButton could be the name of a frame that the movie would go to when the RadioButton is selected.

Or, for example, if you want to set the text of the dynamic text field to be the label of the RadioButton that you click, replace this statement:

```
myInfo.text = event.target.value;
```

with this statement:

```
myInfo.text = event.target.label;
```

When you look at the preceding code, you may be thinking, "Huh?" But it's possible to do a lot of coding in Flash without getting a PhD in ActionScriptology first. You can accomplish a lot by copying existing code, playing with it, and observing the effect.

Using CheckBoxes in a Flash movie

CheckBoxes are square boxes that you can check or uncheck to indicate that an option is selected or deselected. Unlike RadioButtons, more than one CheckBox can be selected at a time.

The following steps describe an example of using CheckBoxes that display a movie clip for each checked box:

1. **Decide which elements of your Flash movie will change when a CheckBox is selected; then add those elements to the Flash movie if you haven't already done so.**

   For example, perhaps you made movie clips of a cat, a tree, and a field, and you want to use CheckBoxes so that users can choose as many or as few as they like. And let's say that you named the instances *cat, tree,* and *field* and the CheckBoxes `catBox`, `treeBox`, and `fieldBox`.

2. **Drag a CheckBox from the Components panel onto the Stage.**

3. **To change the CheckBox's label, click the Value field in the Label row of the Component inspector, type a new name for the CheckBox, and press Enter (Windows) or Return (Mac).**

   The CheckBox's label changes on the Stage.

4. **To change the CheckBox's initial state, click the Value field in the Selected row in the Component inspector and select True or False in the drop-down list that appears.**

   If you choose True, the CheckBox is initially marked. If you choose False, the CheckBox is initially cleared.

5. **To change the CheckBox's label placement, click the Value field in the LabelPlacement row in the Component inspector (as shown in Figure 12-4) and make a selection in the drop-down list that appears.**

6. **To give the CheckBox an instance name, type a name in the Instance Name field in the Property inspector.**

Figure 12-4: Changing the CheckBox's label placement.

You can enter **myCheckBox** (or **treeBox** or **catBox** or **fieldBox**).

7. **Repeat Steps 2 through 6 for each CheckBox that you want to make.**

8. **Choose Window⇨Actions to open the Actions panel if it isn't open already. In the Actions panel, click the Script Assist button to deselect it (if it's selected).**

   This allows you to type code directly.

9. **Select Frame 1 of your Actions layer in the Timeline and enter the following code in the Script pane of the Actions panel:**

```
import fl.controls.CheckBox;
import flash.display.DisplayObject;
import flash.events.EventDispatcher;
tree.visible = false;
cat.visible = false;
field.visible = false;
treeBox.addEventListener(MouseEvent.CLICK, seeTree);
catBox.addEventListener(MouseEvent.CLICK, seeCat);
fieldBox.addEventListener(MouseEvent.CLICK, seeField);
function seeTree(event:MouseEvent):void {
    tree.visible = event.target.selected;
    }
function seeCat(event:MouseEvent):void {
    cat.visible = event.target.selected;
    }
function seeField(event:MouseEvent):void {
    field.visible = event.target.selected;
    }
```

You can replace `seeTree`, `seeCat`, and `seeField` with any names you like. In this example `tree`, `cat`, and `field` are the instance names of your movie clips, and `treeBox`, `catBox`, and `fieldBox` are the instance names of the CheckBoxes. (For information on how to create instances of movie clips, see Chapter 7.)

Statements 1, 2, and 3 in the code import three files to make the application programming interfaces for CheckBoxes, object visibility, and event listeners available to our Flash movie. Statements 4, 5, and 6 make the CheckBoxes for the tree, cat, and field invisible. Statements 7, 8, and 9 add an event listener to each of the three CheckBoxes so that when you select one of the CheckBoxes, Flash executes the corresponding function `seeTree`, `seeCat`, or `seeField`. These three functions are defined in the last lines of the code. As a result, when the user checks the `tree` CheckBox, for example, the `Tree` movie clip appears.

An *event listener* is a little bit of code that checks for events that may be connected to a particular object in your Flash movie (such as our CheckBoxes here) and performs a specified function when they occur. Picture an event listener as a tiny dedicated spy or ear always waiting to hear one particular click.

Using ComboBoxes in a Flash movie

A *ComboBox* is a text box that shows the current selection, combined with a drop-down list of alternate selections. The following example describes how to create a ComboBox that displays the item chosen from a list in a dynamic text box:

1. **Decide what elements of your Flash movie will change when a menu item in the ComboBox is selected. Add those elements to the Flash movie if you haven't already done so.**

   For example, if you decide that the contents of a dynamic text box will change when a menu item in the ComboBox is selected, create a dynamic text box on the Stage and give it an instance name, such as *myInfo2*. (See Chapter 5 to discover how to create dynamic text.) In the dynamic text box on the Stage, type the initial message you want to display. If you plan to change the name of each menu item to the name of a different kind of dance maneuver, you might type "Your dance: Charleston" in the dynamic text box if that's the first dance on your list.

2. **Drag a ComboBox from the Components panel onto the Stage.**

3. **In the Instance Name box at the top of the Property inspector, type a name.**

   For example, type the name **myComboBox**.

4. **To control whether the user can edit the items in the ComboBox's menu list, select True or False from the drop-down list in the Value field of the Editable row of the Component inspector.**

   Selecting True allows the user to rename each item on the menu list. Selecting False prevents that from happening.

5. **To create items in the menu list:**

   a. *Double-click the Value text box in the dataProvider row in the Component inspector.*

   A dialog box appears, as shown in Figure 12-5.

   b. *In the dialog box, click the plus sign to add a menu item or click the minus sign to delete a menu item.*

   When you add a menu item to the list, it is excitingly named *label0, label1, label2,* and so on

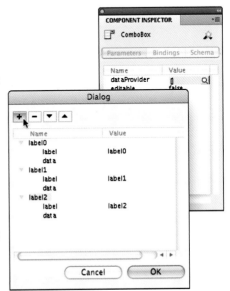

Figure 12-5: Add items in a ComboBox's menu list.

    c. Click the upward-pointing triangle to move an item up the list and click the downward-pointing triangle to move a menu item down the list.

6. **To change a menu item's name from** *label0* **(or** *label1* **or** *label2* **and so on) to something more interesting and meaningful, click the menu item's Value input box in the menu item's Label row and type a more useful name there.**

   For example, you might change the name of each menu item to the name of a different kind of dance maneuver, such as Charleston, Fox Trot, Twist, or Mashed Potato.

7. **Click OK.**

   The dialog box closes.

8. **To change the number of items that can be displayed in the ComboBox without a scroll bar, click the Value field in the Row Count row in the Component inspector and type a new number.**

   The default number is 5.

9. **If you want to make the ComboBox wider so that longer menu items are more readable, choose Modify⇨Transform⇨Scale and pull the handles that appear on the ComboBox's borders.**

10. **Choose Window⇨Actions to open the Actions panel if it isn't open already. In the Actions panel, click the Script Assist button to deselect it (if it's selected).**

    When Script Assist is turned off, you can type ActionScript code directly.

11. **Select Frame 1 of your Actions layer in the Timeline and enter the following code in the Script pane of the Actions panel:**

    ```
    import fl.controls.ComboBox;
    import flash.display.DisplayObject;
    import flash.events.EventDispatcher;
    myComboBox.addEventListener(Event.CHANGE, danceChosen);
    function danceChosen(e:Event):void {
      myInfo2.text = "Your dance: ";
      myInfo2.appendText(myComboBox.selectedItem.label);
          }
    ```

    You can replace danceChosen in the preceding code with any name you like. myComboBox in this example is the instance name of your ComboBox that we mention in Step 3, and myInfo2 is the name of the dynamic text field described in Step 1.

In the preceding code in the definition of the function danceChosen, the two statements that change the text in myInfo2 make the label of the ComboBox appear in the text box.

You could replace these statements with different statements in this function for a different result. For example, you might instead use some ActionScript code that sets the Flash playhead to move to different frame labels in different sections of the Flash movie that correspond to the selected label in the ComboBox.

The first three statements in the preceding code import three files so that the application programming interfaces for ComboBoxes, object visibility, and event listeners are available to our Flash movie. The fourth statement adds an event listener to `myComboBox` so that when you select a menu item in `myComboBox`, the statements in the function `danceChosen` set the text of the dynamic text field to the label of the ComboBox menu item that the viewer selects.

When the user chooses a dance from the list, that dance appears in the dynamic text box. Because the function inserts *You chose:* before the text, the result might be *You chose: Mashed Potato.*

The dance only appears in the dynamic text box if in Step 4 you select False from the drop-down list in the Value field of the Editable row of the Component inspector, so that the user can't rename each item on the menu list. That is probably by far the most common use of the ComboBox. Otherwise the code gets more complicated, which is a bit beyond the scope of this chapter.

If things aren't working when you test your ComboBox, the ActionScript code you typed may contain typos or other errors. Flash often reports these errors in the Compiler Errors panel when you choose Control➪Test Movie. The error messages in the Compiler Errors window may seem obscure, but they can give you an idea of where your problem may be.

Using Lists in a Flash movie

A *List* component in Flash is a scrollable list of selectable items. In the following example, we show you how to create a list that displays the chosen value in a dynamic text box, as shown in Figure 12-6. To use list components in your Flash movie, follow these steps:

1. **Decide which elements of your Flash movie will change when a viewer selects a menu item in the list. Add those elements to the Flash movie if you haven't already done so.**

   Figure 12-6: The three items in this list were created by the three ActionScript statements that call the addItem method.

   For example, if you decide that the contents of a dynamic text box will change when a list item is selected, create a dynamic text box on the Stage and give it an instance name, such as *myInfo3*. (See Chapter 5 to discover how to create dynamic text.)

2. **Drag a list from the Components panel onto the Stage.**

3. In the Instance Name text field at the top of the Property inspector, type a name.

   For example, name the instance *myList*.

4. In the Selection Width field (labeled W) in the Position and Size section of the Property inspector, type a number to change the List box's width, if desired.

   The width should be wide enough to show the desired text. For example, you might want a width of 300 pixels.

5. Choose Window➪Actions to open the Actions panel if it isn't open already. In the Actions panel, click the Script Assist button to deselect it (if it's selected).

6. Select Frame 1 of your Actions layer in the Timeline and enter this code in the Script pane of the Actions panel:

```
import fl.controls.List;
import flash.text.TextField;
import flash.events.EventDispatcher;
myList.addItem({label:"iAXE", data:99});
myList.addItem({label:"Switch Stealth", data: 199});
myList.addItem({label:"Fender Telecaster", data:399});
myList.addEventListener(Event.CHANGE, showPrice);
function showPrice(event:Event) {
    myInfo3.text = "This guitar is priced at: $" +
    event.target.selectedItem.data;
}
```

The labels and data in the `myList.addItem` statements are inside curly brackets that are inside parentheses.

You can replace `showPrice` with any name you like. `myList` in this example is the instance name of your list, described in Step 3, and `myInfo3` is the name of the dynamic text field that we mention in Step 1.

In this example, we use ActionScript to create three list items (as shown in Figure 12-6). However, if you prefer you can instead manually create the list items in the Property inspector. In that case, you don't need to type the fourth, fifth, and sixth statements in the preceding code. To manually create the list items, fill out the list in the way described in Steps 5 through 7 in the preceding section "Using ComboBoxes in a Flash movie."

The first three statements in the preceding code import three files so that the application programming interfaces for List boxes, text fields, and event listeners are available to our Flash movie.

In the next three statements, we use ActionScript to add three guitars to the list. The seventh statement adds an event listener to `myList` that "listens" for a viewer selecting a menu item in `myList`. When the viewer selects one of the menu items, the event listener performs the `showPrice` function, which is defined in the next lines of code. showPrice sets the text of the dynamic text field to This guitar is priced at $, with whatever dollar value is stored in the data field of the list menu item that the viewer selects. You can replace the statement in the showPrice function with other ActionScript code to do other things with the selected values.

Creating a Preloader

If you're ambitious and create a huge Flash file, downloading it to a viewer's browser might take a long time. Your audience won't wait forever. To solve this problem, you can create a *preloader*, which is a tiny movie that loads quickly and tells your viewers to wait.

Creating a nice preloader with ActionScript 3.0 may require more lines of fancy ActionScript code than you may want to deal with if you're new to Flash. For now, you might want to start out with a simple preloader that you can create by following these steps:

1. **Assuming that you've already created your main movie, choose Window➪Other Panels➪ Scene. In the Scene panel, click the Add Scene icon at the bottom left of the Scene panel to add a scene. Drag it above the scene of your main movie. Rename it *preloader*.**

   See Chapter 9 for creating and changing the order of scenes.

2. **In the first scene (the preloader), create a movie clip and put into the movie clip whatever you want your audience to see while the rest of your movie loads, as shown in Figure 12-7.**

Figure 12-7: A preloader animation is useful for inspiring your audience to stick around, by informing them that the movie is loading.

Keep this movie clip simple so that it loads quickly. You might, for example, create a simple, attractive animation that informs the audience that the movie is loading.

3. **If you haven't already placed your movie clip on the Stage of the preloader scene, choose Window⇨Library to open the Library, if it isn't already open, and drag an instance of the movie clip from the Library onto the Stage.**

4. **Choose Control⇨Test Movie to view your movie.**

   Flash loops the movie clip in your preloader scene so that it plays over and over until your main movie is loaded.

When you test your preloader by choosing Control⇨Test Movie, your main movie might load so quickly that you don't even see the preloader. Choose View⇨Simulate Download in the Flash Player window to see how your preloader works while your main movie loads. (See Chapter 13 for more information on testing a movie and analyzing its download performance.) You can also upload your file to a test page on your Web site to see how the preloader works. Make sure that your preloader is long enough for the human eye to see. Remember that one frame is displayed for only a fraction of a second.

Creating an Entire Web Site with Flash

You can use Flash to create your site's complete user interface, along with all the graphics and text. Some Web sites are almost 100 percent Flash (see www.madeinmtl.com, a beautiful Web site for tourists and other explorers of Montreal). Most Web sites with Flash (including www.adobe.com) are a hybrid of Flash and HTML. A Flash Web site may have the following structure:

⯈ An HTML home page that contains the following:

• A user interface (and perhaps other graphics) built into Flash.

• Tests that detect the Flash Player and Player version. (This is provided by default when you publish your Flash movie — see the "Testing for the Flash Player" section later in this chapter.)

• Alternate HTML content for viewers who don't have Flash, and a button that viewers can use to get the Flash Player if they want, as described in the section "Creating alternative sites" later in this chapter.

⯈ Additional HTML pages that, like the home page, utilize a user interface (and other graphics) built into Flash, for all the remaining pages in the Web site. You might want each of these pages to also test for Flash, in case your viewers don't enter the site through your home page.

✓ HTML pages that contain a non-Flash version of the Web site, if you want the site to be available to those who don't have and don't want to install the required version of Flash.

If you create your entire Web site out of one big Flash file, your users can't use their browsers' Back buttons to navigate back and forth through your Flash movie. An advantage of creating multiple HTML pages with Flash on each page is that the browser's Back button still works.

Your opening HTML page is usually the first thing your viewers see and may be the most important page on your site, so be sure to think carefully about your goals for this page. You may want to put lots of useful information or other important material on your home page so that your viewers quickly see that your site is worth exploring.

To match the color of a Flash movie in a Web page to the rest of the page, match the background colors of the movie (by choosing Modify⇨ Document) and the HTML page, as shown in Figure 12-8. (This technique doesn't work if your Web page uses an image for a background.)

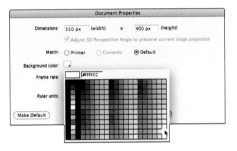

Figure 12-8: Matching the background color of the movie to the rest of the Web page.

Your site probably contains buttons that people can use to navigate through your site, get more information, or contact you. You can create the navigation structure in many ways. Here are three:

✓ Attach event listeners to buttons to trigger the display of movie clips or Flash Player movies (.swf files). See Chapter 10 for an example of a button that plays a movie clip.

✓ Use buttons to trigger the navigateToURL function, to link to other HTML pages on your site. You can, of course, create the HTML pages with Flash. We explain how to do this in the next section.

✓ Use buttons to display information or graphics located on other parts of your Timeline by using the gotoAndPlay or gotoAndStop function. We discuss this option in the upcoming "Using the Timeline to store Web content" section.

You can use combinations of these techniques. For example, you can use an event listener to display information when the mouse cursor is over a button, and you can use an event listener and the navigateToURL function to link to another page when the user clicks the button.

Creating navigation with navigateToURL

Use an event listener to trigger a `navigateToURL` function from a button so the button links to another HTML page. See Chapter 8 to find out how to add an event listener to a button to trigger the `navigateToURL` function.

Using the Timeline to store Web content

In most cases, you use the Timeline to display frames in sequence — in other words, animation. But the Timeline can also store static frames. Create anything on the Stage in those frames and display what is in those frames whenever you want. Use ActionScript to jump to a frame based on a user interaction and stop there until the next user interaction. Different frames on the Timeline can become the equivalent of separate Web pages.

Suppose that you have several buttons on the left side of your page. You want viewers to see different graphics and animation on the right side of the page when they roll the mouse over each button. Perhaps rolling over one button displays a product description and rolling over another button displays a description of a second product.

To create a set of buttons that move the playhead to different sections of the Timeline, follow these steps:

1. **Place instances of your buttons on one side of the Stage (for example, the left side, as shown in Figure 12-9), in separate layers on the first frame of the Timeline of your movie.**

2. **Open the Property inspector if it isn't already open. (Choose Window⇨Properties.)**

3. **Create a new layer and give it a name, such as *Product Views*.**

4. **A few frames out (on Frame 10, for example) on the Product Views layer, create a keyframe.**

5. **In the Name text box in the Label section of the Property inspector, type a label name.**

   In this example, name the frame labels *myFrameLabel1*, *myFrameLabel2*, and so on.

Figure 12-9: Each button will move the playhead to a different section of the Timeline.

6. On the Stage, create graphics and words for the product description or whatever you want displayed when a user rolls the mouse over the first button.

   If you want to display animation when a user rolls over the first button, drag a movie clip from the Library. (Check out Chapter 7 for the scoop on creating movie clips.)

   Place the graphics so that they don't cover the buttons when the graphics appear.

7. Repeat Steps 4 through 6 to create a label and a product description on the Product Views layer for each button, on a new keyframe that is later on the Timeline each time.

   At each new keyframe, delete the previous content, and then add what you want to display for the new product description.

8. Select a button.

9. In the Instance Name text box at the top of the Property inspector, type a unique instance name for the button.

   In this example, name the buttons *myButton1, myButton2*, and so on.

10. Repeat Steps 8 and 9 for each button.

11. On each layer that contains a button, add a keyframe at the same time on the Timeline as the keyframe for the last product description.

    Now your buttons will stay visible when each product description is displayed.

12. Create a new layer and give it a name, such as *myCode.*

13. Open the Actions panel. (Choose Window⇨Actions.) In the Actions panel, click the Script Assist button to deselect it (if it's selected).

14. Select Frame 1 in the myCode layer in the Timeline and enter the following code in the Script pane of the Actions panel:

    ```
    this.stop();
    ```

If you don't do this, your movie simply plays through all the frames, displaying your product descriptions one after another. But you want viewers to see a particular product description only when they roll over a particular button.

15. Select Frame 1 in the myCode layer in the Timeline and enter this additional code in the Script pane of the Actions panel:

    ```
    function menuChoice1(event:MouseEvent):void
    {
        this.gotoAndStop("myFrameLabel1");
    }
    myButton1.addEventListener(MouseEvent.ROLL_OVER,
        menuChoice1);
    ```

`myButton1` is the instance name of the first button that you created in Step 4, and `myFrameLabel1` is the name of the first frame label you created in Step 9.

In the preceding code, `menuChoice` is defined as a function that moves the playhead of the Timeline of the current movie to the `myFrameLabel1` frame and stops. After the function definition is the statement that connects an event listener that "listens" for a rollover to the button that has the instance name `myButton1`. When the mouse rolls over the button, the event listener calls the function `menuChoice1`.

16. **Select Frame 1 in the myCode layer in the Timeline and enter this additional code in the Script pane of the Actions panel:**

```
function menuChoice2(event:MouseEvent):void
{
    this.gotoAndStop("myFrameLabel2");
}
myButton2.addEventListener(MouseEvent.ROLL_OVER,
    menuChoice2);
```

This code connects the second button that you made to an event listener and an event handler.

17. **For each additional button that you made, repeat Step 16 to add more code to Frame 1 in the myCode layer in the Timeline. Substitute the new button's instance name for myButton2. Substitute the new destination frame's label for myFrameLabel2. And substitute a new function name for menuChoice2.**

18. **Choose Control⇨Test Movie to try it out!**

When you roll over a button, the graphics, text, and movie clip animation on the appropriate frame appear.

Figure 12-10 shows a Timeline with frames that are displayed when the mouse cursor passes over buttons. If you use `CLICK` rather than `ROLL_OVER` in Steps 15 and 16, you can display different information when the mouse clicks each button.

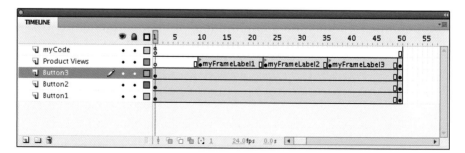

Figure 12-10: When the user moves the mouse over each button, the movie will jump to a different Frame Label on the Timeline.

You can build on this further by, for example, sending the user back to the first frame when the mouse rolls off the button — like this:

```
function menuChoice1A(event:MouseEvent):void
{
    this.gotoAndStop(1);
}
myButton1.addEventListener(MouseEvent.ROLL_OUT[0],
            menuChoice1[0]A);
```

Notice that the new function is named `menuChoice1A` (not `menuChoice1`). It's important that the new function has a new name. For each state of each button, you can add a different function and a different `EventListener`.

Testing for the Flash Player

Although more than 98 percent of the world's Web surfing population reportedly has the Flash Player installed, that's still not everyone, and some have fairly old versions of the Flash Player. For viewers who don't have the Flash Player, it often downloads automatically (as a result of the code that Flash places in the HTML file when you publish your SWF and HTML files, as we describe in Chapter 13). If Flash doesn't download automatically, those users might not be able to view your site.

You can test for the presence of the Flash Player and, perhaps more important, you can test to see which version of the Flash Player they have. If you're using features that exist only in Flash CS4, make sure that viewers have Flash Player 10, because many people might still have Flash Player 9 (or an even earlier version) installed.

Detecting the Flash Player version

You may detect a particular Flash Player version by simply selecting the Detect Flash Version check box in the HTML tab in Flash's Publish Settings before you publish your movie. (See Chapter 13 for specifying Publish Settings.) This does a great job of detecting a particular Flash Player version.

Then when your Web page comes up in a Web browser, if the Flash Player of the specified version can't be found or if the Web browser doesn't have scripting enabled, the resulting HTML code displays the sentence `Alternate HTML content should be placed here` on your Web page. Edit the HTML to replace that sentence with whatever content you want to display.

Creating alternative sites

This alternative HTML content could consist of HTML code for a page in a series of HTML-only, non-Flash pages, if you feel that your audience needs it. Some Flash sites include a complete set of non-Flash (HTML) pages for viewers who don't have the Flash Player and don't want to download it.

If you use features unique to Flash Player 10, you can also create, for example, a Flash 9 site that uses only features available in Flash 9. The overwhelming majority of Web surfers have Flash Player 9 or later. But don't forget how much time you spend updating your Web site now. Imagine updating two or three sites! Make sure you think carefully about who your audience is and the consequences of having so many alternatives.

For detailed information on how many computer users have which versions of the Flash player, check out the latest statistics at www.adobe.com/products/player_census/flashplayer/version_penetration.html. You may be surprised by the statistics.

Using the Movie Explorer

The Movie Explorer is a great tool for analyzing an entire movie. When you start creating complex relationships among several Timelines, you might have trouble remembering what you've done. The Movie Explorer lays out the entire structure of your movie for you to see. The Movie Explorer is also a great tool for troubleshooting problems. By visually displaying your movie's components, you can more easily find where the trouble lies.

Another use for the Movie Explorer is to analyze other people's FLA files. When you open someone else's Flash file, you might wonder where all the action is. It might all be hidden in movie clips and ActionScript that calls other movies and movie clips. The Movie Explorer can help you ferret out the magic behind the animation.

To open the Movie Explorer, choose Window⇨Movie Explorer. The Movie Explorer is shown in Figure 12-11.

Figure 12-11: Explore with the Movie Explorer.

You usually know what you're looking for when you open the Movie Explorer. For example, you might be looking for ActionScript or movie clips. Use the buttons at the top of the Movie Explorer to specify which movie elements are shown in the main window:

- ✓ **Show Text:** Displays all text objects in the movie.

- ✓ **Show Buttons, Movie Clips, and Graphics:** Displays a list of those objects.

- ✓ **Show Action Scripts:** Lists all ActionScript in the movie.

- ✓ **Show Video, Sounds, and Bitmaps:** Lists those objects.

- ✓ **Show Frames and Layers:** Shows each frame and each layer that contains objects.

- ✓ **Customize Which Items to Show:** Opens the Movie Explorer Settings dialog box, where you can indicate which items you want to display by selecting or deselecting them in a list of check boxes. You can also choose to display Movie Elements (showing the elements of your movie organized by scene), Symbol Definitions (a separate listing by symbol), or both. Click OK to close this dialog box.

Movie elements are shown in a hierarchical manner in the Movie Explorer. For example, if a frame has an action attached to it, you see a plus sign (Windows) or a disclosure triangle (Mac) next to the button. Click any plus sign or right-pointing triangle to expand the display — in this case, to reveal the ActionScript attached to that frame. Click any minus sign (Windows) or downward-pointing triangle (Mac) to collapse the display.

In the Find text box, you can type any expression to search the entire movie. Suppose that you want to know whether a movie contains the `navigateToURL` action. Just type **navigateToURL** in the Find text box, and the Movie Explorer displays every instance containing that word.

The Find feature is not case sensitive, but the Find feature is sensitive to spaces. So if the movie contains *navigateToURL* and you type **navigate To URL**, you don't get any results.

You can use the Movie Explorer to select objects on the Stage or frames. Just click the item in the Movie Explorer, and Flash selects the object or frame. (If you select a frame, Flash also includes the frames up to the next keyframe.) If you select a scene, Flash selects the first frame of the scene.

The Movie Explorer contains an extensive menu that you can access by clicking in the upper-right corner of the Movie Explorer panel, or you can right-click (Windows) or Control+click (Mac) inside the Movie Explorer panel.

Some of the more useful features of this menu follow:

- **Show in Library:** Opens the Library (if it isn't already open) and highlights the object that you previously selected in the Movie Explorer.

- **Rename:** Lets you rename the selected object, such as a button instance.

- **Copy All Text to Clipboard:** Copies all the text in the Movie Explorer to the Clipboard so you can paste it into another application.

- **Print:** Prints the entire contents of the Movie Explorer. All items, whether collapsed or expanded, are printed.

If you have difficulty understanding one of the more advanced Flash files from the resource Web sites that we recommend in Chapter 15, try opening the Movie Explorer. Look for actions and movie clips. You might be surprised at what you can discover by using this tool.

Making Your Site More Accessible

Flash includes capabilities that make it possible for you to make Flash more accessible to people with disabilities. Most components in Flash CS4 are designed to be accessible to the visually impaired via *screen readers,* which generate spoken descriptions of the contents of your Flash screens. Screen reader software is widely available from a variety of companies.

Users can also navigate most of Flash's components by using the keyboard rather than the mouse — this is automatically built into the components. And ActionScript has features that can enhance the accessibility of Flash documents.

One of the easiest ways to make your Flash movie more accessible to people with disabilities is to use the Accessibility panel. When you add buttons, movie clips, text fields, input text fields, or components to your movie, you can use the Accessibility panel to make them accessible to screen readers. (Not all components can be made accessible, but most can.) To make a button, movie clip, Dynamic Text field, Input Text field, or component accessible, follow these steps.

1. **Open the Accessibility panel. (Choose Window⇨Other Panels⇨ Accessibility.)**

2. **Select the button, movie clip, Dynamic Text field, Input Text field, or component on the Stage.**

3. **In the Accessibility panel, select Make Object Accessible, as shown in Figure 12-12.**

4. **If you selected a movie clip in Step 2 and you want objects embedded in the movie clip to also be accessible, select the Make Child Objects Accessible check box.**

   For example, select the Make Child Objects Accessible check box if you want to allow text objects in the movie clip to be read by the screen reader software.

5. **In the Name box, type a name for the symbol or component.**

   The screen reader can read this name aloud.

Figure 12-12: The Accessibility panel.

6. **In the Description box, type a description of the symbol or component.**

   The screen reader can read this description aloud.

7. **In the Shortcut box, type a keyboard shortcut that viewers can use to select the object, if appropriate.**

   For instance, if the object is a RadioButton that needs to be selected to receive input, follow this step.

   The screen reader can then use this information to read aloud something like, "The shortcut for this text field is Ctrl+K." (Not all screen readers support this feature.) Typing information in the Shortcut box doesn't actually implement keyboard shortcut functionality. You need to use ActionScript to detect and respond to any shortcut key presses.

8. **In the Tab Index box, you may enter the number corresponding to the object's tab index value, if appropriate.**

   The *tab index* determines how users can use the Tab key to navigate and select the buttons, check boxes, and other controls in your movie. For example, suppose you have three buttons with a tab index of 1, 2, and 3, respectively. When the movie starts, if the user presses the Tab key three times, the button with the tab index of 3 would be selected for input.

If you have the Accessibility panel open when nothing in your movie is selected, the panel offers you the option to Make Movie Accessible, which is selected by default. This allows screen readers to read the different objects in the Flash movie. You definitely want this option selected if you want to make your movie accessible to screen readers and other hardware and software for people with disabilities. Of course, you also have to use the Accessibility panel to name each object for this to be useful.

13

Publishing Your Flash Files

*W*hen your Flash movie is completed, you need to publish it in its final form — most likely an SWF file that you can post on your Web site. In this chapter, we explain how to prepare a Flash movie for publishing and help you determine the ideal publish settings for your needs. We also discuss how to publish to other graphic file formats, such as PNG, in case you want to create a non-Flash site or use your material in another program. We cover all the bases so that you can get your animation up and running.

The filenames of Flash-published movies end with the .swf suffix. The letters SWF originally stood for Shockwave Flash, but nobody uses that term for Flash movies anymore, even though the letters remain the same. So we refer to SWF files as Flash Player files, not Shockwave Flash files.

Flash converts your movie data into a highly compact and efficient form in an SWF file; the SWF file contains only the information needed for playback of your movies. In contrast, when you save your movies by choosing File⇨Save (or File⇨Save As), they are saved with the .fla suffix. They are saved in a format that can be read by the Flash CS4 application, but not the Flash Player. The FLA file contains lots of information about layers, Library items, your video source files, and so on, which you need when you are creating your movies and which the Flash Player doesn't need.

Optimizing Movies for Fast Download

Throughout this book, we offer suggestions for designing a Flash movie with speedy downloading in mind. In this section, we put the suggestions together so that you can review your movie as a whole before you publish it.

Reducing your Flash Player file sizes is no longer so important because many people now have high-speed Internet connections. But not everyone does. So it still isn't a bad idea to spend a little time thinking about shrinking the size of your Flash movies.

Simplifying artwork

By simplifying the artwork in your movie, you can greatly reduce the size of a Flash movie, thereby increasing its speed. Here are the most important techniques:

- **Use symbols for every object that appears more than once.** You can turn any object or group of objects into a symbol. Nest your symbols — for example, turn an object into a symbol and then use it in a movie clip or button. Remember that you can change the color of symbol instances — you don't need to create a new symbol. (Chapter 7 covers symbols in detail.)

- **Group objects whenever possible.** Groups are almost as efficient as symbols. (Chapter 4 explains how to create groups.)

- **Use vector graphics rather than bitmaps when you can.** When you do use bitmaps, don't animate them unless you need to. Bitmaps and bitmap animation can increase your Flash Player file size and thus the download time. However, with the rising adoption of broadband Internet access, bitmaps are an increasingly important part of Flash projects, including the sites referred to in this book, and now Photoshop files can easily be imported into Flash. (Chapter 3 explains how to import a bitmap.)

- **Optimize curves.** (Choose Modify⇨Shape⇨Optimize.) You can optimize curves to reduce the number of lines used to create a shape. This can be tiresome on a large project, but if you really need to reduce the size of your Flash movie, this may help. (Check out Chapter 4 for further explanation.)

- **Use solid lines rather than dashed, dotted, and other line types when possible.** Try to avoid custom line widths. (We explain line types in Chapter 3.)

- **Use the Pencil tool rather than the Brush tool whenever possible.** The Pencil tool uses fewer bytes in your movie.

✏ **Use the Web-safe color palette.** Avoid custom colors. (Check out Chapter 3 for the lowdown on colors.) Custom color definitions are kept with the Flash Player file.

✏ **Avoid using transparency when you don't need it.** Using transparency doesn't make your Flash file bigger, but it can slow down playback because of the extra calculation required. (On the other hand, sometimes transparency effects make your movie look really great.) See Chapter 7 to find out about changing the transparency of the elements in your movie.

✏ **Use solid fills rather than gradients.** Gradients are more complex and make the Flash Player file bigger. However, gradients are also key to the Flash look that is so popular. They help to make vector graphics look less flat.

Optimizing text

Text can consume lots of bytes. Here's what you can do to reduce the byte bite:

✏ **Reduce the number of fonts and font styles (bold, italic) as much as possible.** Use simpler sans serif fonts if you can. You get the best results file-size-wise with the device fonts (sans, serif, and typewriter), although you might find these device fonts boring. Flash doesn't need to store the outlines of device fonts in the SWF file, so these take up fewer bytes. And usually your Flash projects will look better if you don't use too many fonts — avoid using more than two or three fonts in a design, as suggested in Figure 13-1. (See Chapter 5 for more information on fonts.)

Figure 13-1: If you use more than two or three fonts, people may start to think that you're designing a ransom note.

✔ If you create input text fields or dynamic text fields, limit the text and specify any restrictions that you can in the Character Embedding dialog box (shown in Figure 13-2). Choose Window⇨Properties to open the Property inspector if it's not already open, and then (if necessary) click the disclosure triangle to the left of Character in the Property inspector to reveal the Character pane. Then click the Character Embedding button. See Chapter 5 for more info on character embedding. For example, exclude unnecessary character outlines, such as numbers.

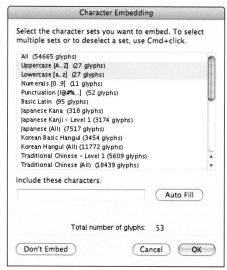

Figure 13-2: Select the character sets you want to embed in your Flash movie.

Compressing sound

You can compress sounds to reduce the file size. When you compress individual sounds in the Sound Properties dialog box, as shown in Figure 13-3, you can fine-tune settings for each individual sound in your movie. Later in this chapter, we review how to compress sound when you publish a Flash movie. Use the MP3 format whenever possible because it compresses well. If you need more information on compressing sounds, check out Chapter 11.

Here are some other ways that you can reduce the size of your sound files:

✔ Adjust the sound's Time In and Time Out points to prevent silent areas from being stored in your SWF file.

✔ Reuse sounds by using different In and Out points and by looping different parts of the same sound.

✔ Don't loop streaming sound.

See Chapter 11 for more information on editing, looping, and streaming sound.

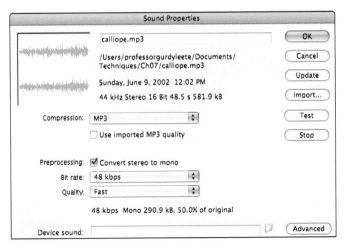

Figure 13-3: Fine-tune the compression settings for each sound in your movie here.

Animating efficiently

One of the most effective ways to reduce file size is to use tweens. (See Chapter 9 for details on this animation technique.) Frame-by-frame animation creates larger files. Keeping animation localized in one area also helps. Small animations (animations where the objects don't move much) produce smaller file sizes than wide-area animations.

Testing Movies

Before publishing your movie, you should test it. The first step is to simply play your animation, as we explain in Chapter 9. But playing the animation on the Stage doesn't provide you with enough information to determine problems caused by file size. To find those kinds of bugs, you have to use the Test Movie command or test your movie in a browser. The following sections tell you how to test both ways.

Flash CS4 is optimized for the tasks that you perform when creating a Flash movie (such as drawing, adding keyframes, showing and hiding layers, and typing ActionScript code). It's not optimized for playing back your animation — the Flash Player is optimized for that. Your FLA file contains lots of information that you need when you're creating your movies — but that the Flash Player doesn't need. The Flash Player plays only SWF files, which you can create when you choose File➪Publish.

Using the Test Movie command

After playing your animation, you should use the Test Movie or Test Scene command. Then you can use the Bandwidth Profiler (and other tools described in the following steps) to provide estimates of downloading speed so you can find bottlenecks that pause your animation. You can also see the results of movie clips and all ActionScript code.

If you're using movie clips, they won't play when you choose Control⇨Play. To see them play you must choose Control⇨Test Movie or Control⇨Test Scene.

To test a movie or scene, follow these steps:

1. **Choose Control⇨Test Movie (or Test Scene).**

   Flash publishes your movie to an SWF file by using the current settings in the Publish Settings dialog box (see the section "Publishing Flash Movies" later in this chapter) and opens a new window. You see your animation run. You can change the settings in the Publish Settings dialog box (choose File⇨Publish Settings) before using this command.

2. **Choose View⇨Download Settings and choose a downloading speed between that of a 14.4 modem (1.2 Kbps) to a T1 line (131.2 Kbps).**

   If you repeatedly change the download settings, you get a better sense of their effect. To specify your own settings, choose Customize, and in the Custom Modem Settings dialog box, enter the menu text that you want to appear on the menu and the bit rate in bytes per second. Click OK. Then open the Download Settings menu again and choose your customized setting, which now appears on the menu.

3. **Choose View⇨Bandwidth Profiler to see the graph that shows the downloading performance.**

   The bandwidth profiler (as shown in Figure 13-4) displays the byte size of each individual frame. Frames whose bars rise above the lower red horizontal line cause loading delays.

4. **To see settings for any one frame, stop the movie by clicking the frame's bar.**

   To the left of the bandwidth profiler, Flash displays the movie's statistics: dimensions, frame rate, file size, movie duration, and the amount of animation to preload in frames and seconds. You also see the size of each individual frame.

5. **Choose View⇨Streaming Graph to see how the Flash movie streams into a browser.**

6. **Choose View⇨Frame by Frame Graph (shown in Figure 13-5) to see which frames contribute to delays.**

   A frame whose bar extends above the red line may cause a bottleneck when the movie downloads at the connection speed you choose in Step 2.

Playback may stop at any frame where the bar extends above the red line, until the whole frame has downloaded.

By default, Flash opens the SWF window in Streaming Graph mode.

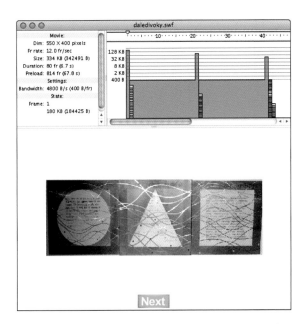

Figure 13-4: When you test a movie, Flash helps you analyze the downloading performance of your movie.

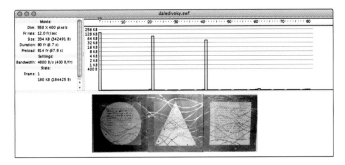

Figure 13-5: In the Frame by Frame Graph, you can see the size of the download for each frame.

7. Choose View⇨Simulate Download if you want to see the Flash movie play as if loading at the speed you choose in Download Settings in Step 2.

8. To close the SWF window, click its Close button.

After you analyze your movie, you can go back and optimize it to eliminate delays. A short delay in the first frame is usually acceptable, but significant delays during the movie result in jerky animation or pauses.

If you have a long movie divided into scenes, you can save time by using the Test Scene command instead of the Test Movie command.

Testing a movie in a Web browser

The final steps of testing a movie are publishing it and viewing it in a Web browser. For a quick view, you can use the Publish Preview command. Flash publishes your movie to an SWF file, creates the appropriate HTML file, and opens the HTML file in your default browser. Viewing your Flash Player file in a browser reveals how the browser will display the movie when you upload it to a Web site.

Flash uses the current settings in the Publish Settings dialog box to create the preview, including the types of file formats that you have selected. To preview your movie in a browser, follow these steps:

1. **Choose File⇨Publish Settings to open the Publish Settings dialog box. Choose the desired file formats and publish settings, and then click OK.**

   See the "Publishing Flash Movies" section, later in this chapter, for more information on the Publish Settings dialog box.

2. **Choose File⇨Publish Preview and choose the desired format from the submenu.**

   Flash opens your browser and runs your movie.

3. **Close your browser to end the preview.**

As with any Web page material, you need to consider the following when testing a Flash Player file:

✐ **The browser that your audience is using:** Preview your Flash Player file in the current version of both Internet Explorer (IE) and Mozilla Firefox, if possible. You should probably try out at least one earlier version of IE, too. And you should test it in Safari on a Mac. Okay, so you probably won't do all this, but don't say that we didn't tell you.

✐ **The resolution of viewers' screens:** Test at least the following common settings: 800 x 600 and 1024 x 768. Remember that the amount of material that appears on the screen changes with the resolution. If you preview at 640 x 480, you can be sure that people with higher resolutions can see your entire movie, but then again, a Flash movie that fits in a 640 x 480 screen may look pretty humble on a 1280 x 1024 screen.

✐ **The color settings of viewers' screens:** Color settings might range from 256 colors to 16 million. If you aren't using Web-safe colors, some viewers might not see them accurately. But almost all viewers now have thousands or millions of colors, which means that it's not so important to test that your movie looks good with fewer colors.

Professional Web site developers take this testing phase seriously. No matter how good an animation looks on your screen, it's not a good animation if it doesn't translate well to your target number of viewers' screens.

Saving Your Work in Flash CS3 Format

If you're collaborating on a Flash project with a group of friends or co-workers and they're still using Flash CS3 (the predecessor of Flash CS4), there is still hope for them. You can save your work in Flash CS3 format.

To save your work in Flash CS3 format, follow these steps:

1. **Choose File⇨Save As.**

   The Save As dialog box appears.

2. **Choose where you want to save your file and then type the filename you want to use.**

3. **Click the Save As Type drop-down list and select Flash CS3.**

4. **Click Save.**

If you're using features new to Flash CS4, a window appears (as shown in Figure 13-6), listing the new features that won't be saved in the Flash CS3 file and asking whether you want to continue. Click the Save as Flash CS3 button if you want to continue. If you do so, some of the data in your file will not be available in this saved version. So be sure to save a CS4 version as well to keep all of your data intact.

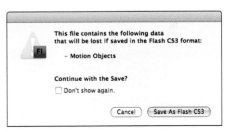

Figure 13-6: Pay attention to this warning message.

Publishing Flash Movies

So you're finally ready to publish your Flash masterpiece. It's time to choose File⇨Publish Settings. This brings you to the Publish Settings dialog box. Don't be overwhelmed by all the options. Typically, you use only a few of them. Start by specifying the settings. Then publish the movie to create the SWF file viewed on a Web page.

After you specify the settings, you can click OK rather than Publish if you want to go back to your Flash movie file and choose Control⇨Test Movie to see the results of your settings. You can try various settings until you're satisfied. Then click Publish to create the final SWF (Flash Player) file. Published files are in the same folder as your FLA movie file by default; you can specify another location if you want. Of course, you can also move the files afterward.

The Publish Settings dialog box lets you easily specify all your settings in one place. Then you click the Publish button, and Flash creates the SWF (Flash Player) file according to your settings. Choose File⇨Publish Settings to open the Publish Settings dialog box with the Formats tab on top, as shown in Figure 13-7.

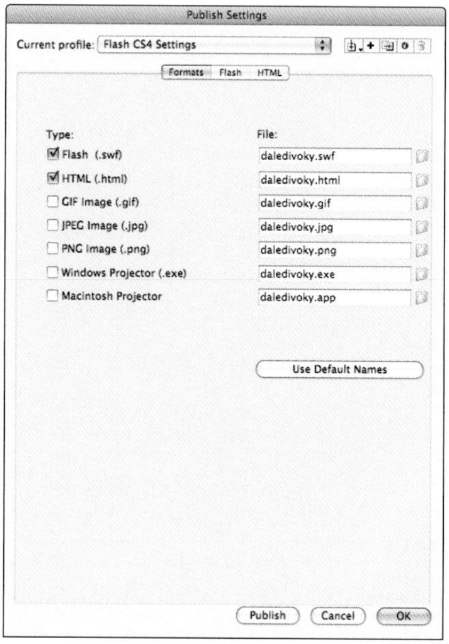

Flash automatically names the files that it creates for you, using the Flash movie's name and adding the appropriate file extension, such as .html and .swf. You can see the names in the Formats tab of the Publish Settings dialog box. To specify your own name for a file, click the File text box and type the new name. To revert to the default filenames, click the Use Default Names button.

Figure 13-7: Your one-stop place for starting to publish your Flash movie.

Most of the time, you need only the Flash (.swf) and HTML formats. But if you want other formats, select them on the Formats tab. When you mark an additional format, the dialog box adds a new tab for that format (except for the projector formats, which don't need one).

After you mark the formats you want, click each tab to specify the settings for that format. The next few sections of this chapter explain each format, why you might want to use it, and how to specify the settings.

After you finish specifying all your settings, click the Publish button. Flash does your bidding, creating the files that you need to put your great creation on the Web.

Publishing to SWF

The second tab in the Publish Settings dialog box (choose File⇨Publish Settings) is the Flash tab, which creates the Flash Player file, also called an SWF file. On this tab, shown in Figure 13-8, you specify settings that affect the SWF file.

Flash gives you options in four categories:

✔ Flash Player and ActionScript version

✔ Settings for images and sounds

✔ SWF settings

✔ Advanced settings

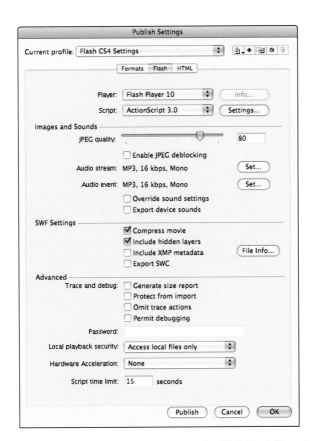

Figure 13-8: Specify how Flash creates the SWF (Flash Player) file.

Flash Player and ActionScript version

In this category, you specify the version of Flash Player that you want to require and the version of ActionScript that you want to use.

- **Player:** Allows you to save in previous version formats for backward compatibility (or in the Flash Lite format for playing Flash movies on mobile phones, or the Adobe AIR format for creating rich Internet applications that can be deployed as desktop applications — but that's a subject for another book). If you use new features but choose an old Flash Player version, Flash warns you of potential problems when you publish your movie.

- **ActionScript version (for Flash Player 6, 7, 8, 9, and 10; and Flash Lite 2.0, 2.1 and 3.0 only):** Specifies whether your movie is using ActionScript 1.0, 2.0, or 3.0. ActionScript 2.0, which was introduced in 2003, added new commands to ActionScript that are mostly of interest to intermediate or advanced programmers who are building applications in Flash that implement new classes and subclasses of objects. ActionScript 3.0 was new in Flash CS3. Fundamental changes in the underpinnings of ActionScript in version 3.0 make it possible for ActionScript 3.0 code to execute up to ten times faster than code from earlier versions.

   In this book, we use the new methods for handling events and other new methods of ActionScript 3.0, so generally, you will want to choose ActionScript version 3.0 in the ActionScript Version drop-down list. You can try choosing ActionScript 2.0 from the ActionScript Version drop-down list and an earlier version of the Flash Player (such as Flash 5 or Flash 6) in the Version drop-down list and then see whether you get a warning when you publish your movie. If you don't get a warning, your published movie will safely play on older versions of Flash; thus, they may reach a somewhat larger audience.

Image and sound settings

In this category, you specify the details for compression of your audio and of your bitmap images.

- **JPEG Quality:** Sets the compression (size) versus quality of bitmaps, if you have any in your movie. You can set the quality anywhere from 0 (the lowest quality and highest compression) to 100 (the highest quality and lowest compression).

- **Enable JPEG Deblocking:** This adds a filter that blends the blocky-looking chunks that can appear if you greatly compress an image in the JPEG file format. This can make low-resolution bitmap images look much better. In some cases, it can make images seem blurry, so enable this option on a case-by-case basis.

✔ **Audio Stream:** Displays and sets the audio compression for *stream sounds* (sounds that use the Stream Sync setting in the Property inspector when a frame with the sound is selected). This setting applies if you haven't set the compression for individual sounds in the Sound Properties dialog box. Also, if you enable the Override Sound Settings check box in the Publish Settings dialog box, this setting overrides the setting in the Sound Properties dialog box. To change the current setting, click Set. The options are the same as in the Sound Properties dialog box. (Turn to Chapter 11 for details on setting sound properties.)

✔ **Audio Event:** Displays and sets the audio compression for event sounds (as set in the Property inspector when a frame with the sound is selected). Otherwise, the compression setting is the same as Audio Stream.

   • *Override Sound Settings:* Select this option to override settings in the Sound Properties dialog box. Then the settings here apply to all sounds in your movie.

   • *Export Device Sounds:* This gives you the option of exporting sounds in formats suitable for playback on mobile devices, such as certain mobile phones and personal digital assistants (PDAs). To do this, you use proxy sound files, a discussion of which is beyond the scope of this book.

SWF settings

In this category, you specify assorted details of your SWF file.

✔ **Compress Movie:** Compresses your Flash Player file, especially text and ActionScript, so that it can download faster. This option is great except that your compressed file doesn't play in Flash Player versions earlier than Flash Player 6.

Your Flash movie probably uses some feature that's been added to Flash after Flash Player 5, anyway, so go for it and compress your movie.

✔ **Include Hidden Layers:** This option is set by default. If you deselect this option, Flash won't publish layers (including layers inside movie clips) that are marked as hidden. Deselecting this option can be useful because then you can test different versions of your document simply by hiding layers.

✔ **Include XMP Metadata:** If you enable this option and click the nearby File Info button, a dialog box appears in which you can input information

about the contents of your movie, and that information will be embedded in your SWF file, available for other search engines or other software
to use. Some of the kinds of information that you can embed include
camera data for photos in your SWF file, the frame rate and shot number
of video footage, the artist name and song title of music in your movie
(as shown in Figure 13-9), and much more.

Figure 13-9: In an SWF file, embed all kinds of information about
the items in your movie.

🡒 **Export SWC:** If you're new to Flash, you can safely leave this option dis-
abled. SWC files are packages of precompiled components. Components
in Flash can be implemented either in an FLA file or an SWC file. The
User Interface components (such as CheckBoxes, ComboBoxes, and
RadioButtons) are implemented as FLA-based components, and the
FLVPlayback and FLVPlaybackCaptioning components are SWC-based.
You can use ActionScript to add SWC-based components while a Flash
Player movie is running so that they can be kept in SWC files that are
separate from your Flash Player file. Because SWC files contain precompiled components, the components appear faster than ordinary movie
clips. If you enable this option, when you publish your file, Flash creates
an SWC file that contains your SWC components and an SWF file that
uses the SWC file.

Advanced settings

In this category, you specify details related to debugging, security, and other
advanced stuff.

✔ **Generate Size Report:** Creates a TXT file that you can use to troubleshoot problem areas, as shown in Figure 13-10. If you enable the Generate Size Report setting, when you publish your movie Flash creates a very useful report on the size of assorted parts of your movie. The report relates the various parts of your movie to the number of bytes that they require in the SWF file.

```
OUTPUT
Scene                   Shape Bytes    Text Bytes    ActionScript Bytes
------------------------ -----------   -----------   -------------------
Scene 1                          0             0                     16

Symbol                  Shape Bytes    Text Bytes    ActionScript Bytes
------------------------ -----------   -----------   -------------------
NextSlide                      122            35                      0
Slide3                           0             0                      0
Slide2                          73             0                      0
Slide4                          74             0                      0
Slide1                          74             0                      0

Font Name               Bytes      Characters
------------------------ ---------  --------------
Arial-BoldMT Bold          418     Netx

ActionScript Bytes    Location
------------------    --------
               1      Scene 1:actions:1
```

Figure 13-10: Enable the Generate Size Report setting when you publish.

The size report can be more useful than the bandwidth profiler in pinpointing the location of the giant-size parts of a movie. It's worth reviewing, and it's interesting (and often surprising) to see the size of the various elements of the SWF file.

✔ **Protect from Import:** Prevents the SWF files from being downloaded from the Web site and imported back into Flash. This feature doesn't provide 100 percent–guaranteed protection, but it helps keep your work from being "borrowed."

✔ **Omit Trace Actions:** Omits special codes used by programmers. *Trace actions* insert into Flash movies the codes used to record and display technical information about a Flash movie's progress in a special window, named the Flash Debugger. Programmers use this information to *debug* (remove errors from) their ActionScript programming. If you added Trace actions to your Flash movie, select the Omit Trace Actions check box to omit these codes from the SWF file, and your file will be smaller.

✔ **Permit Debugging:** Lets you use the Debugger to debug a Flash movie from another computer. If you permit debugging, you can add a password to protect the movie file. Although this option is useful for ActionScript programmers, discussing it is beyond the scope of this book.

✔ **Password:** Allows you to select a password for debugging, if you enable the Debugging Permitted (or Protect from Import) check box. This option prevents viewers from debugging (or importing) the movie unless they have the password.

✒ **Local Playback Security:** If you select Local Access Only, your Flash movie can interact only with files and resources on the computer that it's playing on. If you select Access Network Only, your movie can interact only with files and resources on the network, and not with those on the computer it's playing on. (This separation of local and network access helps make it more difficult for a malicious programmer to create a Flash file that collects data from your computer and transmits it over a network such as the Internet.)

✒ **Hardware Acceleration:** You can enable hardware-accelerated graphics by choosing Level 1 — Direct or Level 2 — GPU from the drop-down list so that Flash uses the computer's graphics card for rendering. However, using these options is tricky. For various technical reasons that are beyond the scope of this book, if you enable one of these hardware-accelerated modes, it will actually slow down your movie in the majority of cases. So if you're just starting out with Flash, you want to leave this option set to None.

✒ **Script Time Limit:** If a Flash movie seems to be stuck in an endless loop, after 15 seconds, the Flash Player will present the user with a dialog box asking whether to continue or quit. Here you can set the limit to a time other than the default of 15 seconds.

If all these settings seem like a bit much, you can always just use the default settings, go with the flow, and check the results.

Publishing to HTML

HTML is the basic language of Web pages. If you work on a Web site, you can write the HTML code from scratch or use an HTML editor. However, many people use a Web authoring program, such as Dreamweaver.

To place a Flash Player file on a Web page, you need the proper HTML code. You probably also want some sophisticated JavaScript code in the Web page that takes care of problems with some versions of IE so that your Flash movies will activate automatically without first requiring that the user respond to a prompt for a click. (*JavaScript* is a programming language that is designed to give Web pages capabilities far beyond what HTML can do.) Luckily, Flash can create all this code for you, in formats suitable for most browsers.

As the result of a patent lawsuit, in 2006 Microsoft released a version of IE that prompts the user with a request for a confirmation click for each Flash file, QuickTime movie, and other ActiveX control in each Web page, to confirm that the user wants to activate it. In November, 2007, Microsoft announced that as a result of license acquisitions, this workaround was no longer needed. In March, 2008, Microsoft released an update that removed the need for the confirmation clicks.

Understanding the HTML code for a movie

Figure 13-11 shows the type of HTML code and JavaScript code that Flash generates when you publish your Flash file by using default settings, as displayed in TextEdit on a Mac. (In TextEdit, before opening your HTML file, be sure to choose TextEdit⇨Preferences and then select the Plain Text option in the New Document Attributes section of the Preferences dialog box.) Windows users can use Notepad to view HTML code created by the Publish command.

If you know some HTML, some parts of this page will look fairly familiar. (And if you don't, you might want to check out *HTML, XHTML, & CSS For Dummies,* 6th Edition, by Ed Tittel and Jeff Noble, from Wiley.) The page starts with the *tags* (codes) that all HTML documents contain, namely <html>, <head>, and <title>. Here's how to understand the code in Figure 13-11:

- After <title>, you see many, many lines of JavaScript code between the <script language="javascript" type="text/javascript"> tag and the </script> tag. This code writes HTML code that your Web browser will display. So the JavaScript code creates the HTML code that creates the Web page that you end up seeing.

- Eventually, you see the </script> tag and the </head> tag, which denote the end of that gigantic chunk of JavaScript code, and next you see the <body tag.

- After <body, you see bgcolor="#ffffff">. This is the background color of the entire HTML page.

```
⬤ ⬤ ⬤                      ▾ Movie of the Year.html
<html xmlns="http://www.w3.org/1999/xhtml" xml:lang="en" lang="en">
<head>
<meta http-equiv="Content-Type" content="text/html; charset=iso-8859-1" />
<title>Movie of the Year</title>
<script language="JavaScript" type="text/javascript">
<!--
//v1.7
// Flash Player Version Detection
// Detect Client Browser type
// Copyright 2005-2008 Adobe Systems Incorporated.  All rights reserved.
var isIE  = (navigator.appVersion.indexOf("MSIE") != -1) ? true : false;
var isWin = (navigator.appVersion.toLowerCase().indexOf("win") != -1) ? true : false;
var isOpera = (navigator.userAgent.indexOf("Opera") != -1) ? true : false;
function ControlVersion()
{
        var version;
        var axo;
        var e;
        // NOTE : new ActiveXObject(strFoo) throws an exception if strFoo isn't in the registry
        try {
                // version will be set for 7.X or greater players
                axo = new ActiveXObject("ShockwaveFlash.ShockwaveFlash.7");
                version = axo.GetVariable("rsion");
        } catch (e) {
        }
        if (!version)
        {
                try {
                        // version will be set for 6.X players only
                        axo = new ActiveXObject("ShockwaveFlash.ShockwaveFlash.6");
```

Figure 13-11: When you publish a movie to a Flash Player file, Flash creates HTML and JavaScript code by default.

By default, Flash makes the background color of the HTML page the same color as the background of your Flash movie, but you might prefer to change it to a different color to help visually define the Flash movie.

✔ Next, you again see the `<script language="javascript" type="text/javascript>` tag, followed by more than a dozen lines of JavaScript code, and then a `</script>` tag.

✔ After the `</script>` tag, you see a `<noscript>` tag. All the code after the `<noscript>` tag is the HTML for the Web page that will appear if users have JavaScript turned off in their browser.

✔ Next ,you see the `object` tag. Microsoft IE requires this tag to display your Flash Player files. The `object` code includes the following:

- Detailed codes (which are required to tell IE how to display your player file).

- The specification of the version of the Flash viewer to look for and where to download it if necessary.

- The width and height of the Flash movie in the browser.

- The name of the file (`value="Movie of the Year.swf"`).

- Parameter settings for local or network access, looping, quality, and background color. You set the background color by choosing Modify➪Document in Flash and choosing a background color in the Document Properties dialog box. (See Chapter 2 for details on using this dialog box.)

- The `embed` code is for Netscape Navigator, Mozilla, and Mozilla Firefox browsers, and it accomplishes the same thing as the `object` code.

✔ Finally, you see the closing `</object>` tag, the closing `</noscript>` tag, and the tags that end every HTML document: `</body>` and `</html>`.

If you want to use the HTML document as is, you can. But if you want to combine your Flash Player file with the elements in another HTML file (as you would for a Flash button, for example), you need to combine the code in the two documents.

One way you can do this is to treat as one unit all the code in the first document (the HTML document created in Flash when you choose File➪Publish), starting with `<script language="javascript" type="text/javascript>` AC_FL_RunContent and ending with `</noscript>`. Think of this unit as your Flash movie code. Then copy HTML from your second HTML document and paste it before or after your unit of Flash movie code to display HTML elements before or after your Flash movie.

If you didn't change your default folder locations in the Formats section of the Publish Settings dialog box, your SWF file will be in the same folder as the HTML file that Flash creates when you publish your movie. In that case, the

HTML `<object>` and `<embed>` tags created by the Flash publishing process reference the SWF file by simply mentioning the filename. For that to work, the SWF file must be in the same folder on your Web site's server as your Web page's HTML file.

If you usually keep image files in a subfolder and want to also place your SWF file in that subfolder, you can specify that location on the Formats tab of the Publish Settings dialog box. Click the small folder icon to the right of the name of the SWF file and navigate to the subfolder where you want it to be placed.

Specifying Flash Player detection and other HTML settings

To create the HTML file, you need to specify the HTML settings on the HTML tab of the Publish Settings dialog box, as shown in Figure 13-12.

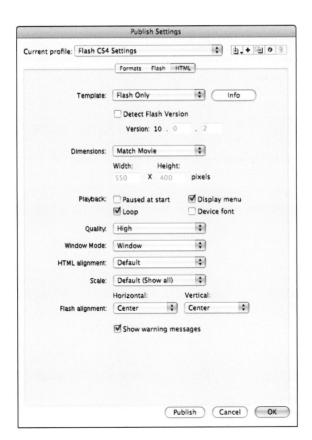

Figure 13-12: Specify how Flash creates HTML code to display your movie.

Template

The first setting, Template, lets you select a *template,* which determines the
format and contents of the HTML file. To keep matters simple, select the
default, Flash Only. Table 13-1 explains the other template options, although
it's very possible that you may never need to use anything other than the
default, Flash Only.

Table 13-1	HTML Template Options
Option	*What It Does*
Flash for Pocket PC 2003	Creates an HTML file with Pocket PC–specific alignment. Can be used with Pocket IE and with desktop IE and Netscape browsers.
Flash HTTPS	Creates an HTML file using the HTTPS protocol to specify where to go to download the Flash Player if necessary. HTTPS is designed to send data over the Web more securely than the standard method (HTTP). It also creates a JavaScript file in your HTML output folder, and this must be uploaded along with the HTML file.
Flash Only (Default)	Creates an HTML file, as we describe in the earlier section "Understanding the HTML code for a movie."
Flash Only — Allow Full Screen	Creates an HTML file and includes support for playing your Flash movie full screen.
Flash with AICC Tracking	Creates an HTML file with support for AICC-HACP tracking when using Adobe Learning Interactions. (AICC is Aviation Industry Computer-Based-Training Committee, and HACP is HTTP AICC Communications Protocol.)
Flash with FSCommand	Used when you have added an `FSCommand` action to your movie to interface with JavaScript.
Flash with Named Anchors	Creates an HTML file with support for Named Anchors so that viewers can bookmark Flash content in Flash Player 6 and later; thus, it uses the Web browser's Back button effectively while navigating within a Flash movie. This could be a great feature — but many browsers don't support it, so it's fairly useless.
Flash with SCORM 1.2 Tracking	Includes support for SCORM (Sharable Content Object Reference Model) version 1.2 tracking when using Adobe Learning Interactions.
Flash with SCORM 2004 Tracking	Includes support for SCORM 2004 tracking when using Adobe Learning Interactions.

Option	What It Does
Image Map	(If you don't know what an image map is, don't worry about this option.) Instead of displaying an SWF player file, it uses a GIF, JPEG, or PNG image (which you need to choose on the Formats tab) as a client-side image map coded in your HTML page.

Below the Template drop-down list is the Detect Flash Version check box. (This option is available only if you choose Flash Player 4 or later on the Flash tab of the Publish Settings dialog box and the Flash HTTPS or Flash Only template.) Select this check box to add browser scripting to detect the Flash Player for the version of Flash you specify on the Flash tab. When this check box is enabled, the Version number text boxes below it are also enabled. If you want to more exactly specify the minimum version required, type revision numbers in the Minor Revision and Incremental Revision text fields there. (*Minor Revision* and *Incremental Revision* appear in tooltips when you move the mouse cursor over the text boxes.)

If you select the Detect Flash Version check box, when you publish your Flash file, the resulting HTML code prints the following on your Web page if the Flash Player of the specified version can't be found or if the Web browser doesn't have scripting enabled:

```
Alternate HTML content should be placed here. This
content requires the Adobe Flash Player. Get Flash.
```

Scripting must be enabled by the Web browser for the Flash Player version detection to work. You can edit the HTML to replace the preceding text with whatever alternative content you want to display when the Flash Player version can't be found.

Dimensions

The Dimensions options control the size allotted to your Flash Player movie on your Web page. You have three options:

- **Match Movie:** Matches the width and height that you set in the Movie Properties dialog box. (Choose Modify⇨Document.)

- **Pixels:** Lets you specify the Width and Height in pixels. Type the desired values in the text boxes.

- **Percent:** Lets you specify the area used by the Flash Player movie as a percentage of the browser window size. The 100% setting is ideal for pages designed to take up the entire page. Type the desired percentage values in the text boxes labeled Width and Height.

Playback

The Playback section determines the values of parameters in the HTML code. You have four options:

- **Paused at Start:** Creates a PLAY parameter whose value is FALSE. The person must start the movie by clicking a button in the movie — the button's instance needs to have a Play action in it. Alternatively, viewers can right-click (Windows) or Control+click (Mac) the movie and choose Play in the shortcut menu, but they might not be aware of this. By default, this check box is deselected, so movies start to play automatically.

- **Loop:** Creates a LOOP parameter whose value is TRUE. The movie repeats over and over. By default, this check box is selected, so make sure to clear it if you don't want to loop your movie!

- **Display Menu:** Creates a MENU parameter set to TRUE. This option enables viewers to right-click (Windows) or Control+click (Mac) the movie and choose from a menu, as shown in Figure 13-13. The menu options in Flash Player 10 are Zoom In, Zoom Out, 100%, Show All, Quality (High, Medium, or Low), Print, Settings, and About Adobe Flash Player 10. Without this option, the only menu items are Settings and About Adobe Flash Player 10. By default, Display Menu is selected.

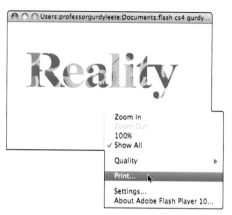

Figure 13-13: Use the Display Menu setting to control whether viewers can bring up the full Flash Player shortcut menu.

- **Device Font:** Applies to Windows playback only. When this check box is selected, the HTML file includes a DEVICE FONT parameter set to TRUE, and Flash substitutes *anti-aliased* (smoothly curved) system fonts for fonts not available on the viewer's system. This applies only to static text you create in Flash. By default, this item is not selected.

Quality

The Quality section determines the quality parameter in the <object> and <embed> tags of the HTML code. *Quality* refers to the level of *anti-aliasing,* which is the smoothing of the artwork so that it doesn't have jagged edges. The lower the quality, the faster the playback. Usually, you want to find a good balance between quality and speed. You have six options:

- **Low:** Doesn't use anti-aliasing (and looks awful).

- **Auto Low:** Starts at a low quality but switches to a high quality if the viewer's computer, as detected by the Flash Player, can handle it.

✔ **Auto High:** Starts at a high quality but switches to a low quality if the viewer's computer can't handle the playback demand. This option should provide good results on all computers.

✔ **Medium:** Applies some anti-aliasing but doesn't smooth bitmaps. This option is a good middle ground between low and high.

✔ **High:** Always uses anti-aliasing for vector art. Bitmaps are smoothed only if the file doesn't contain tweens. (See Chapter 9 for the scoop on tweens.) This setting is the default.

✔ **Best:** Always uses anti-aliasing, including for bitmaps.

Window Mode

Window Mode specifies how the player movie's window interacts with the rest of the page. Here are your options:

✔ **Window:** Plays your movie as an opaque rectangle within your Web page and does not allow your HTML to render other content in that rectangle. This is the default mode.

✔ **Opaque Windowless:** Creates an opaque background for the movie so that other elements in the Web page don't show through when they're behind the movie. This setting does allow your HTML to render content in front of the movie.

✔ **Transparent Windowless:** Makes the Flash background color transparent so that other elements on your Web page show through (or can appear on top of) your Flash content. This setting might slow down playback.

The code for the Transparent and Windowless modes has an effect only in more recent browsers running on Windows or Mac OS X — IE version 5 and later, Netscape version 7 and later, Mozilla 1 and later, Firefox 1 and later, and Opera 6 and later.

HTML Alignment

The HTML Alignment setting specifies the `ALIGN` attribute and specifies how the Flash Player movie is aligned within the browser window. You have five options:

✔ **Default:** Theoretically centers the Flash movie. If the browser window is smaller than the movie, this option theoretically crops the edges of the movie. But in our tests, the default is always left even though it should be center.

✔ **Left:** Aligns the movie along the left side of the browser window. If the window is too small, this option crops the other sides of the movie.

✔ **Right:** Aligns the movie along the right side of the browser window. If the window is too small, this option crops the other sides of the movie.

✔ **Top:** Aligns the movie along the top of the browser window. If the window is too small, this option crops the other sides of the movie.

✓ **Bottom:** Aligns the movie along the bottom of the browser window. If the window is too small, this option crops the other sides of the movie.

Scale

The Scale setting defines how the movie is placed within the boundaries specified by code in the HTML page when (and only when) you set a width and height different from the movie's original size, using the Pixels or Percent options in the Dimensions section of the Publish Settings dialog box. You have four options:

✓ **Default (Show All):** Displays the entire movie without distortion but might create borders on two sides of the movie.

The Show All setting shows all the elements in your Flash movie, even those that you move to the sides, off the Stage.

✓ **No Border:** Scales the movie to fill the dimensions without distortion but might crop portions of the movie.

✓ **Exact Fit:** Fits the movie to the dimensions, distorting the movie if necessary.

✓ **No Scale:** Stops the movie from changing its scale if the viewer resizes the Flash Player window.

Flash Alignment

Flash Alignment determines how the movie fits within the movie window (as opposed to the browser window). It works together with the Scale and Dimensions settings. In other words, it determines how the Flash movie fits within the dimensions you specify. For the Horizontal setting, choose Left, Center, or Right. For the Vertical setting, you can choose Top, Center, or Bottom.

Show Warning Messages

At the bottom of the Publish Settings dialog box is the Show Warning Messages check box. When it's selected, you see warning messages during the publishing process. The publishing process continues, but you know that you might have made an error. For example, if you've chosen a template that requires a GIF or JPEG image but you haven't selected either format on the Formats tab, you see a warning message.

After you choose your settings, click OK to return to your movie or click Publish to publish it.

Publishing to Other Formats

You can use Flash's Publish Settings to generate files in a variety of other formats besides HTML pages and Flash Player movies. These other formats are GIF images, animated GIFs, JPEG images, PNG images, and self-playing Windows and Mac projectors.

Even if you use Flash all day, every day, you might never need to generate GIF images or JPEG images from your Flash movies, so we won't clog up your life by describing the Publish Settings for those formats here.

Creating PNG graphic files

PNG files can display millions more colors than GIF files and support transparency. They offer some of the advantages of both GIFs and JPEGs. To create a PNG image, choose PNG Image on the Formats tab of the Publish Settings dialog box. (Refer to Figure 13-7.) Flash creates a PNG tab in the dialog box, as shown in Figure 13-14.

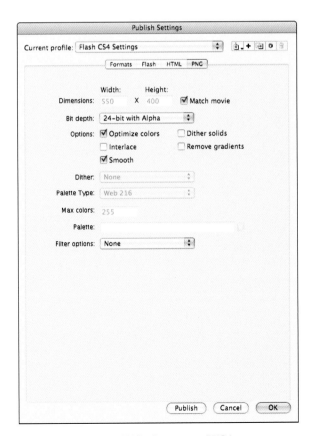

Figure 13-14: Use the PNG tab to create PNG images.

Flash publishes the first frame of your movie unless you label a different frame with the #Static label. (To create a label, click the frame and choose Window⇨Properties to open the Property inspector. If necessary, expand the Label section of the Property inspector to its full size. Type a label name in the Name text box in the Label section of the Property inspector.)

You have the following options:

- **Dimensions:** Lets you specify your own Width and Height settings if you deselect the Match Movie check box. This could be useful if you want to create a thumbnail image to use on a Web page to link to your movie. By default, Flash matches the dimensions of the movie.

- **Bit Depth:** Controls the number of bits per pixel, which in turn means how many colors the image contains. You can select 8-bit for 256 colors (like a GIF), 24-bit for 16.7 million colors, or 24-bit with Alpha, which allows for transparency. When you choose 24-bit with Alpha, the image's background becomes transparent. This is one of the things that designers love about PNG files.

- **Options:** Specifies how the PNG file appears:

  - *Optimize Colors:* Removes unused colors from the file's color table to reduce the size of the file.

  - *Interlace:* Causes a static PNG image to load in incremental resolutions, so the image appears first fuzzy and then successively sharper. Some people like this option because viewers may be able to click the image before it fully downloads, thus reducing their waiting time.

  - *Smooth:* Anti-aliases (smoothes) the artwork. Text usually looks better (and the file size is larger), but occasionally you may get an undesirable halo effect around your art. In that case, turn off smoothing.

  - *Dither Solids:* Does just that — dithers solid colors as well as gradients and images. *Dithering* is a way to approximate colors not available on the color palette by using a range of similar colors. This applies only to files with 8-bit color. See the Dither option, which we describe a few paragraphs from now.

  - *Remove Gradients:* Turns gradients into solids. Gradients may not look good in a Web-safe color table. Nevertheless, Flash uses the first color in the gradient, which may not be the color you want.

- **Dither:** Enables dithering for files with 8-bit color, as we define in the Dither Solids bullet in the Options descriptions. Dithering helps to create more accurate-looking colors but increases file size. Choose one of the three options:

  - *None:* Disables dithering.

  - *Ordered:* Provides a medium amount of dithering and a corresponding medium increase in file size.

- *Diffusion:* Provides the best-quality dithering and increases file size the most. It works only with the Web 216-color palette. (Refer to Chapter 3 for a description of color palettes.)

✔ **Palette Type:** Determines the color palette for the PNG image. This applies only to PNG files with 8-bit color. (Refer to Chapter 3 for a discussion of colors in Flash.) You have four options:

- *Web 216:* Uses the standard 216-color palette that includes only *Web-safe colors* (those that look good on all Web browsers). You can usually get good results for Flash artwork without increasing file size.

- *Adaptive:* Creates a unique color table for your file, based on the actual colors present. You get more accurate color (although these colors may not be Web safe), but the file size may be larger. Use this option if an accurate representation of the colors is most important, as in a photographic bitmap image. You can use the Max Colors text box to specify how many colors you want in the table. The default is 255. Use fewer colors to reduce the file size.

- *Web Snap Adaptive:* Works like the Adaptive option but optimizes the color palette for the Web. Colors close to the 216 Web-safe colors are turned into one of the colors on that palette. Other colors function like the Adaptive option. As with the Adaptive option, you can specify the number of colors on the palette in the Max Colors text box.

- *Custom:* Lets you specify a palette in the ACT format. Click the file folder icon near the Palette text field to browse for a color palette file. (Read the section in Chapter 3 on solid colors for an explanation of how to create a color palette and save it in ACT format.)

- *Max Colors:* This option is enabled only when you choose Adaptive or Web Snap Adaptive, and the Palette option is enabled only when you choose Custom.

✔ **Filter Options:** Controls how an image is analyzed line by line to compress it. You have these options:

- *None:* Applies no filtering. The resulting file is larger than with the other options.

- *Sub:* Filters adjoining pixel bytes (working horizontally). This works best when the image has repeated horizontal information.

- *Up:* Filters in a vertical direction. This works best when the image has repeated vertical information.

- *Average:* Uses a mixture of horizontal and vertical comparison; this is a good first-try option.

- *Path:* Employs a more complex method that uses the three nearest pixels to predict the next one.

- *Adaptive:* Creates a unique color table for your PNG file based on the actual colors present. You get more accurate color, although these colors might not be Web safe. The file size might also be larger. Use this option if accurate representation of colors is most important, as in a photographic bitmap image.

After you specify your settings, click OK to return to your movie or click Publish to publish your PNG image and create the other files you've chosen.

Creating self-playing movies

You can also create projectors in the Publish Settings dialog box. A *projector* is a self-playing Flash movie that doesn't require the Flash Player. All the interactive and animated features of your Flash movie work in a projector. You can use a projector for a Flash movie that you want to burn on a CD-R or DVD-R computer disc. (The projector format is not compatible with the format of a DVD movie disc, though.) Projector files tend to have much larger sizes than their corresponding SWF files.

You can create a Windows or Mac version from either platform. But if you create a Mac version in Windows, you need to use a file translator, such as BinHex, so that the Mac Finder recognizes it as an application.

To create a projector, follow these steps:

1. **Choose File⇨Publish Settings.**

   The Publish Settings dialog box opens.

2. **On the Formats tab, select the Windows Projector check box or the Macintosh Projector check box, or both.**

3. **Click Publish.**

4. **Click OK or Cancel to close the Publish Settings dialog box.**

For Windows, Flash creates an EXE file. For the Mac, Flash creates a Macintosh Projector application. If you create the Macintosh Projector file in Flash while using a Windows computer, the Macintosh Projector file is stored inside a compressed BinHex file (HQX), which can then be uncompressed on a Mac.

Test your movie after you copy it to a CD-ROM or another computer. Try it out with a variety of processor speeds if possible.

Using Publish Profiles

You can save all the settings that you configure in the Publish Settings dialog box as a *publish profile*. You can then duplicate, modify, export, import, and delete your publish profiles and trade them with your collaborators. You can create standard publish profiles, which you use to make sure that all your files are published uniformly, and you can create specialized publish profiles specific to a single project. The following sections tell you how.

Creating a publish profile

To create a publish profile, follow these steps:

1. **Choose File⇨Publish Settings.**

   The Publish Settings dialog box appears.

2. **Click the Create New Profile button (the + symbol) in the upper-right part of the dialog box, shown in Figure 13-15.**

   The Create New Profile dialog box appears.

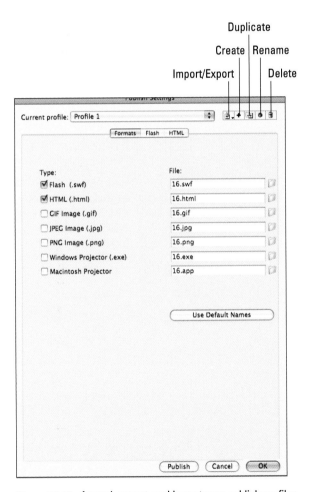

Figure 13-15: Amend, export, and import your publish profiles.

3. Type a name for your profile and then click OK.

   The Create New Profile dialog box disappears, and the name of your new profile appears in the Current Profile drop-down list of the Publish Settings dialog box.

4. Specify the publish settings for your document in the Publish Settings dialog box, as we describe in earlier sections of this chapter, and then click OK.

Duplicating or renaming a publish profile

You might want to duplicate a publish profile to use it as a springboard for new variations. To duplicate a publish profile, do the following steps:

1. Choose File⇨Publish Settings.

   The Publish Settings dialog box appears.

2. In the Current Profile drop-down list (near the top of the dialog box), select the publish profile that you want to rename (or copy).

3. Click the Rename Profile button (or the Duplicate Profile button — the horizontal arrow button), in the upper-right part of the dialog box.

   The Profile Properties dialog box (or the Duplicate Profile dialog box) appears.

4. Type a new name for your profile (or the name for your duplicate profile) and then click OK.

   The dialog box disappears. The name of your renamed profile (or your duplicate profile) appears in the Current Profile drop-down list of the Publish Settings dialog box.

Modifying a publish profile

You might use a particular publish profile as, for example, a standard for your co-workers. As circumstances change, you might want to modify the publish profile, and that's easy to do. To modify a publish profile, follow these steps:

1. Choose File⇨Publish Settings.

   The Publish Settings dialog box appears.

2. In the Current Profile drop-down list (near the top of the dialog box), select the publish profile that you want to modify.

3. Select the publish settings that you want for your document in the Publish Settings dialog box, as we describe in the earlier sections of this chapter, and then click OK.

Deleting a publish profile

To delete a publish profile, follow these steps:

1. **Choose File⇨Publish Settings.**

   The Publish Settings dialog box appears.

2. **In the Current Profile drop-down list (near the top of the dialog box), select the publish profile that you want to delete.**

3. **Click the Delete Profile button (the Trash can) in the upper-right part of the dialog box.**

   A dialog box appears asking you to confirm that you want to delete the profile.

4. **Click OK.**

Exporting and importing publish profiles

To use a publish profile in documents other than the document in which you created it, first you export it from the document in which you created it. Then you import it into the new document.

This makes your work easier if, for example, you're working on a Flash project with a team and need to publish your Flash documents according to a single standard. The entire team can easily share the same publish profile.

To export a publish profile, follow these steps:

1. **Choose File⇨Publish Settings.**

   The Publish Settings dialog box appears.

2. **In the Current Profile drop-down list (near the top of the dialog box), select the publish profile that you want to export.**

3. **Click the Import/Export Profile button (the vertical arrow button in the upper-right part of the dialog box) and select Export in the drop-down list.**

   The Export Profile dialog box appears.

4. **In the dialog box, select a location where you want to save the file and then click Save.**

   The default location is a folder named Publish Profiles, which is located in the Flash CS4 application folder. The file is saved as an XML file.

To import a publish profile, follow these steps:

1. **Choose File⇨Publish Settings.**

   The Publish Settings dialog box appears.

2. Click the Import/Export Profile button (the vertical arrow button in the upper-right part of the dialog box) and then select Import in the drop-down list.

   The Import Profile dialog box appears.

3. In the dialog box, browse to find the publish profile that you want to import and then click Open.

   The name of the imported publish profile appears in the Current Profile drop-down list of the Publish Settings dialog box.

Using Publish Preview

If you want to specify publish settings, see the results, and then go back to tweak your settings, you can use Publish Preview rather than Publish. Publish Preview creates the files specified in the Publish Settings dialog box, just as the Publish command does. The only difference is that Publish Preview automatically displays the requested file, usually the SWF file. The value is in simply saving the steps of manually opening your files in your browser — helpful when you're doing lots of tweaking and going back and forth between your publish settings and your browser to see what works best.

To use Publish Preview, follow these steps:

1. Specify your settings by using the Publish Settings dialog box (as we explain earlier in this chapter) and then click OK.

2. Choose File⇨Publish Preview.

3. In the Publish Preview submenu, choose the file format that you want to preview.

4. When you're finished, close the window or browser.

Posting Your Movie to Your Web Site

After you finish publishing your movie, you probably want to post your SWF file on your Web site, or place it on a CD-R or other media. You can make Mac and Windows projectors and copy them onto a CD-R by using CD-burner software. Then you can view your Flash movie independently of a Web browser, or copy your published HTML and SWF files onto a CD-R along with any external scripts, image files, or text files used by your HTML and SWF files.

Refer to the "Understanding the HTML code for a movie" section, earlier in this chapter, for instructions on modifying the HTML code if you want to place your SWF file on an existing Web page or place your SWF file in a subfolder.

To post your movie to a Web site, upload both the HTML and the SWF file.

If your HTML or SWF files load data from any image files, text files, or external scripts (such as JavaScript or ActionScript files), you need to upload those, too.

Open your browser and load the Web page that contains your Flash movie. We hope it works perfectly and looks great! If not, check out the HTML code, check your publish settings, and make sure that the necessary files are in the proper location on your Web site's server.

Exporting Movies and Images

In addition to publishing, Flash lets you export image files and QuickTime movies. Export a Flash file when you want to use it in another application. For example, you may want to export a frame as a PNG file and insert it into a word processing document. You can use Export Movie to export to a QuickTime movie or create a still image of every frame.

After you export a movie or image, you can then import it into the desired application for further editing or display.

Note that when you choose File➪Export➪Export Movie to export a movie to a format such as GIF, JPG, or PNG, you export a sequence of individually numbered images. That might give you some interesting raw material to import into other graphics applications.

To export a movie or image, follow these steps:

1. **Open the Flash document from which you want to export.**

    See Chapter 1 for information about opening an existing Flash movie.

2. **To export to an image, select the frame that you want to export. Otherwise, skip to Step 3.**

3. **Choose File➪Export➪Export Image or File➪Export➪Export Movie.**

4. **In the dialog box, navigate to the desired location and type a name for your image or movie.**

5. **In the Save as Type (Format on a Mac) drop-down list, select the type of file.**

6. **Click Save.**

7. **Depending on the format that you selected, a dialog box might appear. If so, specify the settings and then click OK.**

    These settings are similar to the kind of settings that we describe earlier in this chapter, in the "Creating PNG graphic files" section.

Table 13-2 lists the types of files that you can export.

Table 13-2			Export File Types
File Type	*Windows*	*Mac*	*Comments*
Adobe Illustrator (AI)	X	X	A vector format.
Drawing Exchange Format (DXF)	X	X	A format that you can import into AutoCAD, although you lose fills.
Encapsulated PostScript (EPS)	X	X	A vector format used in Adobe Illustrator and recognized by many other applications.
Graphics Interchange File (GIF)	X	X	A bitmap format, limited to 256 colors.
Joint Photographic ExpertsGroup (JPEG/JPG)	X	X	A bitmap format that supports 24-bit color.
Flash Video (FLV)	X	X	A video format designed for use with video conferencing and other communications applications.
PICT (PCT)		X	A bitmap format that can be used with most Mac and many PC applications. Supports transparency and variable bit depths.
Portable Network Graphic (PNG)	X	X	A bitmap format that supports variable bit depths and transparency.
QuickTime (MOV)	X	X	The movie file format developed by Apple.
Video for Windows (AVI)	X		A bitmap video format. Files can get large.
Windows Audio (WAV)	X		Exports just the sound.
Windows Bitmap (BMP)	X		A bitmap format. Many applications recognize it. Offers variable bit depths and transparency support. File size is large.
Windows Metafile and Enhanced Metafile (WMF/EMF)	X		A vector format supported by many applications. Creates smaller files than EPS.

Creating Printable Movies

Suppose that you want your Web site viewers to be able to print a form on your Web site that you created in Flash. Or perhaps you want them to print your contact information so that your Web page can become your business card. The Flash Player printing features enable your viewers to print receipts, information sheets, coupons, or whatever else helps you do business on the Web. You can specify certain frames in a movie — including frames in the main Timeline, a button, or a movie clip — to be printable from the Flash Player shortcut menu. Viewers right-click (Windows) or Control+click (Mac) to access the Print command.

Your viewers need instructions on how to print, so place some text somewhere telling them what to do.

Of course, viewers can use their browser's Print command to print, but the result isn't nearly as controllable. When we tried it, our browser printed only the first frame, which was useless in our example. The browser also added the Uniform Resource Locator (URL), the name of the movie, the date, and the page number.

By default, the Flash Player shortcut menu lets viewers print the entire movie, frame by frame. This feature is useless for most purposes. But by specifying which frames are printed and the print area, you can use the Player's Print command to make specific information or forms available to your viewers.

Preparing your movie for printing

If you want a nice, clean result, you need a nice, clean frame. The Flash Player prints all objects on all layers of the movie. If you want to create a form, for example, put it in its own frame and make sure that objects on other layers don't continue into that frame.

Alternatively, you can specify the print area so that you include only the area that you want printed, excluding other objects on the Stage in the frame. But if you specify a small area, this area becomes the entire page size when printing, so the objects in that small area are enlarged to take up the entire printed page. You can control the layout by changing the dimension, scale, and alignment HTML settings (on the HTML tab of the Publish Settings dialog box, as described earlier in this chapter).

Make sure that everything you want to print is on the Stage. For example, if you want to print from a movie clip, it must be on the Stage and have an instance name.

You can make a movie clip invisible by setting its `_visible` property to `false`. (Use the Actions panel.) This capability enables you to instruct viewers to print an item that they don't see on the screen — for example, a form that's formatted differently on paper and on the computer screen.

If your movie displays text instructing users how to print from the printable area, you might want to exclude this text from the printable area. They probably don't want to print the instructions on how to print, right?

Specifying printable frames

To specify which frame or frames you want to print when your viewers choose Print in the Flash Player shortcut menu, follow these steps:

1. **With the movie open, choose Window⇨Properties to open the Property inspector.**

   The shortcut is Ctrl+F3 (Windows) or ⌘+F3 (Mac). If necessary, expand the Label section of the Property inspector to its full size.

2. **Select from the Timeline the frame you want printed.**

3. **If the frame you selected isn't a keyframe, make it a keyframe by choosing Insert⇨ Timeline⇨Keyframe.**

   Turn to Chapter 9 for the low-down on keyframes.

4. **Type #p in the Name text box in the Label section of the Property inspector, as shown in Figure 13-16. Below the Name text box, set the Label Type drop-down list to Name (the default).**

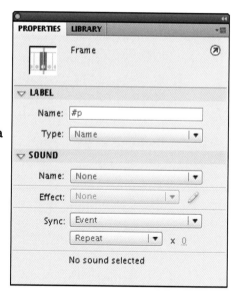

Figure 13-16: Use the Property inspector to label frames for printing.

For each additional keyframe that you want to specify for printing, select the frame and then label it #p in the Property inspector Name text box.

Specifying the print area

Unless you specify the print area, the Flash Player prints the entire Stage. If you have loaded other movies, the Flash Player uses their Stage size. You might, however, want to specify a different area. As we mention earlier in this chapter, you might want to include instructions on how to print, but you may not want the instructions to be printed. You can exclude other objects on the Stage as well.

Choosing a very small print area results in an output of very big objects. The Flash Player sizes your objects to take up the entire printed page.

You create an object, usually a rectangle, to specify the print area. To specify the print area, follow these steps:

1. **Click a frame that you have labeled #p (as we describe in the preceding section).**

2. **Create a rectangle around the area that you want to be printed.**

   You might have to experiment with different sizes of rectangles. See the instructions in the section "Printing movies from the Flash Player," to test the printing of your movie.

   Use the No Fill feature for the rectangle so that you can see the material that you want to print.

3. **Select the rectangle and choose Edit⇨Cut to cut it to the Clipboard.**

4. **Click a frame without a #p label but on the same layer.**

   Using the next frame might be a good choice to keep the printing area rectangle conveniently close to the frame you've specified for printing.

5. **Choose Edit⇨Paste in Place.**

   You now have a rectangle of the right size, but in its own frame — a frame without a #p label.

6. **Select the frame containing the rectangle and choose Window⇨Properties to open the Property inspector.**

   If necessary, expand the Label section of the Property inspector to its full size.

7. **In the Name text box in the Label section of the Property inspector, type #b to signify that the shape in this frame will be used as the boundary for the print area.**

   You can have only one #b label in a Timeline. Also note that if you use a #b label, it must be on the same layer as the #p label.

Printing movies from the Flash Player

Before uploading your printable movie to your Web site, you should test the printing function. To do so, use the Publish Settings dialog box to specify the publish settings that you want, as we explain throughout this chapter. Then choose File⇨Publish Preview⇨Default. Your browser opens, and you see your movie play.

To test-print your movie, right-click (Windows) or Control+click (Mac) in the browser. From the Flash Player shortcut menu, choose Print.

On the Mac, the Page Setup dialog box appears. Choose the printer, paper size, orientation, and scale; and then click OK.

For both Mac and Windows, the Print dialog box appears. Choose the print range to select which frames to print or choose All. In Windows, you can also choose Selection to print the current frame. If only one frame has been made printable, the Pages option appears dimmed. Any option that you choose prints the frame you specified for printing. Click Print.

After you upload your movie onto your Web site, viewers use the same procedure to print your movie.

Place on your page some text that explains to your viewers how to print your movie. Many viewers don't even know that the shortcut menu exists.

Part VI
The Part of Tens

The 5th Wave   By Rich Tennant

"I can't explain it, but every time I animate someone swinging a golf club, a little divot of code comes up missing on the home page."

In this part . . .

In the famous *For Dummies* Part of Tens, we answer the ten most-yasked questions — or at least the ten questions we most wanted to answer. In the chapter on the ten best Flash resources, we manage to give you dozens of Flash resources, such as the many Flash resource Web sites (while convincing our publisher that only ten exist). Finally, to top off the book, we give you our votes for ten great Flash designers. Surf to see the work of all ten and be amazed and inspired by the possibilities!

So dunun invites you to share his experiments and his sound pa:
- **Meetings** : percussionists I have photographed or filmed durin(
- **References** : My performances photographed with the groups 3.
- **Press** : Some press releases.
- **Compose** : Create and experiment rhythms
- **Play !**: Your keyboard changes into a djembe, a dunun or a bal;
Please make your choice in the drop-down menu below.

Ten Frequently Asked Questions

*I*n this chapter, we answer some frequently asked questions about Flash while explaining how to create some cool effects and streamline the process of creating Flash movies.

How Do I Combine Two Flash Movies?

Merging two Flash movies isn't difficult. You simply copy all the frames in each scene in your first movie to new scenes that you create in your second movie. To merge two Flash movies into one, follow these steps:

1. **Choose File⇨Open. In the Open dialog box that appears, navigate to and select the Flash movie you want to copy from.**

   The Flash movie you select appears on the Stage.

2. **Click the Edit Scene button near the top right of the Stage (shown in Figure 14-1). In the drop-down list that appears, choose the scene you want to copy.**

Edit Scene button

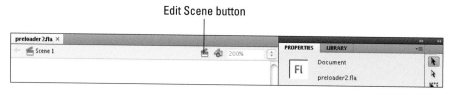

Figure 14-1: Use the Edit Scene button to choose your scene.

The scene you select appears on the Stage.

3. **Unlock all the layers in the scene.**

See Chapter 6 for information on unlocking layers.

4. **Choose Edit⇨Timeline⇨Select All Frames.**

This selects all keyframes and tweens in all layers in the scene.

5. **Choose Edit⇨Timeline⇨Copy Frames.**

This copies all the keyframes and tweens in your scene.

6. **Choose File⇨Open. In the Open dialog box that appears, navigate to and select the Flash movie you want to copy to.**

The Flash movie you select appears on the Stage.

7. **Choose Insert⇨Scene.**

An empty scene appears on the Stage.

8. **Click the first frame in the Timeline and then choose Edit⇨Timeline⇨Paste Frames.**

This pastes the scene you copied from your first movie into your new scene in your second movie.

9. **Repeat Steps 1–8 for each scene you want to copy from your first movie.**

10. **Choose Control⇨Test Movie.**

Your second movie now includes all the scenes you copied from your first movie.

How Can I Sync Sound with Motion?

Suppose you want certain parts of your animation synchronized with specific sounds. For example, you want a bouncing ball to synchronize with the beat of music you imported into Flash. If you don't synchronize the sounds, the sound and the animation might play at different speeds. For example, a faster computer might play the animation faster but won't adjust the length of the sound. Or a slow computer might take its time displaying a transparent ball bouncing, and the synchronization with sound will drift. (For basic information on adding sound to Flash, see Chapter 11.)

To synchronize animation with sound, you need to use a *stream sound*. When you add the sound file to a frame, choose Stream from the Sync drop-down list in the Property inspector. Then adjust the keyframes so that the animation and the sound end at the same time.

To be even more precise, you can synchronize your animation with specific parts of the sound. Choose Modify⇨Timeline⇨Layer Properties, and then choose 200% or 300% in the Layer Height drop-down list. You can also choose Medium or Large for the size of the frames from the drop-down menu in the upper-right corner of the Timeline. Now, as shown in Figure 14-2, you can see the shape of your sound wave more clearly so that you can adjust the keyframes of your animation to match certain parts of the sound.

The playhead

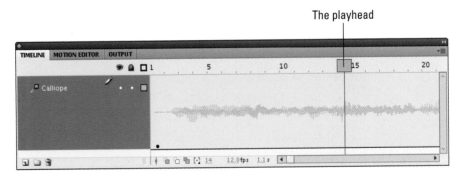

Figure 14-2: Increase layer height in the Timeline to see your sound wave shape more clearly.

One way to pinpoint which frame to use for placing an animation event is to drag the playhead (the red rectangle) just above the Timeline. This technique lets you control the speed of the animation. You can drag left or right until you find the exact frame that you want to work with. You can then move a keyframe to that frame, for example, to move an animation event to a frame that contains a specific portion of your sound.

What's the Best Way to Import Bitmaps?

Maybe you're working on an animation, and you need to include your boss's photograph or a photo of the product that you sell. Or maybe you want an effect in your Flash movie that you can create only in Photoshop. So you need to use a bitmap image. What bitmap format do you use?

You might not have a choice of format. If your information systems department hands you a logo with a solid white background in JPEG format, you probably have to use it.

At other times, you can choose your format. For example, when you scan a photo, most scanner software lets you choose from among several formats. A digital camera might also let you choose the format. Of course, if you create the bitmap in an image-editing program, you can choose from any format that the program supports. (Turn to Chapter 3 for instructions on importing bitmap images. *Hint:* Choose File⇨Import⇨Import to Stage or File⇨Import⇨Import to Library.)

Here are some commonly used bitmap formats as well as their pros and cons:

- ✓ The **GIF** file format can't have more than 256 colors. You can use the GIF format for simple drawings with a limited color palette, but you might be better off using the PNG format, described later in this list.

- ✓ Because **JPEG** files can display many more colors than GIF files, they produce more realistic photos and other complex drawings. However, although JPEG graphics can be highly compressed to reduce file size, they might lose some detail or color fidelity as a result, depending on how much you choose to compress them.

- ✓ **BMP** doesn't lose quality when compressed, but the BMP format results in larger file sizes than GIF or JPEG.

- ✓ **PNG** is a nice compromise between file size and image quality. The PNG format doesn't lose quality when compressed and also allows many more colors than the GIF format. And it provides the capability for transparency. If you want the smallest file size but don't want to compromise quality, the PNG format is a good choice. The Flash image compressor works best and most efficiently with images that haven't been compressed by using techniques that can lose some image quality.

Your final result is the SWF file that you publish. Flash compresses bitmaps (as well as the entire movie) when the movie is exported to an SWF Flash Player file. Therefore, you need to think about the entire round-trip journey that your bitmap will make. You might have to test varying bitmap formats and publish the movie for each one to see the exact results.

When you export, you can set the JPEG quality on the Flash tab of the Publish Settings dialog box. You also set the overall quality on the HTML tab. For that quality setting, only the High and Best settings *smooth* (anti-alias) the bitmaps in the movie. (Refer to Chapter 13 for more information about publishing your Flash movie.)

When you import a bitmap image into Flash, you can take the following steps to ensure good-looking results:

- ✔ **Save your graphics in the highest quality possible.** If you have a photograph, don't import it as a GIF file.

- ✔ **Don't overcompress your original bitmaps.** Find a happy medium. Try saving an image at several compression levels to see the difference in quality and size.

- ✔ **Set the compression type and quality in the Bitmap Properties dialog box.** After you import the image, open the Library (choose Window⬀ Library), right-click (Windows) or Control+click (Mac) the image, and then choose Properties to open the Bitmap Properties dialog box, as shown in Figure 14-3.

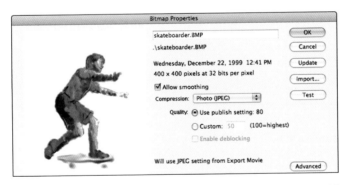

Figure 14-3: Use the Bitmap Properties dialog box to fiddle with your bitmaps.

How Do I Rescale My Movie's Size?

You create a beautiful Flash movie that takes up the entire page. But then your boss says that you need to fit it into an existing HTML page, which translates into reducing the size of the whole thing by 25 percent. What do you do? Get a new boss, if possible. Barring that, you can rescale the size of the movie.

1. Decide the amount of the reduction you need to achieve, such as 25 percent.

2. If you have any locked layers, unlock them.

   See Chapter 6 for all the info on locking and unlocking layers.

3. If you have any hidden layers, right-click (Windows) or Control-click (Mac) the name of any layer and then choose Show All.

   This step ensures that all layers are considered in the reduction.

 4. Click the Edit Multiple Frames button (just below the Timeline).

5. Drag the onion skin markers to the beginning and ending frames of your animation.

   See Chapter 9 for more information on how to use onion skin markers.

6. Choose Edit⇨Select All.

7. Choose Window⇨Transform to open the Transform panel (shown in Figure 14-4).

8. In the Transform panel, select the Constrain check box.

9. In the Width or Height input box, type the new number for your reduction percentage, and then press Enter (Windows) or Return (Mac).

   Flash scales your animations by the reduction percentage.

10. Choose Modify⇨Document.

11. In the Width and Height boxes of the Document Properties dialog box that appears, type new numbers reflecting the reduction percentage size, as shown in Figure 14-5.

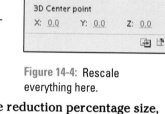

Figure 14-4: Rescale everything here.

Figure 14-5: Type in your new width and height.

Here, you'll have to first do a little math, multiplying the old width and height by the reduction percentage to come up with the new numbers you type in.

You're done! Flash scales your entire movie as you specified. You might have to drag everything so that it fits appropriately within your smaller-sized movie.

Size requirements are key pieces of information to nail down before building a Flash movie to avoid rescaling your movie's size.

What Are the Best Tips for Creating Movies?

Every Flash user collects a number of techniques that make creating a Flash movie easier. Following are a few ideas to help you get started:

- **Save multiple versions of your movie** by choosing File⇨Save As. If a problem arises, you can always go back to a previous version and start again.

- As soon as you have an overall structure, **test your movie in a variety of browsers** (for example, Internet Explorer; Mozilla Firefox; and on a Macintosh, Apple's Safari) and at various resolutions, if possible. It's easier to correct problems early, before your project becomes too complex. Choose Control⇨Test Movie as soon as you develop your animation and continue to test it in this way for each new significant change. It's also a good idea to keep testing your movie with Publish Preview (press F12) to see how it will work in a browser.

- **Add comments** (see Chapter 10) to your ActionScript so that you can figure out what you did when you go back to your movie after your vacation.

- **Use consistent names for symbols.** Many Flash users add the type of symbol after the name: for example, a button called *Contact_btn,* and a movie clip called *Intro_mc.* When you start creating movie clips inside buttons, you might get confused if you don't name your symbols intelligently.

- **Use meaningful names for your instances.** If you have three instances of a button symbol, you need to be able to distinguish which is which. You can name them by their purpose, such as *Email, Services,* and *Clients.*

- When you complete work on a layer, **lock the layer** to avoid making unwanted changes.

- **Give layers meaningful names.**

- **Place related elements in layers that are near each other,** and then put the layers in layer folders to group them.

✔ **If you have ActionScript on a layer, don't put anything else on that layer.** This avoids potential conflicts between items you might have on the Stage and your ActionScript code that references them.

✔ **If your ActionScript code references particular frames, reference them with frame labels rather than frame numbers.** Then if you later move those frames on the Timeline, you don't have to change any frame numbers in your code.

✔ **Organize similar assets in your Library with Library folders,** and give your Library folders meaningful names, as shown in Figure 14-6.

✔ For longer presentations, **use several SWF files in sequence** rather than a series of scenes.

Figure 14-6: Organize Library assets in folders with meaningful names.

Then your audience can download your presentation more quickly in small pieces, one SWF file at a time, rather than having to download the entire SWF file that contains many scenes all at once. On the other hand, if you create lengthy animations, you might want to use scenes in a single, big SWF file so that your audience downloads everything at the beginning, and can then view the lengthy animation without interruption.

Can Flash Do Full 3D?

As you can see in Chapter 9, it's really cool that you can use Flash's new 3D transformation tools to animate 2D Flash objects in 3D space. But is there any way to create and animate fully 3D objects in your Flash worlds? Yes, but you need to resort to additional software packages to do so — or do some pretty fancy ActionScript programming.

Software-wise, check out Electric Rain's Swift 3D (Figure 14-7), which is specifically designed for creating 3D animation for Flash. It's also fairly easy to use, compared to other 3D software packages. Electric Rain also sells software plug-ins that you can use to export 3D animation from the 3D animation software packages 3DS Max and Lightwave 3D into Flash.

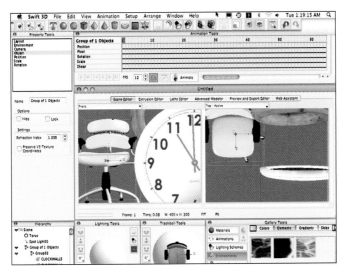

Figure 14-7: Create 3D animations in Swift 3D and import them into Flash.

Those with a high level of programming skill can choose from several increasingly popular, free software programming frameworks to create 3D animation with ActionScript. Papervision3D is one such framework, and you can see an example of its capabilities at `www.papervision3d.org`, shown in Figure 14-8. To learn more about Papervision3D and to see more demonstrations of its capabilities, check out `http://blog.papervision3d.org`.

Other popular 3D programming frameworks for Flash include the Go ActionScript Animation Platform (`www.goasap.org`), Away3D (`away3d.com`), and the Sandy 3D Engine (`www.flashsandy.org`; see Figure 14-9).

Figure 14-8: An interesting example of what Papervision3D can do.

Figure 14-9: Sandy 3D Engine demos, tutorials, forum, and blog are online.

How Do I Center a Flash Movie in a Web Page?

As we discuss in Chapter 13, you can make your Flash movie appear in a Web page by choosing both the Flash and HTML formats in your Publish Settings and then publishing your movie. Flash then generates the HTML code (like the code in Figure 13-11) for a Web page. This Web page appears to contain your Flash movie when you view the Web page in a browser. To make the Flash movie centered in that Web page, you just need to add a little bit of extra code to the HTML page, which you can do with a text editor.

To add the code for centering your Flash movie in the Web page, follow these steps:

1. **After choosing the Publish Settings for Flash and HTML (using the Flash Only or Flash HTTPS template in the HTML tab of the Publish Settings dialog box, as we describe in Chapter 13), choose File⇨Publish.**

   Flash creates a Flash Player (SWF) file and a Web page (HTML) file.

2. **Start a text editor or an HTML editor, and open the HTML page within the editor.**

   You can use an HTML editor (such as Dreamweaver) or a text editor (such as Notepad in Windows; or TextEdit on a Mac).

   In TextEdit, choose TextEdit⇨Preferences. In the Preferences window, on the New Document tab, select Plain Text rather than Rich Text in the Format section. On the Open and Save tab of the Preferences window, deselect the Add '.txt' Extension to Plain Text Files check box in the When Saving a File section.

3. **Find </head> in the file and insert this code before it:**

   ```
   <style type="text/css" media="screen">
       body {text-align: center; }
       div#container {width: 550px; margin: 0px auto;
       text-align: left; }
   </style>
   ```

   Be sure you find </head>, not <head>.

   This code defines some Cascading Style Sheet (or CSS) styles that your Web browser will use to dynamically create margins on the left and right of a Flash movie, 550 pixels wide, so that the movie is automatically centered on the page. If your Flash movie is a different width — say, 200 pixels — just change 550px in the preceding code to 200px.

4. **Find `<script language="javascript"type="text/javascript>` `AC_FL_RunContent` in the file (after `about:internet`) and insert `<div id="container">` before it.**

   Be sure not to put anything between the <script> and </script> tags.

5. **Find `</noscript>` in the file and insert `</div>` after it.**

   Be sure you find </noscript>, not <noscript>.

In HTML lingo, `<div>` and `<style>` (and any other words starting with a bracket [`<`]) are called *tags*. The `<div>` tag defines the beginning of a division or section of a Web page, and the `</div>` tag defines the end of it. By giving the `<div>` an `id` equal to `"container"`, the Web browser uses the style that you define for `"container"` in Step 3 and applies it to everything between the `<div>` and `</div>` tags.

Figure 14-10 shows an example of an HTML file with all the code added. This is the code shown in Figure 13-11, revised with `<style>`, `</style>`, `<div>`, and `</div>` tags, which center the movie in the Web page.

```
                    Movie of the Year Centered.html
</script>
<style type="text/css" media="screen">
    body {text-align: center; }
    div#container {width: 550px; margin: 0px auto;
    text-align: left; }
</style>
</head>
<body bgcolor="#ffffff">
<!--url's used in the movie-->
<!--text used in the movie-->
<!-- saved from url=(0013)about:internet -->
<div id="container">
<script language="JavaScript" type="text/javascript">
        AC_FL_RunContent(
            'codebase', 'http://download.macromedia.com/pub/shockwave/
cabs/flash/swflash.cab#version=10,0,0,0',
                'width', '550',
                'height', '400',
                'src', 'Movie of the Year',
                'quality', 'high',
                'pluginspage', 'http://www.adobe.com/go/getflashplayer',
                'align', 'middle',
                'play', 'true',
                'loop', 'true',
                'scale', 'showall',
                'wmode', 'window',
                'devicefont', 'false',
                'id', 'Movie of the Year',
                'bgcolor', '#ffffff',
                'name', 'Movie of the Year'
```

Figure 14-10: This code centers the movie on the Web page.

6. **In the editor, save the file with the changes you made.**

   Now when you view the HTML page in a Web browser (assuming it's a fairly recent version of a Web browser), your Flash movie appears centered in the Web page.

What Are the Size Limits for a Flash Movie?

Usually, you won't be too concerned about how big of a movie you can create with Flash because one of the reasons to use Flash is that it employs vector graphics, tweening, and other methods to create small files that download quickly over the Web. If you're using Flash to create gigantic projects, that can be great fun and even workable in some cases. Just keep in mind that Flash wasn't primarily designed to do that. On the other hand, more and more studios are using Flash for production animation (including broadcast TV shows), and video is now an important feature of Flash.

In any case, it's interesting to know that other than limits imposed by your computer's RAM, CPU, hard drive, video card, browser, and operating system, there are few limits to the size and complexity of a Flash movie. However, here are at least two limits:

- The minimum size of your Stage is 1 pixel wide and 1 pixel high.
- The maximum Stage size is 2880 pixels wide x 2880 pixels wide.

What Are the Top Tips for Web Design with Flash?

The vast majority of Flash movies end up on Web sites. Here are some tips to help ensure that your Web site is as attractive and useful as possible.

Set your goal

Know why you have a Web site. Write out one main goal and perhaps one or two secondary goals. For example, the main goal of your site might be to sell used music CDs. A secondary goal might be to provide viewers with music reviews so that they can decide which CDs they want to buy. Another secondary goal could be to attract viewers to your site (so that they can buy your CDs). Avoid putting material on your site that doesn't help you reach your goal.

How does your Flash movie help you attain your Web site's goal? Perhaps your movie displays the covers of your most widely sold CDs and plays some of the music, giving viewers an instant understanding of your site's purpose.

Make thumbnail sketches first

This might be the most radical, life-altering advice in this book: After you articulate the goals for your Web site, try out several different designs for each type of page in your site by drawing small sketches of them. For your home page, try out at least a dozen designs.

Keep the sketches really small, so they're the size of a postage stamp. This makes it easier for you to try a lot of different designs quickly. It also forces you to think of the overall design of your site before you jump into the details. This gives you a chance to pick a strong overall design that graphically supports your goals for the site.

Connect the parts to the whole

You found a compelling overall graphic design by drawing your thumbnail sketches, as we describe in the preceding section. Now while you fill in the details of your page, see how you can organize the details of your page so that they fit well into its main graphic theme as captured in your thumbnail sketch. This will help you avoid clutter and will make your pages easier to understand, more powerful, and more attractive.

Clutter and complex structures are usually counterproductive. You can use Flash to create a simple, compelling navigational system that connects the user to every page effortlessly.

Use fewer than four fonts

For maximum coherence and impact, you should probably restrict your Web page design to use two or three fonts at most. It might make visual sense to use one font for the body of your text and one font for the headlines. You could perhaps use a third font for a logo or for some other special item, but this will probably look best if it has some kind of strong visual harmony with the other fonts that you're using.

Test and test again

As we describe in Chapter 13, you undoubtedly need to test your Web site with several browsers, not just the latest version of Internet Explorer. Testing at various screen resolutions (probably at least 800 x 600 and 1024 x 768) is also extremely important. Then have a few friends review your site and navigate through it. Ask them to write down their impressions, moments of confusion, questions, comments, and praise — so that you can view your site from a fresh perspective.

How Do I Dynamically Load Music from the Web?

You can use ActionScript to load music into your movie live from the Web by using the ActionScript `load()` and `play()` methods. (Turn to Chapter 10 to find out more about ActionScript.) To load an MP3 file on the Web into your movie while your movie is playing, follow these steps:

1. **Create a new layer.**

   Chapter 6 explains how to add a new layer.

2. **Click a keyframe.**

   If the frame you want to use isn't a keyframe, right-click (Windows) or Control-click (Mac) it and then choose Insert Keyframe.

3. **Choose Window⇨Actions to open the Actions panel (if it isn't open already). In the Actions panel, click the Script Assist button to toggle it off (if it's enabled).**

   If necessary, click the Actions panel title bar to expand the panel.

4. **In the Script pane of the Actions panel, enter the following code:**

   ```
   var mySound:Sound = new Sound();
   var myChoice="http://ia310140.us.archive.org/0/items/sci2000-11-17.
             matrix.shnf/sci2000-11-17d1/sci2000-11-17d1t1_64kb.mp3";
   var myRequest:URLRequest = new URLRequest(myChoice);
   var myContext:SoundLoaderContext = new SoundLoaderContext(8000, true);
   mySound.load(myRequest, myContext);
   mySound.play();
   ```

   Replace the Web address that follows `var myChoice` in the code with the Web address of the audio you want to play. Or if the audio is going to remain in the same folder as your Flash Player file, you can simply replace it with the name of the file, such as `sci2000-11-17d1t1_64kb.mp3` or `Im_an_Old_Cowhand.mp3`. You can replace `mySound`, `myChoice`, `myRequest`, and `myContext` with any names you like.

Here's a table that shows each statement in the preceding code and what it does. (Each ActionScript statement ends with a semicolon.)

`var mySound;`	Creates an instance of a new sound object with the name mySound.
`var myChoice="http://ia310140.us.archive.org/0/items/sci2000-11-17.matrix.shnf/sci2000-11-17d1/sci2000-11-17d1t1_64kb.mp3";`	Creates a variable and sets it equal to a Web address (a URL).
`var myRequest:URLRequest = new URLRequest(myChoice);`	Creates an instance of a request for an item that has that Web address.
`var myContext:SoundLoaderContext = new SoundLoaderContext(8000, true);`	Specifies how many milliseconds of buffering (in this case, 8000 milliseconds, which equals 8 seconds) to use when loading the sound.
`mySound.load(myRequest, myContext);`	Loads the sound specified in the third statement as a streaming sound by using the buffer size specified in the fourth statement.
`mySound.play();`	Plays the sound.

The preceding code loads your file as *streaming audio.* You hear streaming audio while it's being sent over the Web to you. You don't have to download the entire audio file before you can start hearing it.

5. **Choose Control⇨Test Movie and enjoy the music.**

15

Ten Best Flash Resources

*F*lash is such a flexible program that you'll never stop discovering what it can do. In this chapter, we point you to the many resources you can turn to when you want to increase your knowledge about Flash.

We (of course) think that this book is a great resource on Flash. But much more about Flash is out there, readily available to help you become a great Flash designer and animator.

Check Out Award-Winning Movies

It's both inspiring and instructive to see what the best Flash movies can do, and you can find the best Flash movies on a couple of sites. For example, the Flashforward Conference Web site lists winners in many categories at `www.flashforwardconference.com/winners`. These movies are winners in the conference's annual contest, as shown in Figure 15-1.

Figure 15-1: Find examples of amazing Flash movies here.

Best Flash Animation Site (at www.bestflashanimationsite.com, of course), showcases Flash sites that have been voted the best each week by viewers. This is a good place to find top-notch examples of Flash in a variety of categories, including Applications, Corporate, Experimental, Technical Merit, and Video.

Look on the Flash Web Pages

Adobe maintains large resources for Flash users on its Web site. Go to www.adobe.com/support/flash and www.adobe.com/devnet/flash, where you can find tips, tutorials, support, technical notes, news, and updates.

Good places to check are the Flash Design Center at

www.adobe.com/cfusion/designcenter/search.cfm?product=Flash&go=Go

and the Adobe Design Center Video Workshop at

www.adobe.com/designcenter/video_workshop

Another great resource is Adobe TV (at http://tv.adobe.com, shown in Figure 15-2), which features many high-quality videos on Flash and other Adobe software.

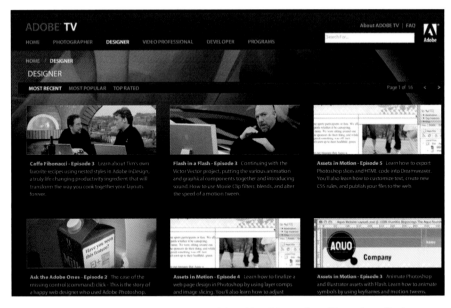

Figure 15-2: Adobe TV features many insightful and inspiring online videos about Flash.

Visit Our Site

Check out the *Adobe Flash CS4 Professional For Dummies* page on the Wiley Web site. You can find the site by surfing to `www.dummies.com/go/flashcs4fd`. It contains sample files from the book, tips, and updates. We hope that you find the site helpful!

Take a Course

Many colleges and universities offer courses in Flash. Sometimes these courses are part of a Web design or graphic arts course, or they might stand alone. To find these courses, call local educational institutions and ask.

The advantage of a course led by a teacher is that you have a chance to ask questions — and receive answers. A teacher also guides the learning process and possibly even gives you lots of tips and hints!

You might also consider taking self-paced courses in Flash offered by Adobe or instructor-led courses at an Adobe Authorized Training Center. Visit `www.adobe.com/training` for more information, including free sample lessons.

Join a Flash Discussion Group

Adobe maintains active Flash support forums, where anyone can ask questions and get answers from other members of the Flash community. To read messages from and send messages to these discussion forums, point your Web browser to www.adobe.com/cfusion/webforums/forum/index.cfm?forumid=15.

Also available are several popular Internet newsgroups for discussing Flash — including one for general technical discussions of Flash and one for discussions of designing entire Web sites by using Flash. You can view messages on these newsgroups by visiting these two sites:

```
http://groups.google.com/group/macromedia.flash
http://groups.google.com/group/macromedia.flash.sitedesign
```

If you have software for reading newsgroups on your computer, you can alternatively go to these two sites to read messages from and send messages to these two groups:

```
news://forums.macromedia.com/macromedia.flash
news://forums.macromedia.com/macromedia.flash.sitedesign
```

Several other excellent active discussion groups reside on Web sites. The best way to tell whether a discussion group is active is to see how many messages have been posted in the past one or two days. You can also check out how many different people are participating. See the following section in this chapter.

You can also subscribe to electronic mailing lists for ongoing discussions sent by e-mail. With more than 3,000 members, the Yahoo! FLASHmacromedia list is one of the largest lists specifically for users who want to discuss Flash techniques. You can ask questions and get answers from the community of Flash users. To sign up or to view the Web archive of messages, go to

```
http://tech.groups.yahoo.com/group/FLASHmacromedia
```

You can find more than 800 other Flash e-mail discussion groups at Yahoo! alone. Find them by surfing to

```
http://tech.dir.groups.yahoo.com/dir/Computers___Internet/
          Software/Multimedia/Macromedia_Flash
```

That's three underscores between *Computers* and *Internet.*

Check Out Flash Resource Sites

A huge Flash community is on the Internet — so vast, in fact, that you'll probably never be able to participate in all its offerings. These Web sites offer news, tutorials, discussion groups, tips, and links to other Flash resources.

Some of these sites are more up to date, lively, and complete than others. The quality of the tips and tutorials varies widely. Some specialize in tips for beginners; others are geared toward advanced users. The following list briefly reviews the ones that we find most useful, in alphabetical order:

- ✔ www.actionscript.org: This site is a well-designed, comprehensive resource on ActionScript. It includes extremely active discussion forums (with more than 100,000 discussions); more than 400 tutorials on ActionScript at beginning, intermediate, and advanced levels; a Library with more than 700 ActionScripts, and more than 1,000 Flash movies; links; and an employment section.

- ✔ www.flashkit.com: Flash Kit is probably the largest Flash site, and it's up to date, having Flash CS4 material within days after it shipped. You can find thousands of FLA files to download and study, more than 1,100 tutorials, dozens of active discussion forums (some with hundreds of thousands of discussions), links, thousands of sounds, more than 1,500 downloadable fonts — if you can think of it, you can find it here.

- ✔ www.flashgoddess.com: Flashgoddess is an informative site showcasing women who do brilliant work with Flash. It includes profiles of and articles on terrific Flash designers, a gallery of work by featured artists, links, and more.

- ✔ www.flashmagazine.com: This site features news and reviews of Flash and Flash-related products.

- ✔ www.gotoandlearn.com: This site contains dozens of terrific, free Flash tutorials on video, developed by Lee Brimelow, a Platform Evangelist at Adobe. The site also includes a forum with thousands of discussions. Lee's blog at http://theflashblog.com is a good place to find out what's new at Gotoandlearn.com. See Figure 15-3.

- ✔ www.kirupa.com: This is Kirupa Chinnathambi's site about Flash and other Web technologies. It contains hundreds of tutorials (many of them on video) and discussion forums with hundreds of thousands of posts.

- ✔ www.ultrashock.com: Ultrashock is a multifaceted site that includes Flash-related news, job listings, and discussion forums with more than 600,000 posts.

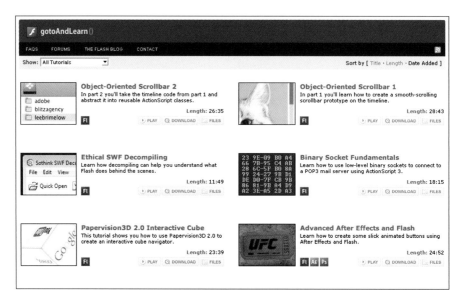

Figure 15-3: Find dozens of terrific, free Flash tutorials on video here.

Check Out Sites That Use Flash

You can get ideas by looking at what others do. (It's interesting, for instance, that simple Flash sites are sometimes the most beautiful and practical.) In Chapter 16, we list sites by ten great designers that use Flash. And many resource sites have showcases of great Flash sites, as Adobe does at

www.adobe.com/products/flash/customers

Attend a Flash Conference

Attending a conference on Flash is an exciting way to find out much more about Flash from an array of experts, see award-winning Flash movies, participate in workshops and seminars, hear the latest news from Adobe, make contacts with others interested in Flash, and generally immerse yourself in the world of Flash. Even just visiting the Web sites of some of these conferences can be instructive. Conferences you might consider attending include the following:

 ✔ **Flashforward (including the Flash Film Festival):** A two- or three-day conference, held two or three times per year in a changing roster of cities that has included San Francisco, Boston, New York, Seattle, and Austin. For information, visit `www.flashforwardconference.com`.

 ✔ **FlashBelt Conference:** A two-day conference in Minneapolis in June. For information, visit `www.flashbelt.com`.

Collect Flash Movies

Many Flash resource Web sites let you download FLA files. You can also trade FLA files with others who you know use Flash. Analyzing FLA files is one of the best ways to see how effects are created. In Chapter 12, we explain how to use the Movie Explorer to ferret out all the hidden details of an FLA file.

Be sure to check out the Library of an FLA file — many of the secrets lie there. And you can use the Movie Explorer to find and study all the actions in an FLA file. You'll soon be on your way to adapting the techniques that you see to your own projects.

Reuse Your Best Stuff

After you create some great Flash movies, you can reuse your best stuff. *Fadeouts* (changing transparency), *glows* (soft edges), and masks are simple effects that you can use again and again. You can also reuse ActionScript on new objects. After you get a technique down, you don't need to reinvent the wheel. If you've created an animated logo, you can have an entirely new animation by merely swapping a symbol.

You can import items from the Library of any movie into your current movie. Choose File⇨Import⇨Open External Library and then choose the Flash file that contains the Library you want to use. Then drag the items that you want from the imported movie Library onto the Stage or into the Library of your current movie. This is a really nifty Flash feature.

Ten Flash Designers to Watch

*T*rying to choose ten of the best designers who use Flash is almost absurd — so many brilliant designers are out there. Nevertheless, in this chapter we give you a shortcut to finding some of the most innovative and skilled Flash designers so that you can check out their work, get ideas, and see the possibilities.

Note that some of the sites they've designed can take a really long time to load if you don't have a broadband connection to the Web.

Joshua Davis

Joshua Davis is one of the most relentless explorers of Flash's capabilities. His legendary PrayStation site, an archive that you may see at `http://ps3.praystation.com/pound/v2`, originally went online in 1997 as a spoof of PlayStation graphics, but it soon morphed into one of the most aggressively experimental Flash sites on the Web. He then moved on to create Once Upon A Forest (which you may see at `www.once-upon-a-forest.com`), a visually poetic series of computer-generated imagery that is easier to experience than describe. (He likes to bury his links, so you may have to search to find anything clickable.) You can see his current work at www. joshuadavis.com. Benek Lisefski's essay on Joshua Davis, at www. pixelinspectors.com/reviews/joshua-davis.html, can help you understand his mysterious work a little more clearly.

Anthony Eden

Australian designer Anthony Eden showcases a fascinating group of Flash experiments at his site, www.arseiam.com, shown in Figure 16-1.

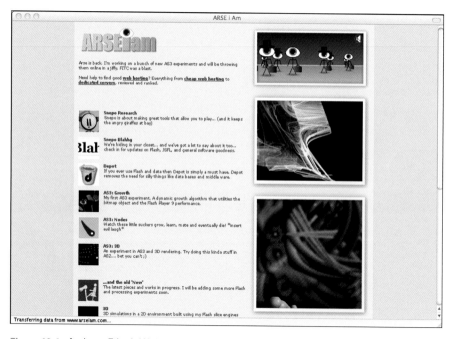

Figure 16-1: Anthony Eden's Web site features numerous interesting Flash experiments.

Andy Foulds

Andy Foulds's clients includes Nike, Miramax Films, Mercedes-Benz, Microsoft, and Yahoo. His Flash portfolio, on view at www.andyfoulds. co.uk, is tremendously inventive and visually intriguing.

Chris Georgenes

Chris Georgenes is a freelance artist and animator whose clients include Cartoon Network, Dreamworks, ABC, NBC, FX, Comedy Central, PBS, and UPN. Check out his online portfolio of many charming animations at www.mudbubble.com (shown in Figure 16-2) and his blog at www.keyframer.com.

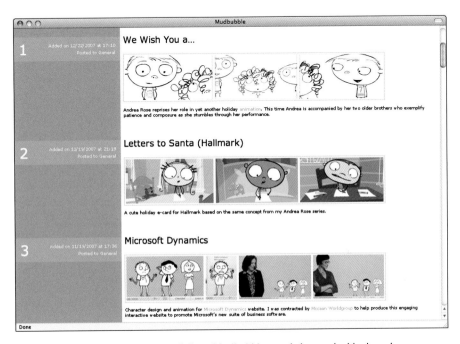

Figure 16-2: Chris Georgenes's portfolio at Mudbubble.com is jammed with charming animated characters.

Ben Hantoot

Ben Hantoot is one of the most, as he says, "over-the-top" animators on the planet. Other Flash sites look positively motionless compared to the site of his studio, www.webfeatsdesign.com. The incessant inventiveness of his work is outrageously delightful.

Seb Lee-Delisle and Dominic Minns

Seb Lee-Delisle is a Flash 3D innovator who has pushed Flash's boundaries in games, physics simulations, and interactive 3D animation. You can see some of his handiwork at his company's site at www.pluginmedia.net (shown in Figure 16-3), which also features charming graphic design by creative director Dominic Minns. Be sure to check out the lab there. Seb's blog (www.sebleedelisle.com) presents lots of interesting and useful material on 3D techniques in Flash.

Figure 16-3: You can see the work of Dominic Minns and Seb Lee-Delisle at their company's site, which features crazed Flash wizards from beyond the stars.

Erik Natzke

Interactive designer Erik Natzke presents some truly spectacular animation at http://play.natzke.com. Erik's online journal at http://jot.eriknatzke.com is also worth visiting.

Micaël Reynaud

At www.dunun.com, the award-winning French Flash designer Micaël Reynaud has created a site full of surprises that, like several of the sites in this chapter, is difficult to describe but charming to experience. For example, his work at www.dunun.com/2002 (shown in Figure 16-4), combines music, imagery, and unusual user-interface techniques to showcase a panoramic view of this artist's multiple skills.

Figure 16-4: Micaël Reynaud uses Flash to create fascinating virtual environments such as the one shown here.

Jared Tarbell

Jared Tarbell uses ActionScript to generate beautiful imagery. Interestingly, his mathematical explorations in Flash often end up in commercial projects. You can see his work (and download his ActionScript code) at www.levitated.net.

Jeremy Thorp

Vancouver artist and educator Jeremy Thorp teaches in Langara College's Electronic Media Design Program, and in the University of British Columbia's Department of Art History, Visual Art and Theory. His clients have included Honda, The Canadian Broadcasting Corporation, FOX, and the LA Kings. At his Web site, `www.blprnt.com`, you can see an award-winning assortment of his beautiful Flash experiments in art and technology.

Index

• *M* •

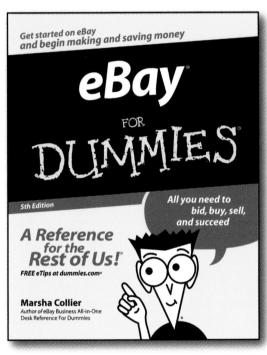
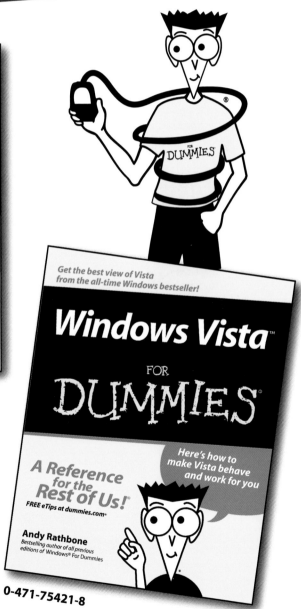